Social Work with Refugees, Asylum Seekers and Migrants

Social Work with Refugees, Asylum Seekers and Migrants

Theory and Skills for Practice

Edited by Lauren Wroe, Rachel Larkin and Reima Ana Maglajlic

Foreword by Debra Hayes

Jessica Kingsley *Publishers*
London and Philadelphia

The names of the authors of the narrative sections have been changed where requested.

First published in 2019
by Jessica Kingsley Publishers
73 Collier Street
London N1 9BE, UK
and
400 Market Street, Suite 400
Philadelphia, PA 19106, USA

www.jkp.com

Library of Congress Cataloging in Publication Data
A CIP catalog record for this book is available from the Library of Congress

British Library Cataloguing in Publication Data
A CIP catalogue record for this book is available from the British Library

ISBN 978 1 78592 344 9
eISBN 978 1 78450 674 2

Printed and bound in Great Britain

100% of the royalties from the sale of this book will be donated to Social
Workers Without Borders and other migrant and refugee organisations.

Contents

Foreword: Part of the Problem or Part of the Solution?   7
Debra Hayes

Acknowledgements   11

Narrative 1: Learning from Henrietta   13

1.   Social Work with Refugees, Asylum Seekers and Migrants   17
Lauren Wroe, Rachel Larkin and Reima Ana Maglajlic

2.   Social Work Without Borders   27
An Interview with Lynn King

Narrative 2: Learning from Mary   39

3.   Black Feminist Diaspora Spaces of Social Work Critical Reflexivity . .   41
Suryia Nayak

4.   Migration and Austerity   57
Lucy Mort

Narrative 3: Learning from Sam   75

5.   Disability and Forced Migration   77
Rebecca Yeo

6.   Learning from Immigration Controversies   95
Natalia Farmer

Narrative 4: Learning from Jan   115

7. Working with Separated Children and Young People
    Seeking International Protection 117
    Jen Ang

8. Asylum-Seeking Children In and Leaving Care 143
    Anna Gupta

✳ 9. Social Work with Survivors of Torture 163
    Jude Boyles, Anna Turner and Katy Tolman

    Narrative 5: Learning from Stella. 185

10. Lessons from Community Work 189
    Hannah Berry

11. Understanding Destitution and Finding Creative Solutions 205
    Rachael Bee

    Narrative 6: Learning from Andy 217

12. Supporting Migrants and Asylum Seekers In
    and Beyond Immigration Detention in the UK 219
    Joanne Vincett

    Narrative 7: Learning from Aida. 237

✳ 13. Age Assessments of Unaccompanied Minors 239
    Elaine Ortiz

14. From 'Translation Machine' to Trusted Colleague. 251
    Annemarie Morsch

    Narrative 8: Learning from Ken 263

15. Concluding Thoughts 267
    Lauren Wroe, Rachel Larkin and Reima Ana Maglajlic

    Contributors. 279

    Subject Index 285

    Author Index 292

Foreword

Part of the Problem or Part of the Solution?

Debra Hayes

I'm humbled to be asked to write a foreword for this important and timely book. In 2004, I co-edited, along with the late Beth Humphries, the first book exclusively dedicated to exploring the issues of immigration and asylum in social work (Hayes and Humphries 2004). I'd like to acknowledge also that Jessica Kingsley Publishers supported and published that work, and is continuing to support this poorly resourced area of social work research and writing by publishing this wonderful book. In 2004, I was lucky enough to work with a range of social workers, social work students, researchers, practitioners, activists and service users to produce that book. Writing this foreword has allowed me to reflect back on the past 14 years and consider where we are now, what has changed and what remains the same for those in some way connected to social work and migration, either as workers or users of services or indeed as activists fighting to sustain or develop services.

In 2004, 'Austerity' had not yet entered popular parlance or academic writing, as a political project cynically manufactured to explain and manage the impact of financial crisis. The onslaught on public finances, and the brutal attacks on those in receipt of even minimal assistance and the poor more generally have accelerated since. That project, though, was only able to capture the moment quite so successfully by building on already established discourses around welfare desirability and deservedness. In 2004, those subject to immigration control were already firmly constructed as part of the problem. The book came in the wake of the 1999 Immigration and Asylum Act, which institutionalised removing asylum seekers from mainstream welfare. In short, we knew a significant corner had been turned and we knew there was urgency concerning exploring the role and function of social work in relation to that group. Events over the last 14 years have embedded further stigmatising and damaging ideas around certain social groups, and migrants have been centre stage throughout as the easiest scapegoat and seemingly obvious target in making the 'Austerity' project function.

Of central importance, both then and now, is the exploration of the relationship between immigration control and welfare delivery. I must acknowledge here the significance of the work of the late Steve Cohen, who I was fortunate enough to work alongside in my early years as a probation officer and subsequently an academic. He more than anyone forced us to look at those controls differently, not simply as mechanisms which operate at borders to exclude or remove, but as *internal* systems policing those who reside, largely legally, on a day-to-day basis in myriad ways. This matters to us here because those internal controls involve not simply police and immigration officials but often welfare agencies and workers.

The previous book explored that relationship between welfare delivery and the functioning of immigration control and showed they are inextricably linked both ideologically and practically. Since 2004, this has become more entrenched and more sophisticated. Technological shifts have dramatically increased the surveillance possibilities for the state, and at every turn welfare agencies are involved in gathering data, gatekeeping resources and facilitating the passage of information from seemingly benign state agencies to systems designed to detain and remove. The 'Austerity' agenda has hardened a set of ideas that it is perfectly reasonable for welfare agencies to contribute to this. It is not accidental that those caught up in the Windrush scandal of 2018, involving the detention and deportation of many Caribbean people who had come to the 'Mother' country over 40 years ago, often hit difficulties precisely when they came to access benefits or medical care.

Since 2004, the local state, in the form of local authorities, has become further embedded in these processes. Recent press reports of Home Office workers sitting in on interviews with destitute migrant families in certain local authorities are a frightening example of where we are in the local state. What has shifted since 2004 and what was foretold and described by Steve Cohen as 'dining with the Devil' has been the creeping inclusion of voluntary sector agencies in this. Agencies we now describe as third sector have had to fight battles to survive these last 14 years, and the privatisation and contracting-out culture has led some agencies to become involved in that machinery of surveillance and control. This book is an important update on where we are and offers new discussions on how we resist and fight for a different type of service provision. The book continues the crucial work of investigating and exposing how welfare agencies are not immune from inclusion in systems of surveillance and control, and must continue to resist this creeping role as unpaid immigration officers.

Alarmingly, further shifts since 2004 involve the increasing confidence of the far right both in the UK and globally. The resurgence of fascist parties, both at government level and on the streets, shows an emboldened far right manipulating the issue of migration, often it seems without resistance from mainstream politicians or the mainstream media. The neo-liberal agenda has nicely fed this and enjoys gorging itself on the consequences, facilitating a real increase in fear, insecurity and violence in the lived experience of migrant communities. What also seems palpable in ways not felt in 2004 is the sense that we live in a world system which is collapsing. In 2004, I believe there was still a sense that the system of global capitalism remained the only way we could organise ourselves. The mass displacement of human beings through war, civil war, environmental disaster or hunger was still mainly seen as a problem at the edge of a largely functioning system. There has been a shift perhaps in levels of acceptance that this particular way of organising ourselves as humans has outlived its usefulness and rationale. The 'Austerity' myth has now been busted and hangs on by a thread. Is it possible then that the profession of social work might extricate itself from that depressing weight of logic that we just have to do things the way we do?

Maybe we are finding some space now for real conversations about a different way, space to find a practice that stands alongside those bearing the brunt of this brutal global system in crisis. This book offers us hope, different models of practice, examples of resistance and inspiring stories of a different social work, a social work which is part of the solution and not part of the problem. It could not be more timely.

References

Hayes, D. and Humphries, B. (2004) *Social Work, Immigration and Asylum: Debates, Dilemmas and Ethical Issues for Social Work and Social Care Practice.* London: Jessica Kingsley Publishers.

Immigration and Asylum Act (1999) Accessed 28/11/2018 at: www.legislation.gov.uk/ukpga/1999/33/contents.

Acknowledgements

This book would not have been possible without the guidance and assistance of a number of experienced, and passionate, individuals and groups.

First, we would like to thank the staff at Jessica Kingsley Publishers for their commitment to our work. We would also like to thank Debra Hayes for her challenging and passionate foreword; her work alongside Beth Humphries in 2004 inspired us to embark on this publication. This book draws on the experience and expertise of a number of voluntary sector organisations that have dedicated their scarce time and resources through their contributions, and we would particularly like to thank Bristol Refugee Rights and all of their members and the Growing Together Levenshulme project for sharing their stories with us. These insights remind us of the human impact of the decisions we make as professionals, and guide us towards good practice based on thoughtfulness, solidarity and care.

Editing a book alongside continued, and increasingly demanding, social work and academic roles is not an easy task. Thanks go to Adam Larkin for assisting with the final proofing of the chapters and to Ratha Kaur Lehall, Elliot Richards and Katy Tolman for transcribing the interviews that formed the basis of the narrative sections of the book.

Personal thanks go to all our family, friends and colleagues who have supported us throughout this process.

Narrative 1
Learning from Henrietta

Seeking asylum is not an easy experience. It is a situation where you know when you start, but you don't know the date it will end. It makes it difficult, a life of not knowing when the process will come to an end.

While in detention you are expected to get a lawyer to represent you, but most of them give you conditions and request documents to prove that you qualify for legal representation. If you are not able to meet them, they are not willing to represent you and you have to go to a private lawyer, who you are forced to pay. Usually you can't afford it because you don't have the money. If you are lucky, friends may be able to pay at the beginning, and as the case continues you can try to apply for the legal representation and provide the right documents so they can assess you.

I would like to see the legal process recognise that asylum seekers don't have money, and provide lawyers without asking for so many documents. These are people who are stranded and depressed and they are asked for so many documents which they cannot give. I think social workers should make people in power understand that asylum seekers don't have money, they don't have documents, or proof of this or that.

I was in detention for ten days, but those ten days felt like eight months. The stress there is like the second part of slavery. It really is slavery. Some of us have avoided the slave trade, but that is what is happening in detention. They drag people on the floor, pull them around in the name of forcing them to work. They are using us as cheap labour. We are not allowed to work, but in detention we are made to work for £1 an hour. They use us. They say they don't want us to work, but they are still using us. That is slavery. For these reasons, we want the detention centres to be shut down.

I have been threatened with deportation. I have also been involved in many anti-deportation campaigns. In detention, your case could be looked into and dismissed immediately, and then you would be deported. This is called fast track. They make you do the interview and everything all at once while in detention, and then they decide whether you will be deported. But campaigns helped to stop this. At least you now have the right to come out of detention and not be on the fast track. Subsequent campaigns like 'Shut Down Yarl's Wood' are continuing, for all the people undergoing stress in detention.

Professionals who help us often don't know what is happening there. It takes someone who has been in detention to know what it is like. Experience is the best teacher, so I would like to see social workers try to go into the detention camps and hear from people directly, to conduct one-on-one interviews with people in detention.

'No recourse to public funds' is another area that needs to be improved. You are given just £36.75 a week which is supposed to be for food, but you are expected to go to different groups and activities to get your evidence for your asylum claim. How do they think we can manage with transport if it wasn't for help from charity groups? When you just stay in the house you are isolating yourself, you are not building your confidence. Some people end up with mental health problems because they are stuck in the house and can't go out. They should increase the amount paid to those with 'no recourse to public funds'. Five pounds a day, which is only enough for one or two meals, is not enough. If asylum seekers cannot access public funds, then the allowance needs to be increased.

I have experienced racism in the asylum process. In asylum groups, people sometimes segregate themselves according to nationality or race. I think we should try to stop this, and welcome everyone as one. Some people see asylum seekers as if they have come to take their money, to take their benefits. But we need to let them know that we have not come to take their benefits, we are here because of the situation in our country. We need to stop racism anywhere we see any trace of it.

My experience with housing was not a good one. Sometimes the toilet would break, and you'd spend weeks calling and calling the landlord. You are not given money for anything other than food, so how are you supposed to call them if you don't have money to top up your phone? Even when you get through to the house keeper, it takes days before they come. Sometimes the heaters would break, the boiler would not work, the taps would stop flowing or there would be a leak in the roof. If there was a problem on a Friday, you had to wait until Monday or Tuesday.

Some asylum seekers find it difficult to register with a GP, which is not how it should be. They should not be asking for so many documents and proof. Some people die because they are too scared to go. If people have not yet claimed asylum, they are dying in their homes. Why? Because they are scared of going to the hospital in case they are arrested. Authorities should work on how they can improve the health of everybody, irrespective of status. Help them. Life is important.

Health is important. You should be able to register with a GP without them asking for so many documents. You are talking about life, and these people are scared.

Community groups like Growing Together really help. You go there, you eat a good meal, you are happy, you are seeing people and they are telling you their story. You go back feeling happy, as if you are not alone. You make new friends and they may be able to tell you about other charity groups you may not know about. That's one thing I like about Manchester. There are eight or nine different groups helping asylum seekers. I appreciate Manchester for that. I stayed in Birmingham during my asylum process and there were no groups to attend. In Manchester, we have many of them. They're really supportive.

I would like to see groups like this continue and have more funding. They provide transport for us, they feed us. I would like to see individuals who have been contributing to these charity groups keep doing so. Depression is reduced, isolation is reduced, because you have somewhere to go. If these groups stopped, it would be difficult for us. Some would go mad stuck at home. If there are groups out there continually providing transport and a good meal, the asylum process is less stressful. Every week I look forward to going to Growing Together.

Getting involved in activities and campaigns really helps. It lets people out there know what asylum groups and organisations do for us. There are people out there who have money and have the heart to help, but they don't know about the benefits of these charity organisations if we don't tell them. If one day there are no more groups like Growing Together, people will go mental, people will get sick. We participate in these campaigns to let people out there know what is happening. It is important that we let people know about our situation, and know about how these groups are really helping us.

Social workers are really helpful for asylum seekers. Some of us don't know what to do or don't speak English. My friend has mental health issues and does not speak English, and her social worker really helped. They book appointments and make calls for them. Social workers really play an important role for asylum seekers.

I would like to encourage people out there to support charity groups. They have done marvellous things and are improving people's lives. For me, they have helped me to build my confidence. Being proud and able to talk how I talk now is because of them. Before I came into Growing Together, I lost my confidence. They are not discriminatory, they don't judge you. They welcome you, they accept you irrespective of your tribe. As a group, they welcome people from different parts of the world, they see everybody as one. I would encourage everyone to do the same. Welcome everybody, accept them, and don't judge them because of their religion, their sex or their beliefs. It is what they are, you can't change them, just accept them for who they are.

Chapter 1

Social Work with Refugees, Asylum Seekers and Migrants

Theory and Skills for Practice

Lauren Wroe, Rachel Larkin and Reima Ana Maglajlic

Social workers are really helpful for asylum seekers. Some of us don't know what to do or don't speak English. My friend has mental health issues and does not speak English, and her social worker really helped. They book appointments and make calls for them. Social workers really play an important role for asylum seekers. (Henrietta, see Narrative 1, 'Learning from Henrietta')

There is racism in social services. They like some people and not others. I feel like my daughter and I have been discriminated against. My daughter stays alone inside my friend's house. They are trying to accommodate my daughter, but not me. I am advocating for us to stay together. (Mary, see Narrative 2, 'Learning from Mary')

These quotes are taken from a series of testimonies contributed to this book by members of Bristol Refugee Rights[1] and the Manchester-based Growing Together Levenshulme project.[2] Both projects provide an example of fantastic, community-based advocacy and support work with people who are navigating the asylum process in the UK. These narratives, shared by their members, are interspersed throughout the chapters of this book; they humanise and bring to life the theories and skills needed for social work

---

1   www.bristolrefugeerights.org
2   www.facebook.com/GrowingTogetherLevenshulme

practice across borders, and are a reminder of the power of social work when it is carried out in accordance with principles of human rights and social justice. This book is premised on the notion that, as Henrietta says, social work does, should and can *'really play an important role for asylum seekers'*.

We are writing at a time characterised by an intensified focus on asylum seeking and immigration in the UK. During the 2014–16 'European migrant crisis' (as it cynically became known), it is estimated that over one million people entered the European Union (EU) to seek humanitarian protection (UNHCR, no date). This movement of people across borders to Europe and the UK had direct implications for social work. Kent County Council saw an increase in the annual number of separated asylum-seeking children arriving in their area, from 180 in 2013 to 333 in 2014. As of 31 March 2016, Kent has seen a 136 per cent rise in the latest year, up to 865 looked-after children – 21 per cent of all unaccompanied asylum-seeking children (George and Abi-Aad 2017). The changing demographic of people crossing borders, from single men to families, women and separated children, brought with it a host of new safeguarding concerns. Opportunities to mitigate these, the Women Refugee Commission warned, were being missed at every opportunity (Women's Refugee Commission, no date). Alongside that, we have seen an intensification of right-wing, anti-migrant activity across Europe and an explicit political commitment to the exclusion of migrants in the UK, implemented through the government's hostile environment agenda.

This book is born out of the work of the UK charity Social Workers Without Borders (SWWB)[3] carried out in response to this 'crisis'. The editors of this book have done this work on behalf of SWWB, as part of the charity's commitment to framing immigration and asylum as a human rights issue on the social work curriculum. SWWB was formed in March 2016 by a collective of social workers returning from refugee camps in Leros and Calais. The book begins with an interview with Lynn King, co-founder of the charity, who talks us through why and how the charity was established in early 2016, and the moral outrage at the situation in Calais that drove the formation of the group. The organisation promotes social work intervention not only to improve the material conditions of the lives of people crossing borders, but also to counter discourses and policies that exclude asylum seekers and migrants from social care provision – specifically, discourses that seek to securitise the issue of immigration (see Farmer 2017; King and Grant 2016; Robinson and Masocha 2017; Wroe 2015, 2018).

---

3   www.socialworkerswithoutborders.org

The contributors to this book build on this work, framing social work with asylum seekers, refugees and migrants as work that is concerned with solidarity and safeguarding, not securitisation. Weaving together the chapters, you can hear the challenges people face when trying to access social care and welfare provision as asylum seekers, refugees and migrants; the devastating consequences for individuals and families (and arguably for the integrity of our profession) when social workers are complicit in the use of care and welfare as instruments of immigration control; and the huge impact that small actions can have when social work is practised from a place of solidarity and care. It is this intersection of immigration policy and welfare provision that makes the issue of borders directly relevant for social workers.

Restricting access to welfare has long been instrumentalised as a mechanism of immigration control, through the denial of public funds, enforced destitution and embedding immigration surveillance into various state agencies. In 2004, Debra Hayes and Beth Humphries explored these ethical challenges for social work in their book *Social Work, Immigration and Asylum: Debates, Dilemmas and Ethical Issues for Social Work and Social Care Practice* (Hayes and Humphries 2004). They were writing five years after the Immigration and Asylum Act 1999 introduced the first legislation to exclude asylum seekers from mainstream welfare provision, introducing lower than subsistence voucher schemes and mandatory dispersal to areas with cheap housing stock. Hayes and Humphries tracked the racism inherent in UK immigration control and the use of welfare exclusion as a means of marginalising and deterring asylum seekers and migrants. They challenged social workers to 'stop and think about the seriousness of this collusion and to consider strategies for resistance, as well as the development of good practice' (Hayes and Humphries 2004, p.11). This book continues that commitment to the development of good practice at the intersection of social work and borders.

Fast-forward 14 years and the political landscape has changed significantly. What has persisted, and indeed intensified, is the encroachment of immigration control into the realm of welfare provision and social care. Alongside that, we are living the reality of a political agenda set to dismantle the welfare state, severe cuts to services following post-financial crash austerity and the construction, both discursively and materially, of an explicitly hostile environment for migrants. As Lucy Mort outlines in Chapter 4, Migrant Families and Austerity:

This hostility is enacted through creating legislative barriers that make it difficult – if not dangerous and impossible – to access service provision. While ostensibly targeting those who do not have a legal right to remain in the UK (though we should seek to challenge the simplistic and unhelpful demarcation of legality versus illegality when it comes to people), the very notion of a hostile environment is one that permeates institutions and encounters between practitioners and those accessing services, so that discrimination based on race and perceived 'foreignness' comes to affect both migrant and non-migrant alike.

This is a problem for social work. Since the Conservative government announced its 'hostile environment' agenda (made possible by years of consecutive, cross-party immigration policy excluding migrants from expanding areas of public provision), we have seen numerous examples of individuals and families being denied care or having their immigration status interrogated while trying to access services. How does a pregnant woman, arrested and questioned about her immigration status while being cared for at a sexual assault referral centre, marry with our values as caring professionals? Or the exposé by London charity Project 17, revealing that local authorities across the UK are refusing to provide care for destitute migrant and 'failed' asylum-seeking families under Section 17 duties, forcing parents into destitution and threatening family separation? Or the embedding of immigration officials in local authority 'no recourse to public funds' (NRPF) teams? Excellent practice is evident across the social work profession, but it is clear that the fear of deportation and family separation is increasingly being weaponised to prevent people from attempting to access services.

It is timely to remind ourselves of the International Federation of Social Workers' (IFSW) global definition of social work:

Social work is a practice-based profession and an academic discipline that promotes social change and development, social cohesion, and the empowerment and liberation of people. Principles of social justice, human rights, collective responsibility and respect for diversities are central to social work. Underpinned by theories of social work, social sciences, humanities and indigenous knowledge, social work engages people and structures to address life challenges and enhance wellbeing. The above definition may be amplified at national and/or regional levels. (IFSW 2014)

The International Association of Schools of Social Work (IASSW) also reminds us that, as a profession, we have a responsibility to promote social justice and equality, to challenge discrimination and to maintain (and defend) our professional integrity (IASSW 2018). Is it possible to marry the 'promotion of human rights', 'respect for diversity' and 'access to equitable resources' (IASSW 2018) with social work complicity in welfare restriction, used as an instrument of immigration control? By bringing together the myriad of voices that form this book, we hope to amplify another version of social work – one that is committed to social and economic justice.

We can start this journey by creating a lively and critical conversation on social work across borders, and by forming professional coalitions committed to ethical practice. This will arm us with the theory and skills to confront the challenge of practising social work in an environment that is not just hostile to migrants, but hostile to the very notions of care and solidarity that underpin our work. The Docs Not Cops[4] and Schools ABC[5] campaigns are brilliant examples of professional resistance to advancing immigration enforcement. Both campaigns take an ethical position, prioritising need over compliance with the hostile environment. They raise their professional voices and engage in campaigning work, to defend their profession and the rights of patients and pupils. Lessons can be taken from this, to inform and support social work practice as the pressure to collude inevitably intensifies.

This book, then, is about defending the rights of migrants *and* defending the values that underpin social work: it is about defending our right to care. Reni Eddo Lodge, in her fantastic educational podcast *About Race*, reminds us of the voices of the Queensland Aboriginal activist group: 'If you have come here to help me, you are wasting your time. But if you have come because your liberation is bound up with mine, then let us work together' (Queensland Aboriginal activist group, cited in Lodge 2018). Defending the rights of asylum seekers, refugees and migrants, then, is just as much about defending the autonomy of our profession to deliver services to all who need it, as it is about opposing immigration control. While we are keen to acknowledge the harms being caused by political systems that rely on the 'othering' of migrants to justify a politic of inequality and competition, we are also keen to celebrate a profession that is dedicated to, and importantly *skilled* to, challenge this agenda. As Suryia Nayak asks us in her chapter Black Feminist Diaspora Spaces of Social Work Critical Reflexivity:

---

4   www.docsnotcops.co.uk
5   www.schoolsabc.net

How can a politics of location (Boyce Davies 1994 p.153), where feelings, in the practice of social work, refuse to be dis-placed, dis-membered and dis-located but are asserted to the foreground as information and as intelligence, serve as a resource? How can social work provide human-rights-based and empathy-based advocacy for service users if it cannot provide this for itself?

The chapters that follow are a celebration of critical thinking and practices of solidarity and are rich with examples of the theories and skills needed to navigate social work at 'border spaces'. They are interwoven with the stories of those with lived experience of seeking refuge in the UK, foregrounding the humanity of practitioners and those they seek to support, as they collectively battle oppressive political agendas.

Following the interview with **Lynn King**, co-founder of Social Workers Without Borders, the opening chapters powerfully explore how cultural and political climates can work to exclude, and dehumanise, particular groups of migrants, and they call for collective responses to address this. **Suryia Nayak** begins with a clarion call for social workers to recognise the inherent racism in the ways that migrant bodies are constructed. Writing from a black feminist perspective, she calls on the profession to make a choice about where it stands in relation to people positioned in border spaces, and to develop a language of solidarity rather than one of exclusion. In her chapter on austerity, **Lucy Mort** gives us a similarly compelling account of how economic inequality and the 'hostile environment' create precarious everyday lives for certain migrants. She argues that practitioners could take strength from a collective, transnational approach that challenges the inequalities which exclude and marginalise.

The potential outcome of such marginalisation is powerfully described by **Rebecca Yeo**, who writes about the death of Kamil Ahmad, a disabled man seeking asylum who was murdered in Bristol in 2016. Rebecca's personal and sometimes harrowing account illustrates how someone can be left unprotected when they are framed as less deserving than others, and invisible to systems designed to support them. These themes of deserving and undeserving are taken up in **Natalia Farmer's** chapter, where she explores how law and policy can create destitution for families left with 'no recourse to public funds'. Drawing on her own research she asks highly pertinent questions about the role of social work in this context and the potentially oppressive use of professional authority. In the following chapter, **Jen Ang** also describes the importance of practitioners understanding the possibilities and limits of the law, as she considers the legal frameworks which shape social work with children and young people who migrate.

The middle section of the book explores particular areas of social work practice with the diverse range of people who migrate into the UK. **Anna Gupta** skilfully explores the role of the social worker with separated young people. She identifies the ways in which relationship-based work, and a human-rights approach, can positively impact on young people's lives, but she also calls for practitioners to challenge discriminatory practice when it occurs. **Jude Boyles, Anna Turner** and **Katy Tolman** similarly adopt a human rights lens to consider their work with people who have survived torture. They take a strengths-based approach that resists framing survivors as 'victims', and argue for reflective use of power which reduces, rather than reinforces, inequality and difference.

The book explicitly calls on expertise from professions and practices outside social work, as community-based and voluntary sector organisations boast a wealth of knowledge, expertise and innovation when it comes to working across borders. **Hannah Berry**, founder of the Manchester-based Gender Participation Unit, describes a successful, group-based intervention for asylum-seeking women and explores how this way of working enables women to use their voice and take an active role in when and how they access support. **Rachael Bee** developed a voluntary organisation that hosts homeless migrants and she has been a host herself. In her chapter, she writes passionately about the need to retain a value-base in social work, reminding us that social work has always been a contested profession and that other approaches are possible.

The final chapters offer important perspectives on social work practice from colleagues within other agencies. There are examples of positive work here, but also critiques of some practice approaches. These critiques may sometimes be hard to hear but they have to be acknowledged if we are going to address them. In her chapter on detention, **Jo Vincett** offers a rare lens on the hidden world of the UK Immigration Removal Centre and the experiences of those detained there. She highlights the emotional impact of being detained without timescale, arguing that well-trained and well-supported mentors are needed to support those being detained. **Elaine Ortiz** reflects on her experiences of advocating for young people going through age assessments as an appropriate adult and advocates for social workers to rethink their role in the age-assessment process. **Annemarie Morsch's** chapter considers the ways in which good practice with interpreters can be supported and undermined by organisational cultures, individual practice and power-dynamics within each relationship. She challenges us to examine more robustly our practice in this area, if we are to better hear the voices of service users. The book ends with some concluding remarks from the editors, pulling out the major themes and laying the foundations for further work, both theoretical and practical, to progress social work without borders.

We are hugely grateful to all the contributors who took the time to share their knowledge and skills within these chapters, and thank them for sharing both their struggles and their motivations to continue with this complex work. We would like to particularly thank the people who shared their personal stories of migration, and who told us about their lives in the UK in the hope that it would help social workers and others to stand with them in their fight for more easily liveable lives.

References

Farmer, N. (2017) '"No Recourse to Public Funds", insecure immigration status and destitution: the role of social work.' *Critical and Radical Social Work*, 5, 3, 357–367.

George, A. and Abi-Aad, G. (2017) *Looked after Children – Children in Care*. June. Accessed 28/11/2018 at: www.kpho.org.uk/__data/assets/pdf_file/0006/71691/LAC-Children-in-Care.pdf.

Hayes, D. and Humphries, B. (2004) *Social Work, Immigration and Asylum: Debates, Dilemmas and Ethical Issues for Social Work and Social Care Practice*. London: Jessica Kingsley Publishers.

IASSW (International Association of Schools of Social Work) (2018) *Global Social Work Statement of Ethical Principles*. Accessed 26/11/2018 at: www.iassw-aiets.org/wp-content/uploads/2018/04/Global-Social-Work-Statement-of-Ethical-Principles-IASSW-27-April-2018-1.pdf.

IFSW (International Federation of Social Workers) (2014) 'Global Definition of Social Work.' Accessed 26/11/2018 at: www.ifsw.org/what-is-social-work/global-definition-of-social-work.

Immigration and Asylum Act (1999) Accessed 28/11/2018 at: www.legislation.gov.uk/ukpga/1999/33/contents.

King, L. and Grant, K. (2016) 'Meet the social workers supporting refugees in Calais.' Accessed 25/11/2018 at: www.communitycare.co.uk/2016/08/24/meet-social-workers-supporting-refugees-calais.

Lodge, R. (2018) *About Race: The Big Question*. Accessed 26/11/2018 at: www.aboutracepodcast.com/9-the-big-question.

Robinson, K. and Masocha, S. (2017) 'Divergent practices in statutory and voluntary-sector settings? Social work with asylum seekers.' *British Journal of Social Work*, 47, 5, 1517–1533.

UNHCR (Office of the United Nations High Commissioner for Refugees) (no date) 'Operational Portal: Refugee Situations.' Accessed 28/11/2018 at: https://data2.unhcr.org/en/situations/mediterranean.

Women's Refugee Commission (no date) 'Women and Girls in the European Refugee Crisis.' Accessed 28/11/2018 at: www.womensrefugeecommission.org/gbv/resources/1358-refugee-women-europe.

Wroe, L. (2015) 'Social workers have a duty to speak up about the humanitarian crisis in Calais.' Accessed 25/11/2018 at: www.theguardian.com/social-care-network/2015/aug/04/social-workers-humanitarian-crisis-calais.

Wroe, L. (2018) '"It really is about telling people who asylum seekers really are, because we are human like everybody else". Negotiating victimhood in refugee advocacy work.' *Discourse and Society*, 29, 3, 324–343.

Chapter 2

Social Work Without Borders

An Interview with Lynn King, Founding Member of the UK Social Work Charity Social Workers Without Borders

Introduction

In 2015, resulting from the ongoing conflict in Syria, the Arab Spring and escalating global inequality and political crises, an unprecedented number of people crossed the borders of the EU to claim asylum in Europe. Notably, an increasing number were children, and many of those who made it across Europe to the border of the UK often found themselves trapped at the UK border in France, at the now infamous, unofficial Calais refugee camp. Before the camp was demolished in late 2016, it was estimated that over 1600 (*The Telegraph* 2016) were living in the camp, with minimal oversight or support from the British and French authorities.

Social Workers Without Borders (SWWB) is a UK charity established in early 2016 by a small group of social workers responding to these events at the French and UK border. In this interview, the editors of the book explore why and how SWWB was set up, what the challenges were to practising social work in the unofficial refugee camp in Calais and, crucially, what theories and skills for practice SWWB has drawn on to establish its work.

Lauren: How did UK social workers become involved in Calais? And how did this initial involvement lead to the establishment of Social Workers Without Borders?

Note: Ideas and responses to the interview were formed by Lynn King and Lyndsey Kramer, who also volunteers with SWWB.

Lynn: When myself, and my colleague Louise Morgan, first went to the Calais refugee camp it was February 2016. We didn't have a plan other than to raise our professional voice of concern about what was happening in Calais, based on what we had read in the papers. The Calais refugee camp in northern France had become known as 'the Jungle' and was deemed to be an unofficial settlement. There were an estimated 4000 refugees living in the camp by February 2016, including an undocumented number of unaccompanied children, yet there was no effective statutory social services response provision from the French or British state.

Although it may seem obvious that any human being living in these conditions would be affected physically, emotionally and socially, we felt that the truly appalling incompatibility of this situation with basic principles of human rights was not causing sufficient levels of outrage or action on behalf of the social work profession. At this point, we were thinking of the International Federation of Social Workers global definition of social work (see Chapter 1) and our commitment to social justice. We also thought about the work by Williams and Briskman (2015, p.3), which proposes that 'addressing contraventions of human rights and social justice issues demands an emotional connection with the nature of injustice'. It really was this emotional response to the injustice in Calais, this 'moral outrage', that fuelled us and built the momentum for the work we went on to do.

We found it difficult, initially, to slot into the network of informal provision at the camp as there was definitely some mistrust and suspicion of social workers. It was our view at the time that this was probably related to the negative public perception of social workers but, also connected to that, that social work had become increasingly disconnected from the communities it operates in.

To counter the initial negative response, we decided to keep coming back to the camp, to show consistency in our desire to work alongside the existing non-governmental organisations and volunteer networks. We also altered our use of social work terminology. It really felt as if this was causing a barrier to partnership working, that the language of social work might seem elitist to other volunteers and, not only that, it would likely be incomprehensible to the people living in the camp. Talking about 'empowerment' and 'seeking a dialogue with refugees' was not only jargonistic but it also jarred with the reality of people's lives there.

What do we mean by empowerment in such circumstances, and how would it be achieved? Could we not just say that we wanted to talk with people in the camp to understand their lives and needs, to figure out together how to best help, and to ensure that we told their stories to our colleagues in the UK who didn't understand and sometimes doubted them? We discussed this during the course of our weekly visits and decided we needed to create a clear, stripped-back language. This required a group analysis of our understanding of what 'social work' meant in the circumstances we faced. It was not actually an easy task. Many of us relied on a language that was based on our academic learning, and practice environments that had become over-laced with jargon about service provision and service users.

We wanted to ensure that we were helping practically and materially in the camp. When we first arrived, we gave out our contact details to the volunteer legal shelter and offered our support. We went to the camp every weekend and we helped out at the Jungle Books Kids Space, a makeshift shelter in keeping with the rest of the camp, that had been set up by volunteers to provide a space for the children at the camp to play and eat. We volunteered in the Jungle Books space and did activities with the kids, helping out the other volunteers to take the pressure off them. We wanted to know what was happening directly from the frontline and to understand the context for the lives of people in the camps. We referred to the work by Nelson, Price and Zubrzycki (2017), who seek to reconnect social workers with the key professional values of social justice and human rights. They propose that, to apply this ethic to work with unaccompanied asylum-seeking children, we need to develop a critical awareness of the cumulative impact of hostile discourses on the lives of migrant children. They also remind us that we need to engage with change on a social level. By having a presence in the camp, we were able to feed back to our social work colleagues in the UK about what we were seeing there.

We drew on ideas from Friere's (1970) critical pedagogy, to think about how we positioned ourselves as an organisation. With no resources and no jurisdiction as statutory social workers, we were forced to reposition ourselves in alignment with the volunteers and residents at the camp and, importantly, we did this by speaking out against the injustice people were facing, as opposed to coming in as charitable, benevolent or professional helpers. It was this solidarity approach that emerged as central to the ethos of SWWB. We wanted to highlight the conditions in the camp, not by focusing on the victimisation of individuals and families, but by shining a light on the lack of political will to safeguard people arriving at the UK border. The British and French governments needed to be held to account for abandoning the needs and rights of children and families on their territory.

Months later, after we had been travelling to the camp from the UK every weekend, we got a call from the Calais legal shelter asking us to be involved in some 'best interest' assessments for family reunification claims under Dublin III.[1] These were the cases that weren't straightforward. For example, there were problems proving the children's identity or family connection. Lots of young people didn't have the right paperwork to meet the requirements of the bureaucratic process, or they had cousins in the UK and not close family members. The Calais legal shelter contacted us, as they needed additional input from social workers to make a case under Dublin III. And that's where we started.

Lauren: Was there an assessment model in place for SWWB volunteers to complete these assessments? Were there challenges to conducting these assessments in a refugee camp, assumedly a very different context to where you had been used to practising social work?

Lynn: The legal shelter didn't have a pro forma for conducting 'best interest' assessments. I had worked in adult services in the UK, so I developed an assessment template based on what I knew from adult social work and included domains relating to health, education and so on. Then I tailored it to what I knew would be the concerns for the children in the camp. I added a few prompts and a social work rationale, and summary section at the end so that a clear conclusion could be put forward. I was working as a best interest assessor in adult services, so I was keen to set out how we would evidence our assessment, referencing both the young person's voice but also cross-referencing with other organisations in the camp that had been working with the young person.

We began using this assessment template and then suddenly we had to do a lot more assessments very quickly. Just as the camp was being demolished, a UK legal firm, Duncan Lewis, approached us and asked us to carry out assessments for the young people they were representing in the camp. They needed an assessment format to be drafted that evening! I added in the Convention of the Rights of the Child (CRC) articles, for example the best interests of the child (Article 3), health (Article 24), education (Article 28), emotional and behavioural development (Articles 23, 31), identity (Article 27), family and social relationships (Articles 18, 21, 22),

---

1   Dublin III is an EU regulation that determines the state responsible for deciding an asylum claim lodged in an EU member state, Iceland, Norway, Switzerland or Liechtenstein. The current Dublin III Regulation was adopted in June 2013 as Regulation (EU) No.604/2013.

self-care, parenting provision of basic care, ensuring safety, providing emotional warmth, guidance and boundaries and provision of stimulation (Articles 18, 19, 20, 21, 22). We then cross-referenced that with what we had already in the assessment pro forma. As we went on we have adapted the assessment a bit, based on feedback from our social work volunteers, but on the whole the assessment pro forma has remained as it was in those early days.

I used the *UNHCR Guidelines on Determining the Best Interest of the Child* to create the assessment framework and that was crucial for shaping what exactly it was that was being assessed. We had to adapt the guidance slightly as we weren't able, for example, to pull together a panel of decision makers – it wasn't possible in that crisis situation. But we followed the other guidelines, for example ensuring that it was professional practitioners who were conducting and overseeing the assessments.

At that point, the young people were in a camp with no parental supervision, just the support networks they had drawn up around them, in horrendous circumstances and with no support from French or UK social services, and they didn't want to stay in France as a result of that experience. The UNHCR Guidelines (2008, p.70) remind us that:

> For a child who is severely distressed as a result of past events, such as through serious violations of their fundamental rights, no decision that could cause even more distress to the child can be considered to be in their best interests.

So, really, most of the time it wasn't difficult to come to a decision about the best interest of that young person. If you looked at the options of the young person coming to the UK on the bottom of a lorry, or coming legally to the UK, it was always going to be the latter.

Lauren: As a social worker for adults, how did you navigate this new context, not only the refugee camp but in the work with children, in an acutely stressful and rapidly changing environment?

Lynn: If I had been on my own I wouldn't have been able to make that transition, but the very first social worker who came with me was a social worker in an unaccompanied asylum-seeking children's (UASC) team. We discussed what was happening in Calais and then very quickly, within a month, we were going to the camp one day every weekend with a car full of social workers from across the UK.

The volunteers who came with us were from children's teams, some were from adult teams, some were from disabled children's teams, child-in-need teams, child protection teams. It was incredible to have the support, and to share ideas for practice, between such a diverse group of professionals. I had never had the opportunity to work with such a wide range of social workers. We had the assessment pro formas with us and we would discuss them and look at what could be added and refined; we discussed practice and theory and skills in the car on the way over to Calais. I was able to draw on an incredible body of knowledge from all of the volunteers! On one occasion when we were going to do an assessment, there was a social worker from an adult social care team and she was worried about doing the assessment as social worker coming from adult services, but collectively we talked it through with her and she did the assessment. Not only that, but she stayed in touch with the young man, engaged with the French social worker at the accommodation centre he had been dispersed to, and between her and the French social worker they supported the young man to claim asylum in France. It really is amazing what social workers can achieve when they have the confidence and support of others!

Lauren: Clearly, SWWB volunteers had to quickly identify, learn and practise a new set of ideas and skills in relation to their social work practice. What were the major differences between practising as a social worker in the UK and applying these skills and ideas in Calais? What did you need to do to work across this difference?

Lynn: At first, we though that it was incredibly liberating, and that we were working outside the state and were free from any sort of bureaucracy! This is kind of a bit laughable, now that we've spent weeks doing General Data Protection Regulation (GDPR) policies.

Quite quickly, we realised that in order to conduct the assessment work we had been asked to do we were going to need some practice guidance, policies on how we planned to work, data protection registration, a secure database for storing assessments and so on. At this time, the organisation was growing and we joined forces with other social work groups who were trying to raise the profile of what was happening in Calais and at borders across Europe. We needed to start to formalise the organisation and we spoke to the British Association of Social Workers (BASW) about how to do this. We needed to know if it was legal for us to practise as social workers outside the UK. What guidance did we need to follow? At the same time, we consulted the Health Care Professions Council (HCPC), which advised us that we were able to do what we were doing as long as it was legal and in line with our registration.

We took this on board but we were still tentative; we didn't want to take any risks with our volunteers that might cause problems for their registration or careers. We contacted Lawyers Without Borders, which advised us that practising as social workers in France was a grey area, as we were working in Calais as volunteers, not professionals, and the assessments we were carrying out were for the UK, not the French, courts and the Home Office. Eventually, we were advised that on this basis it was within the law and within the boundaries of our professional registration to complete this work and we didn't need to be registered as social workers in France. It took a long time to confirm this and that was one of the major challenges.

Lauren: What did you have to do to formalise SWWB's work and to build a social work charity in the UK?

Lynn: We began the process of establishing ourselves as a charity by seeking guidance from a number of different organisations that support groups wanting to form as charities. The initial feedback that we received was that they couldn't believe we were already doing so much! By this time, we had also begun delivering seminars at universities about our work, we had contributed to some local authority training for social workers, had sealed a book contract to document our work and pull together examples of best practice in social work across borders, and we had been engaging in campaigns around the treatment of immigration detainees at Brook House and a number of other issues.

Like a lot of the organisations working in the Calais camp, we were responding to an immediate need. We started by doing what was needed, and then we backtracked and thought about how to structure and organise what we were doing. Knowing what I know now, there is a way to set up a charity and this is not it! But, like all the groups in the camp, we were responding to a situation that we felt needed an immediate response, so I wouldn't change that – we needed to do it that way. When it came to formalising the organisation we registered with the Charity Commission as a charitable incorporated organisation, we registered with data protection, created a secure website, wrote numerous policies on safeguarding, the media, volunteers and so on (there are always new ones!), purchased public liability and professional indemnity insurance, formalised our recording using a secure database for client information, set up secure email accounts and generated a seemingly endless number of passwords! It really felt as if we started to grow up as an organisation.

Now that the Calais camp is largely dispersed, we predominantly work in the UK. At the time that the camp was being demolished, we were working a lot with Duncan Lewis, and the firm continued to contact us to request best interest assessments for children and families in the UK. We also began to receive requests from other solicitors who told us that they were not able to access pro-bono social work assessments from anywhere else. These were particularly required where families were not entitled to legal aid; for example, those who were appealing decision on their immigration status based on their Human Rights Act (1989), Article 8 right to private and family life. So we were filling a gap that existed on the grounds of very hostile immigration rules.

By August 2018 we had completed 31 assessments in the UK. We are now working with Bail for Immigration Detainees (BID), providing assessments for families where a parent is facing deportation, and Kids In Need of Defence (KIND), which provides legal advocacy for young people who have been in the UK for over seven years. We carry out the same kind of assessment we did previously, using largely the same format. It can be more complicated, as sometimes the children are known to statutory services and there may be ongoing concerns, so we're liaising with our colleagues in statutory services to complete these assessments and this has normally always been a good experience of working across agencies.

Completing the assessments in these contexts has required consideration of what the remit of our assessment is, and what we can and cannot say based on the limitations of our involvement with the family. For example, we don't make recommendations about who a child should live with or what the contact arrangements might be; our assessment is focused on the likely impact to that child or children of a parent being removed from the UK and no longer able to sustain a relationship with that young person. We've had to be really clear, to ourselves and others, about the parameters of what we are doing, as SWWB.

Lauren: Given that there is evidently such a high level of need for these assessments, why do you think there is no statutory provision for this work, when young people's families are being separated due to immigration decisions?

Lynn: That's what we've been asking ourselves too! The cases we work on for BID, where a parent is detained with a view to deportation, statutory services may submit a report to the courts but this will detail where the child should live, it does not comment on the impact on that young person of a parent being deported. That's where our assessment fills the gap. That is solely what we're focusing on, giving that issue consideration where it is otherwise not being considered. We have worked on cases where whole families face removal – they're not known to statutory services and there is no requirement for statutory services to be involved regarding the impact on the children if the family is removed. We plan to join with BID to raise the profile of this issue, that when children are being removed from the UK by the Home Office, they need to commission an independent best interest assessment before the removal takes place.

Lauren: What opportunities does SWWB offer for social work to be practised in a value-based way, one that can contribute to ideas for transforming and expanding how we think about what it means to do social work?

Lynn: SWWB is an organisation of social workers shaping our own practice. I often read articles or new stories in Community Care, for example, about 'reclaiming' and 'transforming' social work but often this is still within a managerialist model. What we decided is that 'social work without borders' means not only working across national borders, or those imposed by immigration control, but also transcending those borders imposed by liberalist ideologies and market-led approaches. It's quite a leap to move away from that way of thinking and it is great to be able to have those discussions within SWWB as part of how we operate as an organisation.

An example from today, as we conduct this interview, is that we have decided not to take part in a social work award event due to issues around unethical sponsorship. We were able to make that decision from an ethical standpoint based on the values we have agreed as an organisation. We didn't have to think about publicity or funders, that didn't factor, we just made a decision in the steering group based on our ethical position and then decided how we would communicate that. With regard to the referrals we decide to take, there is an element of resources, because we only have a finite number of volunteers and case coordinators, but there's no consideration about whether legal aid funding is available or whether we will do it for free. We are able to work with very few funds as long as we have enough money to reimburse our volunteers for their costs. We can make decisions based on need.

Now that we're a registered charity we have four trustees, three of whom are social workers and one is a lawyer we worked with initially in Calais.

We are looking to expand our trustee committee and to include members with experience of seeking refuge. We now have 18 steering group members, both social workers and social work students, and decisions are made using a consensus decision-making model. There are certain decisions that the trustees might be accountable for, but most decisions take place via consensus with the trustees and the steering group members, and three of the trustees are also steering group members. It works well.

Going back to an earlier question, regarding how statutory practice and practice within SWWB mould together, it has made me question whether or not social workers should be employed directly by local authorities, or whether social work should operate as a more autonomous profession. This is an ongoing debate regarding the autonomy of the profession in general. It has made me very aware of how much of my statutory practice is governed by non-social workers, or people who do not think and act in alignment with social work values. This is reflected in our assessments and our policies. The assessments we use in adult services involve a lot of tick boxes and are prescriptive, as is the eligibility criteria it in the Care Act 2014. It becomes increasingly difficult to justify the work you are trying to do with an individual or family, as there can be raft of funding panels just to put one foot in front of the other. That is what we are liberated from when we practise within SWWB. If we want to do more with an intervention we can, we can have those discussions and look at what the need is. I don't know if that could ever happen within statutory services?

Practising in this way, I feel confident and competent again as a social worker, and I am proud to be social worker for the first time in my life. I don't mumble any more when people ask what I do for a living, I can look at them directly and say that I am a social worker, because I am proud of what we have done and what we can do.

References

Care Act (2014) Accessed 28/11/2018 at: https://services.parliament.uk/bills/2013-14/care.html.

Freire, P. (1970) *Pedagogy of the Oppressed*. London: Penguin Books.

Human Rights Act (1989) Accessed 13/05/2019 at: https://www.legislation.gov.uk/ukpga/1998/42/schedule/1/part/I/chapter/7.

Nelson, D., Price, E. and Zubrzycki, J. (2017) 'Critical social work with unaccompanied asylum-seeking young people: Restoring hope, agency and meaning for the client and worker.' *International Social Work*, 60, 3, 601–613.

Telegraph, The (2016) 'Nearly 700 Jungle kids expected to apply for British asylum as remaining 1,600 leave Calais'. 2 November. Accessed 27/11/2018 at: www.telegraph.co.uk/news/2016/11/02/last-group-of-calais-refugee-children-evacuated-from-camp.

UN Convention on the Rights of the Child (1989) Accessed 13/05/2019 at: https://downloads.unicef.org.uk/wp-content/uploads/2010/05/UNCRC_united_nations_convention_on_the_rights_of_the_child.pdf?_ga=2.11957300.16 76377525.1556805005-1660326016.1553782227.

UNHCR (2008) *UNHCR Guidelines on Determining the Best Interest of the Child.* Accessed 27/11/2018 at: www.unhcr.org/4566b16b2.pdf.

Williams, C. and Briskman, L. (2015) 'Reviving social work through moral outrage.' *Critical and Radical Social Work,* 3, 1, 3–17.

Narrative 2
Learning from Mary

The experience with social services was very difficult for my daughter and me; it seemed like they were against me. As I didn't have the right papers, I didn't think the social workers were truthful with me and they didn't give me back the important documents that I needed. I did live in a house, which was okay, until I was threatened by a male in the house who said he would kill me. Social services didn't do anything, they just said they would document it. I called [a local support group] and they came and supported me by taking me to the police station. Nothing changed. I really needed help. He did the same to another lady and she was removed and given another house. I was scared so I decided to take my daughter and myself away from the house. I was asked to leave and authorities saw it as me making my daughter and myself intentionally homeless. My daughter is vulnerable and has a learning difficulty – she is deaf. At this point [another charity] stopped supporting my daughter. I now stay with my niece and my daughter stays with a friend. My daughter and I have been separated by the circumstances.

There is racism in social services. They like some people and not others. I feel like my daughter and I have been discriminated against. My daughter stays alone inside my friend's house. They are trying to accommodate my daughter, but not me. I am advocating for us to stay together.

The Home Office says I am lying about my asylum claim. The priest knows I am not lying. My daughter can't hear and can't talk. She is really vulnerable. The doctor wants to keep my daughter here and send me back to [my country of origin]. I felt like she was after something. She said I was bossy. I didn't feel safe in my house, there were lots of people coming and going and everyone had keys.

There are consequences when certain professionals write things down and information is shared and other people see it. If people, for example doctors, share the wrong information, lots of damage can be caused. I was accused of stealing the doctor's wedding ring; this was said to cause confusion. The doctor is spoiling our names. I tried to book an appointment with the doctor, but was told the GP is not available. The doctor is always unavailable and the practice never called me back to arrange a new appointment. I never received any call to rearrange an appointment. I don't know why they can't arrange an appointment with another doctor; they refuse to see me.

I feel down and I take medicine for depression. When I went to the doctors they said I don't have depression and I am lying. I told them I used to hear voices. My daughter now sits and cries. I called [a mental health support service] who said to go to my GP and gave me other places to contact for help. When I called the GP when my daughter was really sick they never looked at her. I am not taking any medication at the moment because the doctors say I am lying. If I hear a voice I go and check who is talking. I am managing my own mental health. I don't recognise the voices, I hear people talking against me but I can't see the people. I have never been referred to any mental health services to help me with the voices I hear. I have type 2 diabetes and at one point my blood pressure was really high. I take tablets for this.

There are lots of things that are making my life difficult. There are a lot of bad things against me. I came here in 2007. I have appealed my immigration status. I made a fresh claim and social services would not give me new evidence.

There is a lack of listening and understanding from professionals. Family should not be separated, but people are trying to separate my daughter and me. People are treated differently and our rights have been neglected. I would never go to [local group] again. They did nothing, that's why I stopped going there.

This country, according to the Geneva Convention, says everyone should be safe. I came here to this country to help my brother. I have been asked to return to my country, but it is not safe. There is nothing there and people are killing each other.

Social services have failed to help us (my daughter and I). I ask myself why I came to [this city]. I am not coping. It's getting worse and worse.

Chapter 3

Black Feminist Diaspora Spaces of Social Work Critical Reflexivity

Suryia Nayak

Working with issues of migration brings social work practitioners into close proximity with the predicaments and possibilities of position, location and residence where:

> The Politics of location brings forward a whole host of identifications and associations around concepts of place, placement, dis-placement; location, dis-location; memberment, dis-memberment; citizenship, alienness; boundaries, barriers, transportations; peripheries, cores and centers. (Boyce Davies 1994, p.153)

This chapter offers a black feminist model of social work critical reflexivity that draws on Brah's (1996) concept of 'diaspora space'. Configured on the predicaments of place, location and boundaries, black feminist diaspora spaces of critical reflexivity trouble comfortable, taken-for-granted professional territories of social work practice. The proposal is that the content of social work with dis-placed, dis-located and dis-membered people and communities provides the basis for a method of black feminist diaspora spaces of social work reflexivity. Diasporic journeys are purposeful, and critical reflection needs to share that same sense of purposefulness, and as such:

> if this is the case, we will have to do something quite extraordinary: Will have to go to great lengths. We cannot go on as usual. We cannot pivot the center. We cannot be moderate. We will have to be willing to stand up and say no with our combined spirits, our collective intellects, and our many bodies. (Davis 2016, p.145)

Black feminist diasporic spaces of reflexivity recognise and track the mutually constitutive relation between method (the how) and content (the what). Therefore, based on the fact that '[op]pressed groups are frequently placed in a situation of being listened to only if they frame their ideas in the language that is familiar to and comfortable for a dominant group' (Hill Collins 2000, p.vii), this chapter only cites black feminist scholarship. Black feminist scholarship has and continues to be dis-placed, dis-located and dis-membered within social work education, practice and research. It is by no coincidence that black women social workers, black women, and girl service users have and continue to be dis-placed, dis-located and dis-membered within social work, including social work education, practice, theory and research. In defiant affirmation of black women social workers and black women and girl recipients of social work, this chapter places the activism of black feminist theory as central to social work without borders. Black women have a proximity to borders that makes black feminism particularly relevant for the construction of diasporic spaces of reflection; black women are positioned in the borderlands of oppressive social constructions. Black women are limited by bordered thinking and are discriminated by borders of prejudice. Thus, it is not surprising that the concept of borders and boundaries frame many black feminist texts, for example: *Borderlands/La Frontera: The New Mestiza* by Gloria Anzaldúa (2007); *Feminism Without Borders: Decolonizing Theory, Practicing Solidarity* by Chandra Talpade Mohanty (2003); *Elsewhere, Within Here: Immigration, Refugeeism and the Boundary Event* by Trinh T. Minh-Ha (2011). For further examples of black feminist scholars and scholarship that develop the theory of location to function as methodology see Nayak (2017).

Black feminist concepts of the interdependency of theory and practice troubles constructed borders between practice and academic learning, which plague social work and form blockades to rigorous reflexivity. In other words, framing the notion of praxis as the co-production of theory and practice enables a social work epistemology constituted in and through lived experience. Stated another way, black feminism is a methodological theory born out of the intersectional experiences of racism in order to contest intersectional experiences of racism. Boyce Davies (2013, p.6) explains her approach as the 'move between the autobiographical and the conceptual, the experiential and the theoretical, in order to disrupt the logic of exclusionary academic discourse that often denies the personal'.

If the effects of macro social injustice are felt through the micro aggressions of social injustice in the minutiae of exhausting day-to-day hardships of lived experiences, it follows that a black feminist model of social work critical reflexive praxis for liberation from these hardships cannot collude with 'the logic of exclusionary academic discourse' (Boyce Davies 2013, p.6). The challenge for social work is how to inhabit the borderlands or 'diaspora space' between being agents of social control and agents of social justice. The challenge amounts to social work choosing, for it is a choice, whether to stand by waiting for liberation to happen or to be instrumental in the struggle. In short, social work 'cannot wait to start working on those problems until the great day in the future when the revolution somehow miraculously is accomplished' (Beale 2005, p.109).

Border consciousness

The situation of social work with migration and diaspora shines a light on the trauma of borders on multiple intersecting geo-political, structural, conceptual, psychological and physical axes. Paradoxically, the process of bumping up against borders demonstrates their existence, but conversely, facilitates a conscious proximity that can enable a deconstruction of borders to open up spaces of border consciousness as the basis for anti-oppressive social work practice, for example opening up consciousness about the ways in which the representations of 'the migrant' and diasporic experiences mirror aspects of the representation of those who are positioned in the margins of society regardless of nationality. Thus, the experience of being silenced, invisiblised, vilified, an outsider, not belonging and being stripped of social assets characterises the experience of many disenfranchised national-born citizens, who may then dare to have the audacity to embark on a journey of social mobility. The vicarious trauma experienced by social workers in working with the inhumanity of migration creates a hypervigilance of borders that can be put to use in recognising, rather than disavowing, hidden and taken-for-granted borders that scaffold oppressive discursive practices. The work of black feminist diasporic critical reflexivity is the arduous task of seeking out and deconstructing our own internalised borders. Here, Mohanty's work on 'feminism without borders' reveals the complexity of the task, whereby, in regards to social work practice, the deconstruction of borders, or social work without borders, is not an argument for a 'border-less' social work. Mohanty (2003, p.2) explains that:

> Feminism without borders is not the same as 'border-less' feminism.
> It acknowledges the fault lines, conflicts, differences, fears, and

containment that borders represent. It acknowledges that there is no one sense of a border, that the lines between and through nations, races, classes, sexualities, religions and disabilities, are real – and that a feminism without borders must envision change and social justice work across these lines of demarcation and division…in order to draw attention to the tension between the simultaneous plurality and narrowness of borders and the emancipatory potential of crossing through, with, and over these borders in our everyday lives.

Social work has to inhabit the tension whereby 'the high wall that keeps out is the same wall that keeps in' (Minh-ha 2011, p.3). Translated into practice, examples of these tensions can be found in the wall between an individualistic and collective social work approach; between pathology and context; between a single or intersectional axis of heritage, legacy and time; between thinking and feeling; and between provider and recipient of social services. Social work would do well to adopt the black feminist approach of:

> La mestiza [who] constantly has to shift out of habitual formations; from convergent thinking, analytical reasoning that tends to use rationality to move towards a single goal (a Western mode), to divergent thinking, characterized by movement away from set patterns and goals and towards a more whole perspective, one that includes rather than excludes. (Anzaldúa 2007, p.101, emphasis in original)

Anzaldúa's concept of mestiza consciousness forms the bedrock of the black feminist diaspora model of critical reflexivity offered in this chapter. It is a model that many black women social workers will find a home in; however, to leave it at that would be to fall into the trap of territorialisation that constructs insider/outsider positions. Black feminist models of social work are a 'diaspora space' for all anti-oppressive practitioners whereby 'diaspora space' (as distinct from the concept of diaspora) is 'inhabited' not only by diasporic subjects but equally by those who are constructed and represented as 'indigenous' (Brah 1996, p.16). In black feminist diaspora spaces of critical reflexivity, space is more than a physical environment; space is a process. Black feminist diaspora spaces of critical reflexivity are flexible processes that function on simultaneous temporal and spatial dimensions; diasporic spaces inevitably disrupt and (re)construct constitutive contexts. Black feminist diaspora spaces of critical reflexivity create 'a ground that belongs to no one, not even the "creator"' (Minh-ha 1991, p.71) in order to destabilise problematic positions of provider/recipient. To be clear, the invocation of fluidity in destabilisation does not amount to an insider/ outsider indeterminacy that equates to one foot in and one foot out of the door; anti-oppressive social work requires full commitment with corresponding risks, sacrifices and costs.

A black feminist diaspora model of critical reflexivity

The logics of black feminist social work critical reflexivity are as follows:

- The logic of the collective and connectivity rather than western individualised logics that constitute social work casework approaches and interventions. The logic of the collective needs to underpin the interlinking of specialised social service provision, such as mental health, children and families, disability and older people. Davis (2016, p.127) reminds us that 'there is one principle, we should remember. This principle is associated with Dr. Martin Luther King and should be the slogan of all our movements: "Justice is indivisible. Injustice anywhere is a threat to justice everywhere."'

- The logic of time, that resists the 'historical amnesia that keeps us working to invent the wheel every time we have to go to the store for bread' (Lorde 1980, p.117). The logic of time includes heritage or individual, community, national and racialised gendered histories and ancestral inheritances. The logic of time formulates temporal and societal dimensions as relational to include the importance of intergenerational, ancestral, collective consciousness rather than generational fragmentation.

- The logic of context recognises context as instrumental in the production of the issues, pathologies and impairments that become fastened to individuals, communities and societies. In the logic of context, the attention of social work shifts from casework with individuals and families to casework with contexts: the context of poverty, patriarchy; class, racism, capitalism and oppressive constructions.

- The logic of the erotic is an evidence-based practice 'question of how acutely and fully we can feel in the doing' (Lorde 1978, p.54). The logic of the erotic resists the Descartesian dualism of mind and body and 'the dichotomy between the spiritual and the political' (Lorde 1978, p.56).

The logic of the collective

The aphorism 'there is strength in numbers' points to the weakness of individualism. The idea of strength in numbers points to the reason why survival, growth and resilience is dependent on collective working. On a biological, social, economic, discursive, ideological level, humans are relational. The logic of collectivity sustains the human race on macro and micro dimensions. The relational bonds of human connection are integral to well-being and therefore it makes sense to build a model of reflective practice on a foundation of the collective. The logic of collective interlinking refuses the isolation that prompted Jordan (1976, p.61) to write:

> I know I am not alone. There must be hundreds of other women, maybe thousands, who feel as I do. There may be hundreds of men who want the same drastic things to happen. But how do you hook up with them? How can you interlink your own struggle and goals with these myriad, hypothetical people who are hidden entirely or else concealed by stereotype and/or generalities of 'platform' such as any movement seems to spawn?

Here, Jordan calls for a mode of interlinking that can be the basis for black women social workers to move out from the generality of a profession/ discipline that conceals their worth. Jordan suggests a mode of interlinking that can be the basis for social work interventions, for example, on issues of poverty and domestic violence, whereby service users 'hook' up others who 'want the same drastic things to happen'. Black feminist diaspora spaces of critical reflexivity are where the connections that constitute collectivity can be recognised and joined up. In 'The Transformation of Silence into Language and Action', Lorde (1977) tells us that the principle of Ujima, which characterises the third day of the feast of Kwanza, is 'collective work and responsibility – the decision to build and maintain ourselves and our communities together and to recognize and solve our problems together' (Lorde 1977, p.43).

Here, Lorde juxtaposes the concepts of collective, responsibility and maintaining ourselves, but, and this is the point, Lorde is clear that the togetherness in collective work has to be deliberate in terms of 'the decision to build and maintain'. So, while collective, relational connections are the foundations of attachment, growth and resilience, there is a building and maintaining task to be sustained in a conscious purposeful way. A black feminist diasporic approach to social work critical reflexivity might prompt the following questions:

- How and why do benign discourses of autonomy, independence and self-determination mask the terror of dependency in social work practice? What is so wrong with dependency? If all phenomenon and existence is in a relational interdependency of production and function, then the concept and issue of dependency is a priority space of critical reflection.

- How might the removal of the partitioned units of 'social worker' and 'service user' transform relationship-based empowerment models? By what yardstick has the partition of positionality between provider and receipt in social care been drawn? Who has not been a service user?

- How might professional boundaries be re-imagined to challenge the pathologisation of social workers who 'bring their work home'? If anti-oppressive practice is a vocation and way of life, how can it be boxed off to certain hours of the day? The political imperative for liberation within social work cannot be relegated to a demarcated office space, work badge or uniform. The professional body of social work codes of conduct has no clocking on and off times and applies equally on the dance floor as in the office!

- How might a community mobilisation approach to empowerment enable social work to move beyond casework with individuals as partitioned dislocated units of risk and problem? How can global community development models be utilised to marshal collective responsibility, action and support? How can social work learn from black feminist community mobilisation approaches used by organisations such as Southall Black Sisters and Imkaan?

- What might an intersectional approach to social work look like, where people are seen within their intersectional experiences of race, gender, age, (dis)ability, class, sexuality in the matrix of the contexts of power structures that they inhabit? How can social work learn to inhabit and apply the emotional component of intersectionality from the black feminist diasporic critical reflexivity of the Combahee River Collective (1977)?

- How might connections, alliances and bridge building, with grass-root activist groups for social justice, expand parochial social work practices of inter-professional and multidisciplinary working?

- How might the concept and experience of 'collective consciousness' be harnessed within social work epistemology and practices as an energy and resource for building stainable capacity for social justice?

Hill Collins emphasises that in the decade between writing the first and second editions of *Black Feminist Thought: Knowledge, Consciousness, and the Politics of Empowerment* (2000), it became clear that black feminist diaspora spaces must be collectively connected to social justice. In the preface to the second edition, Hill Collins (2000, p.xi, emphasis in the original) writes:

> In this edition, I also place greater emphasis on the connections between knowledge and power relations. I have always seen organic links between Black feminism as a social justice project and Black feminist thought as its intellectual center. ... These links continue, but as social conditions change, these ties must be rethought.

The logic of time/heritage

The past, present and future produce each other in a mutually constitutive relationship. The past, present and future are interdependent and this equation has and always will be pivotal to revolutionary change for social justice and transformational empowerment. In other words, the temporal symbiosis between past, present and future is a vital component of anti-oppressive social work practice. Davis (2016, p.135) talks about time as a methodology:

> Our histories never unfold in isolation. We cannot truly tell what we consider to be our own histories without knowing the other stories. And often we discover that those other stories are actually our own stories. This is the admonition 'Learn your sisters' stories' by Black feminist sociologist Jacqui Alexander. This is a dialectical process that requires us to constantly retell our stories, to revise them and retell them and relaunch them.

However, unfortunately, far too often, the temporal dimensions of lived experiences of individuals, families and communities within social work are framed as an indictment. Heritage as an indictment is a foreclosure of the 'dialectical process' that Davis speaks of, where the transformational aspect of the legacy of stories is supressed. Heritage as indictment functions to frame, position and represent care leavers as a/at risk; to frame, position and represent a teenage pregnant daughter of a mother who was in care and a grandmother who grew up in an orphanage as a/at risk; to frame, position and represent the raging asylum seeker as too unstable, too angry, too risky for therapeutic interventions on offer; to frame, position and represent the victim of domestic and sexual violence who, unable to comply to the conditions of refusing her violent intimate partner, is placing her children at risk. Preventative social work based on heritage as an indictment is regulation not anti-oppressive practice. In 'Old Stories: New Lives', Jordan offers a critical framing of heritage that challenges internalised despair and negativity. Jordan (1978, p.81) asks:

> Can we not learn from our children because we cannot believe that we are capable of having created a new life that may save our own? Are we bankrupt of self-love to the degree that we cannot have faith in the innocence and the willingness and the tenderly discovering and perpetual energy and excitement of our young people?

Black feminist diaspora spaces enable inherited narratives to be retold, revised and relaunched. A black feminist diasporic approach to social work critical reflexivity might prompt the following questions:

- How do theories of the cycle of abuse, biological traits and learned behaviours of addiction and mental illness function to regulate the trajectories of people through essentialism? What can be learned from black feminist trauma-informed models that trace patterns of behaviour and outcome to reposition shame and blame from the realm of genetics and the individual to the imprinted impacts of oppressive social constructions?

- How might current restricted notions of historic abuse be amended to encompass and reflect the lived experiences of adults? In other words, survivors of sexual and domestic violence testify that the temporal dimension of the trauma of abuse is fluid and non-linear, and can present as a crisis at any time and anywhere, so why do statutory service, legal and policy responses perpetuate discrete abuse time zones?[1]

---

1   See Nayak 2015, pp.43–44, and 2013, for an elaboration on the timeframe of the emotional impact of rape.

- How are socially constructed moral panics, such as the war on terror and the risk of Islam manifestations of colonial heritage, legitimised in and through imperial hegemony and empire?

Lorde (1982, p.139) reminds us that:

> We do not have to romanticize our past in order to be aware of how it seeds our present. We do not have to suffer the waste of an amnesia that robs us of the lessons of the past rather than permit us to read them with pride as well as deep understanding.

The logic of context

There is nothing without context and yet the fetish of dividing people from the context they inhabit persists as predominant. This ingrained habitual tendency, especially evident in social work, to separate people(s) from the conditions they live in is tantamount to 'context' as something dangerous! The logic of context, which foregrounds the constellations of social constructions that produce risk, impairment, dysfunction, abnormality and crisis, is dangerous because such a focus troubles the status quo. Stated another way, context is pivotal to liberation from oppression. The logic of context draws on, and brings together, the logic of time, heritage and the collective, for example in the context of ancestral collective consciousness of colonisation. A black feminist diasporic critical reflexivity would consciously work with the fact that 'women carry with them incorporated traumas swallowed whole, trauma that manifest themselves as continuing symptoms and traces where the anti-colonial struggle is still so new and relevant' (Khanna 2003, p.230).

In other words, the co-production of social work with Muslim women needs to start from their contextual experience of 'anticolonial struggle... still so new and relevant'. The impact of the context of colonialism should form an integral aspect of social work practice in giving name to and raising consciousness about the micro aggressions of appropriation that constitute the living conditions of service users. Understandings of context need to move beyond physical environment to incorporate the ideological, emotional, psychological, the spiritual and imagined, yet to be realised spaces of existence. In the logic of context, context becomes both method and content and both process and outcome. A black feminist diasporic critical reflexivity is mindful of Minh-ha's (1991, p.73) question, '[i]f you can't locate the other, how are you to locate your-self?'; in other words, context is the relational location of self and other. Context is the location of power and as such the gaze on context is threatening to unequal power relations.

A black feminist diasporic approach to social work critical reflexivity might prompt the following questions:

- How might the black feminist concepts developed by Hill Collins (2000) of 'situated knowledge' (ibid., p.270), 'situated knowers' (ibid., p.19) and situated standpoints (ibid., p.25) call 'into question the content of what currently passes as truth and simultaneously [challenge] the process of arriving at that truth' (ibid., p.271)?

- How might social work practices for liberation from oppression be transformed by understanding context as a method rather than a location, where contexts, conditions and circumstances form the contingency of interventions?

- What is so dangerous about context and why? How might the denial and disavowal of context be transformed into the basis for collective mobilisation of protest, empowerment and transformation for social justice?

- How might conventional social work casework, recording, assessment and methods of intervention be transformed by replacing the names of service users with the names of the conditions they live in? In other words, how might a focus on the contexts that produce intersecting constructs of risk and failure, such as capitalism, patriarchy, heteronormativity, ableism and ageism, rather than individuals, families and communities, enable a revolutionary social work for liberation?

The logic of the erotic

The erotic is rarely mentioned within social work. The idea that social work practices encompass the logic of the erotic frequently invokes an interpellated defensive reaction against an imaginary accusation of contravening professional codes of conduct and values. The problem with this split position is that it rests on a one-dimensional sexualised concept, feeling and experience of the erotic framed in patriarchy, which Lorde (1978, p.54) explains in the following way:

The erotic has often been misnamed by men and used against women. It has been made into the confused, the trivial, the psychotic, the plasticized sensation. For this reason, we have often turned away from the exploration and consideration of the erotic as a source of power and information, confusing it with its opposite, the pornographic. But pornography is a direct denial of the power of the erotic, for it represents the suppression of true feeling. Pornography emphasizes sensation without feeling.

The erotic in social work practice is often equated with the abuse of power and transgression of professional boundaries, and, while the codes of practice and value base of social work must be quite rightly, and strictly, adhered to by social workers, perhaps a black feminist framing of the erotic can allow the feeling part of social work practice to flow through as a resource. Perhaps the shared experience of the co-production, partnership, collaborative energies of social worker and service user in achieving reparation, rehabilitation, recovery and realisation of resilience is a form of 'eros, the personification of love in all its aspect' (Lorde 1978, p.55). The logic of the erotic and the logic of the collective intersect to form 'a bridge between the sharers which can be the basis for understanding much of what is not shared between them, and lessens the threat of their difference' (ibid., p.56).

The logic of the erotic positions empathy, compassion, identification and proximity of feelings as crucial to the therapeutic, transformational potential of relationship-based social work to remove the shackles of disempowerment. The logic of the erotic requires social work to develop a language for the rigour of feeling that provides emotional containment, an experience of attachment, separation and loss that is reparative. The logic of the erotic is recognition of the feelings of vicarious trauma, vulnerability, exhaustion and despair that social workers endure in order to feel the joy, privilege and inspiration of their work with oppressive contexts and conditions. The logic of the erotic calls for spaces of clinical supervision where counter-transference, projective identification, the weight of emotional containment, feelings of doubt, despair, exhaustion, feelings that need to be articulated, shared and examined can find a supportive, secure, trusted and consistent place of expression. In the logic of the erotic, clinical supervision is a diasporic space of critical reflexivity. The logic of the erotic recognises that the intersectionality of axes of differentiation, such as race, gender and class, translates into different experiences, positions and representations of people in the context of social work, including, for example, black women social workers. The logic of the erotic recognises the need for specific spaces of support for specific people in the axes of differentiation and as such is supportive of diasporic spaces of critical reflexifity in order to interrogate the impact of oppression. Lorde (1978, p.57) defines the logic of the erotic as:

> a lens through which we scrutinize all aspects of our existence, forcing us to evaluate those aspects honestly in terms of their relative meaning within our lives. And this is a grave responsibility, projected from within each of us, not to settle for the convenient, the shoddy, the conventionally expected, nor the merely safe.

A black feminist diasporic approach to social work critical reflexivity might prompt the following questions:

- How can a politics of location (Boyce Davies 1994, p.153), where feelings, in the practice of social work, refuse to be dis-placed, dis-membered and dis-located, but are asserted to the foreground as information and as intelligence, serve as a resource? How can social work provide human-rights-based and empathy-based advocacy for service users if it cannot provides this for itself?

- How might a logic of the erotic, whether through clinical supervision or diasporic spaces of critical reflexivity for social workers and service users, enable all to 'become less willing to accept powerlessness, or rather those other supplied states of being...such as resignation, despair, self-effacement, depression, self-denial' (Lorde 1978, p.58)?

Conclusion

In recognition that content and method are mutually contingent and constitutive, meaning that what we do and how we do it co-produce each other, this chapter has advocated for a diaspora model of critical reflexivity based on black feminism. A black feminist lens on social work without borders calls for a new discourse. The apolitical discourse of non-judgemental person-centredness isn't fit for the job of revolutionary collective community mobilisation that refuses to be dislocated from context, including the context of heritage. Very rarely does the word 'solidarity' figure in social work education, textbooks, methods of intervention, assessments or configurations of service provision. This needs to change, and social work needs to develop a language of solidarity! Black feminist diaspora spaces of social work critical reflexivity are necessary spaces of rigour, inclusion and deconstruction because:

> If our history has taught us anything, it is that action for change directed only against the external conditions of our oppressions is not enough. In order to be whole, we must recognize the despair oppression plants within each of us – that thin persistent voice that says our efforts are useless, it will never change, so why bother, accept it. And we must fight that inserted piece of self-destruction that lives and flourishes like a poison inside of us, unexamined until it makes us turn upon ourselves in each other. (Lorde 1982, p.142)

References

Anzaldúa, G. (2007) *Borderlands/La Frontera: The New Mestiza* (third edition). San Francisco, CA: Aunt Lute Books.

Beale, F. (2005) 'Double Jeopardy: To Be Black and Female.' In T. Cade Bambara (ed.) *The Black Woman: An Anthology* (second edition), pp.109–122. New York, NY: Washington Square Press.

Boyce Davies, C. (1994) *Black Women, Writing and Identity: Migrations of the Subject.* London: Routledge.

Boyce Davies, C. (2013) *Caribbean Spaces: Escapes from Twilight Zones.* Chicago, IL: University of Illinois Press.

Brah, A. (1996) *Cartographies of Diaspora: Contesting Identities.* Abingdon: Routledge.

Combahee River Collective, The (1977) 'A Black Feminist Statement.' In J. James and T.D. Sharpley-Whiting (eds) (2000) *The Black Feminist Reader*, pp.261–270. Oxford: Blackwell Publishers Ltd.

Davis, A.Y. (2016) *Freedom Is a Constant Struggle: Ferguson, Palestine, and the Foundations of a Movement.* Chicago, IL: Haymarket Books.

Hill Collins, P. (2000) *Black Feminist Thought: Knowledge, Consciousness, and the Politics of Empowerment* (second edition). London: Routledge.

Jordan, J. (1976) 'Declaration of an Independence I Would Just as Soon Not Have.' In J. Jordan (1989) *Moving Towards Home: Political Essays* (third edition), pp.61–6. London: Virago Press.

Jordan, J. (1978) 'Old Stories: New Lives.' In J. Jordan (1989) *Moving Towards Home: Political Essays* (third edition), pp.74–81. London: Virago Press.

Khanna, R. (2003) *Dark Continents: Psychoanalysis and Colonialism.* Durham, NC: Duke University Press.

Lorde, A. (1977) 'The Transformation of Silence into Language and Action.' In A. Lorde (1984) *Sister Outsider: Essays and Speeches*, pp.40–4. Trumansburg, NY: The Crossing Press.

Lorde, A. (1978) 'Uses of the Erotic: The Erotic as Power.' In A. Lorde (1984) *Sister Outsider: Essays and Speeches*, pp.53–9. Trumansburg, NY: The Crossing Press.

Lorde, A. (1980) 'Age, Race, Class, and Sex: Women Redefining Difference.' In A. Lorde (1984) *Sister Outsider: Essays and Speeches*, pp.114–123. Trumansburg, NY: The Crossing Press.

Lorde, A. (1982) 'Learning from the 60s.' In A. Lorde (1984) *Sister Outsider: Essays and Speeches*, pp.134–144. Trumansburg, NY: The Crossing Press.

Minh-ha, T.T. (1991) *When the Moon Waxes Red: Representation, Gender and Cultural Politics*. New York, NY: Routledge.

Minh-ha, T.T. (2011) *Elsewhere, Within Here: Immigration, Refugeeism and the Boundary Event*. New York, NY: Routledge.

Mohanty, C.T. (2003) *Feminism Without Borders: Decolonizing Theory, Practicing Solidarity*. Durham, NC: Duke University Press.

Nayak, S. (2013) 'The Activism of Black Feminist Theory in Confronting Violence Against Women: Interconnections, Politics and Practice.' In I. Testoni, A. Groterath, M.S. Guglielmin and M. Wieser (eds) *Teaching against Violence: Reassessing the Toolbox: Teaching with Gender*, pp.31–60. European Women's Studies in International and Interdisciplinary Classrooms. Budapest, New York, NY: The European Association for Gender Research, Education and Documentation, Utrecht & Central European University Press.

Nayak, S. (2015) *The Activism of Black Feminist Theory: Race, Gender and Social Change*. Abingdon: Routledge.

Nayak, S. (2017) 'Location as method.' *Qualitative Research Journal*, 17, 3, 202–216.

Chapter 4

Migration and Austerity

Lucy Mort

Introduction

This chapter looks to foreground the experiences of refugees, asylum seekers and migrants in a context of austerity. In a globalised – and unequal – world, many are on the move and are seeking safety and security in new countries. However, the revision of the 2007/08 global financial crisis – brought about by an ill-regulated financial sector – into a problem of 'paternalistic' government and social spending has meant that safety nets, for migrants already here and for new arrivals, have become increasingly stretched and tattered.

Drawing on qualitative doctoral research and practice experience with refugees, asylum seekers and migrants in the voluntary sector, this chapter will explore the dual impacts of austerity and a hostile immigration system. The importance of looking at experiences with a transnational awareness (Withaeckx, Schrooten and Geldof 2017), and building an understanding of the multiple and intersecting inequalities faced by many, is highlighted. The chapter goes on to focus on the impact of precarity on the mental health of refugees, asylum seekers and migrants, with particular attention given to the hierarchical rights afforded by legal immigration status and the gendered nature of inequalities. In concluding, we return to consider implications for practice and a call is made for the social work profession to recognise the plight of refugees, asylum seekers and migrants in anti-austerity campaigning, so that we might mobilise for social justice and social change.

Methodology

Following a post-qualifying period where I worked in a voluntary sector organisation that supported refugees, asylum-seeking and migrant families, my doctoral research was concerned with exploring and narrating the experiences of migrant families in a time of increasing scarcity and anti-migrant rhetoric. To capture this, the research adopted a case-study approach, using ethnographic methods including participatory observation in a voluntary organisation that supported migrant families in a city in the North of England, and which was facing severe funding cuts. The study also involved conducting in-depth interviews with both those that provided support services and the families that accessed the services. During the research, 18 participants (12 migrants and six support workers and managers) were interviewed about their experiences and understanding of austerity. Narrative analysis sought to address the multiple ways in which austerity could be understood. Critical attention to the intersections of 'race', gender, class, disability, nationality and immigration status highlighted the structural influences on the narratives told by participants. This chapter will draw on the narratives of participants interviewed, grounding the work in the experiences of refugees, asylum seekers, migrants and those who work on the frontline with them.

Austerity

> I spoke to the letting agency to save some money for my living expenses, but the rest they take to pay the rent. I was very limited in how much I could spend, with things I wanted... I could only use so much so that I could pay the debts as quickly as possible. (Adriana, EU migrant, originally from Angola)

> People come here and they are crying because of benefit sanctions and ask, 'what will I do now?' (Ibrahim, family support worker)

'Austerity' has dominated the political and social landscape for almost a decade, and the effects it has had on those most vulnerable and marginalised are familiar to most studying and working in the field of social care and social work. These effects include the harms of welfare reform, benefit sanctions, punitive workfare conditions and an increasingly precarious labour market. Many, at the mercy of a profligate private rental sector, are threatened by rent arrears, eviction and homelessness. We hear the stories of those who are forced to decide between the most basic and fundamental of essentials: eating or heating. The public and voluntary sectors have faced unprecedented funding cuts, and organisations have radically 'restructured' and reduced their services, made staff redundant, or – in some instances – closed their doors completely. Indeed, the social work profession has responded to these crises, with the British Association of Social Workers (BASW) and Social Work Action Network (SWAN), for instance, leading campaigns to resist austerity.[1] Despite this professional voice against the injustice of austerity, social work has less often and, I argue, insufficiently, foregrounded the everyday experiences of refugees, asylum seekers and migrants living in the UK.

When thinking about the experiences of refugee, asylum-seeking and migrant communities in relation to austerity, it is necessary to not only consider the very tangible effects, such as the retrenchment of the welfare state and the loss of funding to social care organisations, but also the narrative effects of austerity. Austerity is driven by a powerful story. This story ensures that austerity is seen as the common-sense economic solution to out-of-control debt, excessive public spending, and a profligate welfare system. It does this through the dichotomic imagery of the deserving and undeserving, often the 'striver' versus 'skiver', but also through the 'deserving citizen' and 'undeserving migrant' (Vockins 2013). Immigration and welfare are the two areas at which the narrative of austerity is most directed. Both those who migrate here (and who are poor), and non-migrants who are benefit claimants, are impoverished by the retrenchment of supportive structures. It is perhaps unsurprising then that these groups are pitted against one another, and this enforced competition for scarce resources leads to an anti-migrant sentiment that, beyond material deprivation, causes additional hardship in the everyday lives of many refugees, asylum seekers and migrants.

Finally, in thinking about the crisis of austerity, it is important to understand that welfare has historically been organised in ways that mirror and reproduce inequalities along lines of race and nationality. That is to say, many migrants have faced oppression, marginalisation, inferior welfare provision and crisis since long before 2007/08. For evidence of this, we might look to the beginning of the 20th century and the implementation of the Aliens Act 1905, which discriminated against (poor) Jewish migrants fleeing Eastern Europe. In more recent years, the Immigration and Asylum Act 1999 introduced no-choice dispersal and the provision of welfare through

---

1   See, for instance, the Boot Out Austerity campaign led by BASW: https://www. basw.co.uk/what-we-do/campaigns/anti-austerity-and-anti-poverty, and SWAN on the role of austerity in the Grenfell Tower disaster: https://socialworkfuture. org/2017/07/04/swan-statement-on-the-grenfell-disaster-social-work-must-critique-policy-not-simply-deliver-it

the National Asylum Support Service (NASS), whose role, Cohen (2004) argued, was more about the *withholding* of welfare than the provision of it. This is substantiated by the depreciating value of asylum welfare payments, once set at 70 per cent of Income Support. The government refusal to increase these in line with inflation has resulted in asylum payments that are 50 per cent lower than mainstream benefits (Refugee Action 2017). While crisis, then, is not necessarily new for most refugees, asylum seeking and migrant groups, it is their existing insecurity which makes the risks associated with a depleting public and civil sector more virulent (Emejulu and Bassel 2015).

In the next section, we look further at the contemporary racialisation of welfare through the commitment of the Conservative administration to creating a 'hostile environment' for those subject to immigration control.

Hostility

The time when they wanted to deport us was the worst probably. That was a few years ago. Our barrister saved us like in the last minute and we returned… They came and took us to the airport. Heathrow? I think. From Manchester. From our old house to Heathrow… It was very hard [to recover]. We used to think the door was ringing again. (Extract from an interview with a young woman, Fidan, and her mother Zeynab. Both had discretionary leave to remain)

Hostility towards migrants has been mobilised through legislation and political rhetoric. It is also a pervasive atmosphere that has long saturated the political and societal approach towards Britain's migrant population. Since the Conservative/Liberal Democrat government that came to power in 2010 there has been an explicit political movement, spearheaded by the Prime Minister Theresa May, towards creating a really 'hostile environment' for those dubbed 'illegal' migrants (*The Telegraph* 2012). This hostility is enacted through creating legislative barriers that make it difficult – if not dangerous and impossible – to access service provision. While ostensibly targeting those who do not have a legal right to remain in the UK (though we should seek to challenge the simplistic and unhelpful demarcation of legality versus illegality when it comes to people), the very notion of a 'hostile environment' is one that permeates institutions and encounters between practitioners and those accessing services, so that discrimination based on race and perceived 'foreignness' comes to affect both migrant and non-migrant alike.

The 'hostile environment' is both performative and highly punitive. For instance, Jones and colleagues (2017), in their analysis of the 'Go Home' vans that toured diverse areas of London in 2016, emphasise how the vans were viewed by many as an empty – yet highly provocative – promotion of 'tough' immigration enforcement for the benefit of the electorate. However, the vans also transported a pervasive sense of fear and anxiety around the streets of London, as many saw them as legitimising xenophobia and racism in their communities.

The intense heightening of detention and deportation as mechanisms of immigration control in recent years is a salient example of the tension between austerity (the need to save government money) and hostility (the need to return and deter migrants). In 2006, 2540 people were detained in a detention centre (Sales 2007) and by 2016 this had increased to 28,900 people (Silverman 2017). The detainment of an individual for a year costs the government over £30,000 (McGuinness and Gower 2017), and this money goes to multinational corporations, such as Serco and G4S. Detention centres have been deemed immensely harmful to the well-being of those detained, and it is also ineffective by government standards, as over half are released without deportation (Refugee Council 2015), emphasising their arbitrarily punitive nature. Above, Zeynab and Fidan (mother and daughter, with discretionary leave to remain) indicate the fear that a deportation attempt instils.

Recent legislation, the Immigration Act 2014 and its 2016 amendment, has brought the control of borders more prominently into the sphere of everyday life. Under this Act, enforcement of the border is not only about spectacle, but is propagated by employers, National Health Service (NHS) staff, the Driver and Vehicle Licensing Agency (DVLA), letting agents and landlords – all of whom require documentation to be provided before admitting access to their services. In a move reminiscent of the recent screen adaptation of *The Handmaid's Tale*, banks will be able to freeze the account of anyone who is seemingly in breach of immigration rules. The Joint Council for the Welfare of Immigrants (2016) has highlighted that these measures risk reinforcing and driving further underground labour exploitation; deterring landlords from renting to anyone who does not have a British passport; removing legal safeguards and homes from those – perhaps incorrectly – identified as without leave to remain; and buttressing the already-existing discrimination faced by black and minority ethnic communities who may be targeted for additional checks on the basis of skin colour, language, accent and name.

'Memorandums of understanding' that facilitate the sharing of personal data between services and the Home Office further jeopardise migrants in their everyday encounters with service providers. In January 2018, the NHS was ordered by a Health Select Committee to stop sharing data with the Home Office for the purposes of immigration enforcement – data which in 2017 enabled the tracing of 5854 individuals (Matthews-King 2018). Policies such as these act as a deterrent to accessing healthcare, causing such fear that already vulnerable individuals will not seek help, as was reported in the aftermath of the Grenfell Tower disaster.

Through the Immigration Acts, and utilising the narrative of austerity, the government has further legitimised the near state abandonment of some asylum seekers (those without further appeal rights) and migrants (those with 'no recourse to public funds' and/or who are undocumented). Those made destitute may turn to their local authority social services department for subsistence and support. A hostile atmosphere is present here too. A study by the North East London Migrant Association (2017) found that 69 per cent of families that sought support from social services experienced intimidation, blame, disbelief or hostility during the interview process. For those without leave to remain and without an application with the Home Office, this rose to 88 per cent of families facing such hostility. Such studies indicate that within some domains of social work the work of supporting migrants is second to gatekeeping provision and, in this way, social workers contribute to the processes of exclusion that vulnerable asylum seekers and migrants encounter. In short, social workers risk contributing to mechanisms of immigration control, and enacting hostility over empathy.

The supposed intentions of the 'hostile environment' are to encourage irregular migrants to return to their country of origin, and to deter potential migrants from coming to the UK. Evidence shows that this is rarely the outcome of retreating state provision. Instead, many will become destitute, disappear and live under the radar, risk exploitative living and working conditions, and rely on a waning third sector or on faith-based organisations. Moreover, the rhetoric of hostility extends beyond those without leave to remain, to detrimentally affect relations between the state and anyone who may be constructed as 'other'. Hostility cements the chasm between those deemed deserving and undeserving, putting many at sustained risk in their daily lives.

In the next section, austerity and hostility are situated within a global context, and the importance of approaching social work with refugees, asylum seekers and migrants with a transnational and intersectional lens is highlighted.

Global focus

The children do not have a good future [in Spain], there is no work for children, there is lots of discrimination. People that immigrate there, they have degrees, but no jobs, no future. They are sitting at home, doing nothing. (Hamid, EU migrant, originally from Morocco)

The contemporary context in the UK must be situated in a world that appears to be in a constant state of crisis. These crises are particularly notable at the borders, in the attempts of many to traverse them and in the intolerance shown by governments with jurisdiction over them. Despite the risks and loss associated with moving from one country to another, and despite the often hostile reception and stasis that many find once in their destination, many *do* move. To understand the experience of austerity in the UK, we need to have an awareness of what is going on globally: what factors influence the decision to migrate, and how are expectations of life in the destination country (particularly in relation to welfare) shaped by past experiences?

First, austerity is not only something that many find when they come to the UK, but something from which to escape and which influences a decision to migrate. Several participants in the doctoral research had migrated from Southern European countries such as Spain and Portugal. These countries, along with Greece, have been subject to particularly harsh austerity measures that have been mandated by international institutions (known as the *troika*).[2] Consequently, and as Hamid found (see above), unemployment rates are high. Hamid touched on the additional barriers experienced as a migrant. Though Hamid and Laila had been in the country most of their adult lives, they perceived that this, coupled with the discrimination directed at the Moroccan community, was so severe that there were few prospects in Spain for the family and so austerity had its role to play in facilitating onward migration. Hamid hoped that in Manchester his children would have a 'brighter future'.

Second, global crises – such as war, conflict, poverty, discrimination and natural and man-made disasters – have produced the movement of people on a mass scale. Migration is not a new phenomenon, and it is one which is heavily steeped in the legacies of colonialism and imperialism. However, increased global instability and its intersection with the Eurozone crisis has

---

2   Conversely, in the British context, austerity was widely viewed as a political choice made by the national government without international pressure to do so.

seen record numbers of people attempt to enter Europe,[3] and a devastatingly high number of lives lost in doing so.[4] This too has an influence on how life in the UK, and the support received, are experienced. Experiences in countries of origin, and other countries resided in (participants in my study rarely had a linear A–B migration, and this is fairly typical of contemporary migration practices), were inevitably a frame of reference for expectations of, and engagement with, welfare provision in the UK. In interviews, this often played out, initially, as an idealised vision of life in the UK – one in which austerity may appear to be less of a threat to the well-being of the family. For instance, one participant stated that in the UK 'nothing make me feel unsafe here' and that 'there's nothing bad to say about Manchester'. Sara, for example, made these distinctions in comparison to the discrimination and oppression that she had fled as a Kurdish woman in Turkey.

Below, the cracks within this 'idealised' narrative are explored, as participants also spoke of their experiences of precarity and (often poor) mental health in the UK. Before that, I briefly turn to consider the importance of understanding these migrant narratives within a transnational and intersectional framework.

Transnational social work

Transnational social work practice is a developing field of study and one that is responding to the reality of a world which is interconnected and on the move. Social work needs to critically engage with global inequalities, brought about through historical and contemporary layers of neo-liberal policy, colonialism and imperialism, and pre-existing inequalities of 'race', gender, class, religion and caste (Deepak 2011). In a call for a social work profession that is premised on notions of solidarity and resistance, Anne Deepak (2011, p.790) advocates for an engagement with structural forces and for teachers, students and practitioners to 'use consciousness raising and praxis to…make the connections between personal suffering and structural oppression on a global level'. She highlights that a global outlook starts locally, through an understanding of 'the local realities and struggles people are facing' (ibid.). Further, Withaeeckx and colleagues (2017) highlight the

3   Though it should be noted that the majority (67%) of displaced people continue to reside in Asia, the Middle East and Africa (www.unhcr.org/uk/figures-at-a-glance.html).
4   See: https://missingmigrants.iom.int

need to develop a 'transnational awareness'. To summarise the key points of the article, this awareness might consist of:

- recognition of specific migratory trajectories and how these create vulnerabilities

- how migratory trajectories intersect with 'race', class, gender, legal status (and disability)

- exploration of previous experiences and how these shape lives and needs

- recognition of the continuing role of transnational networks (both positive and negative).

Below, narratives from the doctoral research will be put into dialogue with such a transnational awareness.

Intersectionality

Implicated in having a 'transnational awareness' is an understanding of how multiple markers of identity and positionality – such as race, gender, class, nationality, legal status, disability, sexuality and age – come together in shaping experiences of inequality. Intersectionality, a concept that emerged out of black feminist movements in the 1970s, has been adopted more universally in recent years. At the root of the idea is the understanding that race, gender and class are inseparable in analyses of inequality and oppression. Placing these analyses within the context of global capitalism – and recognising the disparity between the Global North and Global South – is important for understanding the factors that might lead to migration and the experiences of migrants once in the UK.

By way of an example, we might consider how poor, black and minority ethnic migrant women who participated in the doctoral study described how difficult it was to access English language classes and the effects this had on their ability to feel settled in the UK. It is the relationship between the multiple ways in which they are positioned that excludes them from access to vital services. That is, their *racialised* status as migrants (migrants are positioned as undeserving of declining state resources and their legal status determined whether or not they were eligible to access limited provisions), their *class* status (participants were unable to self-fund language classes and at times the only available provision in their local area clashed with their employment), and their *gender* (migrant women – in this instance, all mothers – were more likely to have substantial caring responsibilities for children that meant they could not access provision which did not have childcare facilities).

If social workers are interested in promoting social justice, then theory – such as intersectionality – is imperative for critical reflection on power relations and to understand how inequality, oppression and exploitation are experienced in daily life. In the next section, I explore how these dynamics came together in the precarity, and the resulting mental distress, experienced by participants.

Precarity

To be precarious is to be in a position of uncertainty and insecurity. In a neo-liberal context, many are increasingly finding themselves in such positions. However, the extent to which one is precarious is delineated by structural inequalities, including race, class, gender and legal status. Waite (2009, p.421) highlights that the benefit of the term *precarity* over 'risk' and 'vulnerability' (two terms with which social work can be argued to be more familiar) is that it 'more explicitly incorporates the political and institutional context in which the production of precarity occurs rather than focusing solely on individualised experiences of precarity'. That is, the term 'precarity' emphasises the structural factors that lead to uncertainty and insecurity and, accordingly, it is more effective in making claims to social justice. Precarity is most often understood in terms of labour conditions. Thinking about precarity with an intersectional lens, below I consider the precarity afforded by legal immigration status, and the way in which precarity is gendered, particularly how it is implicated in care work and relationships.

Much work on precarity focuses on the experiences of migrant labour exploitation. Several participants in this study spoke of the physically intensive, yet ostensibly low-skilled work that they did, and the low earnings and security that they received in return. For instance, Hamid told me:

> I've spent all my life doing carpentry, since I was ten years old. I love to do this… There are no jobs in here. I was a carpenter in Spain and I work in a car wash in the UK. I work three days a week. I got the job through a Kurdish-Iraqi man that I met at college when I was doing ESOL [English for speakers of other languages]. He introduced me to the job. I am not happy. It's not the kind of job I'm interested in. It is unclean. (Hamid)

For many migrants, they find their labour is devalued, their qualifications delegitimised, and they face deskilling and downward mobility in the UK.

Hand car washes, such as the one in which Hamid worked, are often sites of labour exploitation, with many working long hours for much less than minimum wage (Clark and Colling 2017).

Hamid's precarity in the workforce had consequences for the entire family, and his wife Laila described how they struggled to afford gas and electricity on the expensive pre-payment meter in their rented home. The difficulties that Laila faced at home, such as being unsure whether to use her kitchen appliances for fear of using up all the electricity, were illustrative of the strong sense of uncertainty that she had about the future. Having worked informally in Spain mending and sewing clothes, she had not found comparable work in the UK. She was further isolated as she could not speak English and, as described earlier, she was impacted by the crisis in English language provision that meant she could not find a class locally that did not have an 18-month waiting list.[5] Moved to tears, Laila confided that these issues coalesced to 'make me wonder why I'm in this country'.

The role of legal migration status in creating precarity was also conveyed in participant narratives. Earlier Zeynab and Fidan were quoted, sharing how an attempt to deport them had continuing and lasting effects that made them feel unsafe and insecure in their home. In striking resemblance to austerity research that has pointed to the distress caused when receiving the 'brown envelope' of official welfare correspondence (Garthwaite, Collins and Bambra 2015), Fidan spoke of how seeing the Home Office logo on a letter caused the family to become distressed: 'We thought they were deporting us again, so we started crying.' The pair also spoke of the difficulty of the transitional period between claiming asylum and being granted discretionary leave to remain. Though Zeynab and her husband were at that point *legally* able to claim benefits and take employment, substantively it was a different story. With her father unable to find work and without benefits for three months, Fidan explained how they managed: 'When my mum and dad were together, my dad borrowed money from someone, so we had that, and my mum had some jewellery here, so we sold that.' Informal lending from peers and the sale of personal possessions in times of austerity are just some of the ways that families described getting by when benefits were delayed or stopped, and when low pay and under-employment proved insufficient. With few (and treasured) possessions due to the nature of migration, and

5   In 2016, David Cameron announced a £20 million ESOL fund that rhetorically targeted Muslim women; however, this was preceded by an almost 50 per cent reduction in ESOL funding between 2008 and 2015 (Court 2017).

often with small friend-and-family networks in the UK, these responses can be said to be unsustainable solutions to structural problems.

Similarly, the precarity experienced by Sara belies her insistence that there was nothing hard about life in the UK. While seeking asylum, Sara was dispersed around the North West five times, including while pregnant. A report by Maternity Action and the Refugee Council (Feldman 2013) asserts the substantial risk of dispersal for the health and well-being of mother and baby. A combination of complex social factors, such as existing poor physical and mental health, experiences of sexual and physical violence and trauma, female genital mutilation, fear of the asylum process, language barriers, unfamiliarity with available provision, poverty, destitution and inadequate support, means that dispersed women seeking asylum need *more* rather than less support during their antenatal care. Sara explains how, when giving birth to her youngest child some years later, she came to recognise the injustice she faced when she had been dispersed:

> I went to birth with my little one. I had my partner next to me [and] my friend, she's next to me, but I just been crying. Not from pain…it just like hurt me, you know when I birthed my other one, no one's next to me, so I just been crying. But not of pain…just it hurt me. I saw how I just birth my other one: I didn't know English, I didn't know anything. This really hurt me. (Sara)

Experiences such as Sara's point to the ways in which hostility and precarity are woven into the fabric of the immigration regime, and that these have differential effects dependent on one's social positioning. Narratives such as this also indicate the difficulty of isolating the harms of austerity from the harms of a hostile immigration system, and the artificiality of attempting to do so.

No recourse to public funds

Participants in the doctoral study by and large had recourse to public funds. However, it is also important to highlight the increasingly prominent condition of 'no recourse to public funds' (NRPF) and how this intersects with austerity and hostility. To have NRPF means that one is restricted from access to welfare, social housing and homelessness support. The NRPF condition can be applied to a variety of legal status and affects both those who do have leave to remain and those who are undocumented. Three key groupings of people often with NRPF are as follows:

- non-EEA (European Economic Area) migrants on a family, student or work visa

- undocumented and irregular migrants – those who have come to the end of their asylum appeal rights and/or whose status has not been regularised

- some EEA migrants who are un- or under-employed and subsequently determined not to have a 'right to reside'.

The deprivations that those with NRPF face have been described by Farmer (2017, p.8) as putting people at risk of 'dangerous and exploitative situations'. The relationship between NRPF status and austerity, though difficult to quantify, is clear. In a time when local authority budgets have been cut so deeply following the comprehensive spending review, provision for these families (such as by Section 17 payments for 'children in need'), perhaps deemed undeserving through hostility rhetoric, is highly politicised and contested.

Women with NRPF and who experience domestic abuse are in exceptionally precarious circumstances, as they face both institutional and intimate violence. The option to leave such relationships is made harder by an inability to access housing benefits that could facilitate safe refuge. While the Destitute Domestic Violence (DDV) Concession[6] has been devised to provide one route out of such circumstances for women on a spousal visa, this does not meet the needs of all those with NRPF who may experience domestic abuse and, moreover, the standard of evidence necessary for a successful application is so high as to be restrictive for some. The way in which the NRPF condition and domestic abuse coalesce highlights the inequalities experienced at the intersection of race, class, gender and legal status. Migrant women – often from the Global South – who do not have the material means to leave a violent situation, who are threatened with and fear deportation, and who seek support in a context of universal de-funding of women's refuges, face severe restrictions in seeking safety and protection.

---

6   The Destitute Domestic Violence Concession is a scheme provided by the Home Office and the Department for Work and Pensions to women who have entered the UK as a partner of a British person or a person with settled status and whose relationships have broken down due to domestic violence and who are destitute without accommodation or means to support themselves. It enables women to apply for indefinite leave to remain and to access public funds for a period of three months while their case is considered.

Furthermore, examples such as this highlight the need for social work to be a part of challenging such injustice. This necessitates a transnational awareness, as outlined above, but also a political commitment to social change, to heed the imperative to think *and* act – locally *and* globally (Furman, Negi and Rommel 2010). Finally, we turn now to briefly address the impact that the inequalities described above can have on the mental health of refugees, asylum seekers and migrants.

Mental health

Given the experiences of many refugees, asylum seekers and migrants, it is perhaps unsurprising that they experience mental distress and poor mental health. Critical approaches to mental health research and practice emphasise the structural factors that affect individual psychology. As Lynne Friedl (2009, p.iii) notes:

> Levels of mental distress among communities need to be understood less in terms of individual pathology and more as a response to relative deprivation and social injustice, which erode the emotional, spiritual and intellectual resources essential to psychological wellbeing.

The narratives introduced above are commensurate with this reading of how poor mental health outcomes are derived. The loss of home, of family and friends, the impact of trauma, poverty and discrimination, of insecure and low-paid work, of being deskilled and undervalued, with limited or no access to welfare and formal support structures, facing disbelief and non-recognition when reporting gender-based violence, and a hostile immigration system that has increasingly filtered into everyday relations, all coalesce in shaping the mental health of refugees, asylum seekers and migrants. Taking account of experiences throughout the migration process – that is, in the country of origin, on the journey, in countries of temporary stay, and finally in the UK – can help social workers to appreciate mental distress as a consequence of inequality. Moving away from a pathological understanding of mental distress enables a critical outlook, and a move towards solutions that are cognisant of structures and not solely individualistic in nature.

Participants in the doctoral study were asked to talk about their lives in the UK, and despite their relative security – in that they all had recourse to public funds – all of them spoke of facing distress at some point since their migration. Laila spoke of her isolation – both physically and linguistically – and how because of this, she felt 'stressed and depressed'. Two participants spoke of having felt suicidal post-migration. This was in the earliest days of their settlement, when both had extensive caring responsibilities, fractured/non-existent support networks, little income or material safety net, and had not yet met the professionals (from voluntary organisations) who would support them to address the inequality, trauma and isolation (to name a few) that they had experienced.

In a context of austerity and funding cuts to the voluntary sector – and especially to those organisations that support refugees, asylum seekers and migrants – the simple question that is left to ask is: who will provide support and care to those facing hostility, precarity and mental distress? In these recent times of economic crisis, it is known that suicides have increased, and this has been particularly attributed to punitive and stigmatising welfare conditions (Mills 2017). Earlier in the chapter, it was noted that detention as a tool of immigration control has increased more than tenfold in the last decade and in these centres, suicide attempts are catastrophically high, with 393 people detained attempting suicide in 2015 (O'Hare 2017). Making these connections between hostility towards welfare claimants and towards migrants, we can see how austerity and hostility are implicated in constructing some lives as more expendable/less valuable than others. While the transnational and intersectional narratives of refugees, asylum seekers and migrants highlight the inequalities that lead to mental distress, an awareness of the material worsening of welfare provision – including mental health services – in a time of austerity can also illuminate the pervasive inequality in mental health outcomes for these groups.

Conclusion

> [It] was difficult because you'd be thinking about the thousands of families that we'd work with... You'd think about the staff, that could potentially lose their jobs, you're thinking about your own security, and it was just...it was so much pressure. (Kirsty, manager at migrant family support project)

Using examples from empirical research with migrant families and a voluntary sector organisation, this chapter has shown how the policy narratives of austerity and hostility affect the everyday experiences of refugees, asylum seekers and migrants living in the UK. To advocate for a transnational and intersectional approach, I situate individual narratives within a structural and global context, as opposed to inequality being attributed to individual deficit. I argue that such an approach is imperative for enacting a social work that understands – and places importance on understanding – the entirety and the complexity of journeys and experiences of those it meets in the provision of services, and on working in appropriate ways with diverse groups. Finally, the ways in which economic inequality and tropes of the deserving and undeserving come together to create precarity in daily life, and consequently mental distress, have been explored.

Practising in super-diverse contexts necessitates engaging with communities which have been marginalised and often demonised. As social workers, being guided by ethical action is a professional imperative. In the service of migrants with uncertain or insecure immigration status, this ethical imperative is too often waylaid (North East London Migrant Association 2017). For this reason, it is important to interrogate our own biases but, in concluding, I argue that it is also important to recognise that individual actions are unlikely to be the panacea for structural inequality. To affect real, substantive change, oppressive structures need to change.

In austere and hostile times, how do social workers (in the broadest understanding of the profession) go the extra mile to support refugees, asylum seekers and migrants? It would be remiss not to mention the potential risks to workers. As summarised by one manager in a voluntary organisation, trying to maintain funding was an overwhelmingly difficult undertaking. Migrant families in my research spoke of the care and support they had received, usually from one key person and often from a voluntary organisation. However, with austerity and funding cuts, it is likely that the opportunities for such support are reduced.

Austerity and the 'hostile environment' also place some of those working with refugees, asylum seekers and migrants (sometimes migrants themselves) in precarious positions too. Collectivisation, alongside migrants, is the best way of creating sustainable change and support for one another. Of course, we need to not equate the inequalities faced by those who access social work provision with those providing it, and we must maintain awareness of often unequal power relations and work to reduce these.

Social work has a vital role to play in campaigning to challenge unjust policy. There are existing campaigns such as Docs Not Cops and Against Borders for Children that challenge the 'hostile environment' in a multitude of ways, and which social workers might organise alongside. Looking to our local area and the existing organisations and campaigns is one way to act locally *and* globally. For instance, in Manchester there is the

These Walls Must Fall campaign, and organisations such as Safety4Sisters campaigning for migrant women's rights to safety. Social Workers Without Borders similarly has groups across the UK, and where there is not a group, interested parties can be supported to set one up. Professional associations, such as the British Association of Social Workers, also have a role to play. In challenging austerity and funding cuts, the organisations and networks that support refugees, asylum seekers and migrant must also be protected.

In promoting justice for refugees, asylum seekers and migrants, the extra mile must be conceived of as a collective endeavour, not an individual one.

References

Aliens Act 1905 (5 Edw. VII. c. 13). Accessed 28/11/2018 at: https://www.legislation.gov.uk/ukpga/1905/13/pdfs/ukpga_19050013_en.pdf.

Clark, I. and Colling, T. (2017) 'Work in Britain's informal economy: Learning from road-side hand car washes.' *British Journal of Industrial Relations*. Doi: 10.1111/bjir.12286.

Cohen, S. (2004) 'Foreword: Breaking the Links and Pulling the Plug.' In D. Hayes and B. Humphries (eds) *Social Work, Immigration and Asylum: Debates, Dilemmas and Ethical Issues for Social Work and Social Care Practice*, pp.7–10. London: Jessica Kingsley Publishers.

Court, J. (2017) '"I feel integrated when I help myself": ESOL learners' views and experiences of language learning and integration.' *Language and Intercultural Communication*. Doi: 10.1080/14708477.2017.1368137.

Deepak, A. (2011) 'Globalisation, power and resistance: Postcolonial and transnational feminist perspectives for social work practice.' *International Social Work*, 55, 6, 779–793.

Emejulu, A. and Bassel, L. (2015) 'Minority women, austerity and activism.' *Race & Class*, 57, 2, 86–95.

Farmer, N.J. (2017) '"No recourse to public funds": Insecure immigration status and destitution: the role of social work?' *Critical and Radical Social Work*, 5, 3, 357–367.

Feldman, R. (2013) *When Maternity Doesn't Matter: Dispersing Pregnant Women Seeking Asylum*. London: Maternity Action and the Refugee Council.

Friedl, L. (2009) *Mental Health, Resilience and Inequalities*. Copenhagen: World Health Organisation.

Furman, R., Negi, N.J. and Rommel, S. (2010) 'An Introduction to Transnational Social Work.' In N.J. Negi and R. Furman (eds) *Transnational Social Work Practice*, pp.3–19. New York, NY: Columbia University Press.

Garthwaite, K.A., Collins, P.J. and Bambra, C. (2015) 'Food for thought: An ethnographic study of negotiating ill health and food insecurity in a UK foodbank.' *Social Science & Medicine*, 132, 38–44.

Immigration Act 2014 (c.22). Accessed 28/11/2018 at: http://www.legislation.gov.uk/ukpga/2014/22/pdfs/ukpga_20140022_en.pdf.

Immigration Act 2016 (c.19). Accessed 28/11/2018 at: http://www.legislation.gov.uk/ukpga/2016/2019/pdfs/ukpga_20160019_en.pdf.

Immigration and Asylum Act (1999) Accessed 28/11/2018 at: www.legislation.gov.uk/ukpga/1999/33/contents.

Joint Council for the Welfare of Immigrants (2016) 'What's next for the Hostile Environment: The Immigration Act 2016 and the Queen's Speech.' Accessed 21/02/2018 at: https://jcwi.org.uk/blog/2016/05/23/what's-next-hostile-environment-immigration-act-2016-and-queen's-speech.

Jones, H., Gunaratnam, Y., Bhattacharyya, G., Davies, W. *et al.* (2017) *Go Home!: Immigration Controversies and Performative Politics*. Manchester: Manchester University Press.

Matthews-King, A. (2018) 'NHS told to stop handing over patient data to Home Office for immigration enforcement.' *The Independent.* Accessed 21/02/2018 at: www.independent.co.uk/news/health/nhs-patient-data-home-office-immigration-enforcement-illegal-asylum-seekers-healthcare-a8186746.html.

McGuinness, T. and Gower, M. (2017) *Immigration Detention in the UK: An Overview.* Briefing Paper 7294. London: House of Commons Library.

Mills, C. (2017) 'Suicides linked to austerity: From a psychocentric to a psychopolitical autopsy.' Discover Society, 1 February. Accessed 27/02/2018 at: https://discoversociety.org/2017/02/01/suicides-linked-to-austerity-from-a-psychocentric-to-a-psychopolitical-autopsy.

North East London Migrant Association (2017) 'NELMA Section 17 accompanying stats reveal…what we already knew, but the LAs persist in denying.' North East London Migrant Action, 22 August. Accessed 01/09/2017 at: https://nelmacampaigns.wordpress.com/2017/08/22/nelma-section-17-accompanying-stats-reveal-what-we-already-knew-but-the-las-persist-in-denying.

O'Hare, L. (2017) 'Death in detention: Suicide attempts soar in the UK.' *Al Jazeera*, 12 February. Accessed 21/02/2018 at: www.aljazeera.com/indepth/features/2017/02/death-detention-suicide-attempts-soar-uk-170205114101287.html.

Refugee Action (2017) *Slipping through the Cracks: how Britain's Asylum Support System Fails the Most Vulnerable.* London: Refugee Action.

Refugee Council (2015) *Detention in the Asylum System.* Accessed 16/07/2017 at: www.refugeecouncil.org.uk/assets/0003/3990/Detention_in_the_Asylum_System_March_2015.pdf.

Sales, R. (2007) *Understanding Immigration and Refugee Policy.* Bristol: The Policy Press.

Silverman, S. (2017) 'Immigration detention in the UK.' Accessed 01/09/2017 at: www.migrationobservatory.ox.ac.uk/resources/briefings/immigration-detention-in-the-uk.

Telegraph, The (2012) 'Theresa May interview: "We're going to give illegal migrants a really hostile reception".' Accessed 19/02/2018 at: www.telegraph.co.uk/news/uknews/immigration/9291483/Theresa-May-interview-Were-going-to-give-illegal-migrants-a-really-hostile-reception.html.

Vockins, D. (2013) 'Framing the economy.' New Economics Foundation. Accessed 01/09/2017 at: http://neweconomics.org/2013/09/framing-the-economy/?lost=true&_sf_s=+publications+++framing+the+economy+the+austerity+story.

Waite, L. (2009) 'A place and space for a critical geography of precarity?' *Geography Compass*, 3, 1, 412–433.

Withaeckx, S., Schrooten, M. and Geldof, D. (2017) 'Thinking and acting globally and locally: Developing transnational social work practices in Belgium.' *Transnational Social Review*, 7, 2, 143–157.

Narrative 3
Learning from Sam

My wife has severe mental health needs and I am her only carer. I came on a student visa in 2002, she followed me in 2005. She was hospitalised for more than seven months after witnessing the London Bombing in 2005. Since then, I have cared for her 24/7.

We have been married for 37 years. Sometimes she refuses to take her medication, which makes her psychotic. I wait say, 20 minutes for her to calm down and then encourage her to take it. I cannot leave her unattended for more than a few hours. I know the times of day she will kick off and what upsets her. We cannot use public transport because she gets agitated. My wife sleep walks and often at night, she just can't get to sleep – that stresses me out too. I was meant to go on a course yesterday but couldn't because she was too unwell.

We have never received any help from the social services. We were assessed in 2015 but the social workers said, 'We cannot help you because you have no recourse to public funding.' We cannot access anything because we don't have the right status. Our asylum-seekers' claim was refused and we were told to go home. But she is deemed 'not fit for travel' so we have been on 'section 4' support for two years.

When you are on a 'section 4', it's like being a prisoner in your own house. You are stopped from working immediately. So we have no access to cash. We used to be able to go out using taxis because we can't use public transport as my wife gets very distressed. But I have no money to pay for these now so we stay at home. You can't go anywhere without cash. I even had to borrow £5 from my friend to get to this interview today and I have no idea how I will pay them back. I have not been able to work for seven years now. This is how we became 'destitutes'.

We are only allowed to buy things from the supermarkets accepting the card you are given. This is where it's different for refugees with mental health needs because, for example, my wife doesn't understand this system. I have to keep explaining why we can't buy certain foods she likes.

We were moved to here from another city. My brother and sister lived in the other city too and helped me care for my wife. I tried to explain this to the Home Office but they didn't pay attention and just said, 'You are going to [city name].' My wife found the move distressing because new places upset her.

There are some people who are carers but because they have the right papers, they are paid something for looking after a relative – that's what I hear. But for me, I don't get anything at all. There is nothing the social workers can do because we don't have a stake in the country.

My wife's mental health is getting worse and it's getting too much for me. I feel like I've wasted my years. Sometimes I think about running away. How long do you think I can cope with her on my own?

Chapter 5

Disability and Forced Migration

Rebecca Yeo

Some parts of this chapter were previously published in an article for *The Cable*.[1]

Introduction

Kamil Ahmad was a disabled man, who had fled his home in Kurdistan, Iraq, having been tortured and imprisoned. He arrived in Bristol in 2011, hoping to find peace and safety. Instead, his application for asylum was refused, and on 7 July 2016, four years after arriving, he was murdered.

I met Kamil in 2012, soon after he arrived in Bristol. At that time, I was trying to bring together a group of disabled asylum seekers as part of a bigger project with the UK Disabled People's Council. My first hurdle had been finding people. I spoke to the disabled people's organisations that I knew, but found none that were aware of asylum seekers among their members. I rang a major charity working with refugees and was told 'disabled asylum seekers…don't really exist'. I had been involved in the disability movement for many years, I was prepared for the routine barriers and disregard for disabled people's needs. I am the daughter of a refugee, and grew up with stories of the trauma of fleeing violence and losing one's home. I had been volunteering in the asylum sector and was prepared for the deliberate hostility of asylum policy. However, I was not prepared for the casual denial of people's very existence, even within organisations designed to

---

1   Yeo, R. (2018) 'Long read: Two years after Kamil Ahmad's murder, there is cause for hope and anger.' Accessed 27/11/2018 at: https://thebristolcable.org/2018/08/long-read-two-years-after-the-murder-of-disabled-asylum-seeker-kamil-ahmad-there-is-cause-for-hope-and-anger.

provide support. I found that where the experiences of disabled asylum seekers were acknowledged at all, they were dismissed as if insignificant minority concerns. A Home Office employee explained that the system is designed for the needs of 'the able-bodied' or as an NGO employee put it, the needs of people who are '*normal*, single, fit and healthy' (my emphasis, Yeo 2017a, p.666).

What Kamil and others taught me about the impact of such disregard became the motivation for the doctorate that I am working on. As part of this, I have interviewed people in the immigration sector and the disability movement – including disabled asylum seekers and refugees, people working in asylum support and disabled people's organisations, campaigners, legal representatives, Home Office staff and politicians. This chapter draws on what I have learned from this work. I argue that fundamental systemic change is needed to address the injustice faced by disabled asylum seekers. Moreover, I suggest that while some recent initiatives may appear better than nothing, they risk distracting from, or even reinforcing, the inequalities at the core of the problem.

Kamil's experiences

A murder trial in October 2017 and a review by Bristol Safeguarding Adults Board (2018) have investigated the circumstances of Kamil's death. It is important that lessons are learned from that time, but the ways in which Kamil was failed started considerably earlier.

In 2012, four years before he was murdered, Kamil explained, 'everywhere is closed for me'. He drew a picture of what he wanted people to understand about his life. He told me, 'This is my heart that has been stabbed with a dagger. The Home Office did this, I am bleeding and no one can stop it' (Yeo 2017b). Kamil was not predicting what he thought was going to happen, he was describing what he felt was already happening.

At that time, Kamil had no secure place to live, no source of income, and no knowing if, or when, this situation would improve. What he did have was vast quantities of medication. He talked about doctors asking why he was taking his tablets on an empty stomach. He explained, 'I don't have money, I don't have food.' He asked why doctors could prescribe tablets but not food. Comparing his experiences in the UK with those in Iraq, he recalled, 'When I was in Iraq the people smashed my head by stones, they laughed at me, they hit me, abused me.' In a tragically ironic show of relative trust in the British system, he went on to say, 'In this country they don't hit you...but they do mentally… Is it the human right if somebody is a disabled person to be treated in this way?'

As a refused asylum seeker, Kamil had no right to housing or financial support. At that time, his survival depended on voluntary donations in Bristol. Unlike many people in this situation, he was lucky enough not to be street homeless; instead, he was staying in a shared house, supported by volunteers. However, he spoke of his sense of isolation: 'I can't see anybody to talk to… There are some people, they don't have my illnesses; they don't have my problems.' It became increasingly difficult for his mental health support needs to be met in this setting. Volunteers lobbied for him to receive a Care Act assessment from social services.

Under Section 18(1) of the Care Act 2014, local authorities are obliged to meet eligible needs for care and support if 'the adult is ordinarily resident in the authority's area'. Asylum seekers need to be 'assessed by the local authority in whose area they are present at the time the potential care need is ascertained' (Home Office 2018). If someone appears to need care, then an assessment must be carried out 'regardless of their likely eligibility for state-funded care' (SCIE (Social Care Institute for Excellence) 2014). In practice, however, intense lobbying from the voluntary sector seems to always be needed before an asylum seeker is provided with an assessment, let alone receives community care. Furthermore, although anyone with suspected care needs is eligible for an assessment, asylum seekers are exempt from receiving support, under paragraph 21 of the Care Act 2014, if their 'needs for care and support have arisen solely (a) because the adult is destitute, or (b) because of the physical effects, or anticipated physical effects, of being destitute' (ibid). People whose asylum claims have been refused may also be exempt from eligibility for care, 'except where, after assessment, the local authority decides to provide support to avoid a breach of Human Rights' (Home Office 2018). Kamil's needs were assessed as not being solely the result of destitution. He was assessed as having 'significant and ongoing physical, psychological and mental health needs' and was eligible for care. He was therefore provided with space in a hostel for people with mental health support needs. It felt like some small success. Some of his basic needs were being recognised.

However, soon after he moved in, a fellow resident took a dislike to him. This person repeatedly talked openly about plans to kill him. Over the next few years, Kamil reported being verbally and physically attacked by this man many times. Insufficient attention was paid to Kamil's calls for help and he was murdered on 7 July 2016. The injustice that Kamil experienced cannot be attributed solely to the perpetrator of the murder. He was failed on many levels.

Despite having escaped torture and imprisonment in Iraq, Kamil's asylum claim was refused soon after arriving in the UK. He was trying to submit a new claim, but his mental health conditions, including post-traumatic stress disorder and obsessive compulsive disorder, made it difficult for him to concentrate, remember and provide the necessary evidence of the minute details of his experiences. This is not an unusual experience. Jane Herlihy and Stuart Turner (2007, p.275) write of how 'an understanding of memory processing…dissociation and disclosure, is crucial to a fair and equitable treatment of people seeking protection from persecution'.

Kamil made multiple complaints to the police, the accommodation provider and mental health services, regarding the threats and abuse he was receiving. The Bristol Safeguarding Adults Board Review (2018) refers to language barriers and lack of interpreters, as if this were an excuse rather than a fundamental failing on the part of the agencies concerned. Writing in response to the Safeguarding Review, Ellen Clifford, Mike Steel and Rebecca Yeo (2018) suggest that 'the structures and attitudes of a system that disempowers service users are so ingrained that even now, the report authors are not able to recognise the ways in which Kamil was failed'.

At the time when Kamil was murdered he was also being threatened with eviction; according to social services his support needs had reduced. As disabled people (citizens or migrants) know too well, if appropriate support is provided and barriers are removed then conditions may improve; if support is removed, the situation can deteriorate. The Bristol Safeguarding Adults Board Review (2018) reported that staff were unaware of how traumatic the threat of eviction was for Kamil. This suggests puzzling levels of ignorance, or lack of empathy. As a refused asylum seeker, if Kamil had been evicted, he would have been street homeless without support. Knowing the impact this would have had on his physical and mental health, with the help of friends and supporters, he fought to stay. The eviction decision was overturned the morning *after* Kamil had been murdered.

The problem

The way a problem is understood determines what solutions are developed. It is therefore important to consider the nature and scale of the problem in some detail. Many of the ways in which Kamil was failed are neither unusual nor the result of oversights. *The Guardian* newspaper published footage of a Home Office official explaining to an asylum seeker:

> We are not here to make life easy for you…my aim at the end of the day, to make it a challenging environment for you… You're telling me it's pissed you off. There you go, I've done my job. (Taylor 2018)

The hostile environment is designed to be hostile.

The current situation needs to be understood in relation to historical developments. After the Second World War, the United Nations made multiple commitments designed to prevent such atrocities from recurring: the Universal Declaration on Human Rights (1948); the UN Convention on the Status of Refugees (UNHCR)(1951); the International Convention on the Elimination of All Forms of Racial Discrimination (1969). Overt support for racism became increasingly taboo outside the most extreme political right. Even President Trump must declare that he is not racist, while openly supporting white supremacist values. This is not to suggest that racism ever ended. As David Goldberg (2015, p.3) writes, the idea that we are in an age of 'postracism' results in 'racial outbursts' being 'treated like curses on the road: roll up the window and drive on by'. The structural nature of racism and discrimination is obscured.

I suggest the evil status attributed to the term 'racist' is ultimately unhelpful in preventing racism. Drawing on Lacanian notions of enjoyment, the term 'racist' can serve to make 'us' feel better about ourselves, proving that we are not as bad as 'them'. Benjamin De Cleen, Jason Glynos and Aurelien Mondon (2018, p.656) write of the 'affective investment' of labelling oneself as among those who are 'enlightened' or 'educated' in comparison with those who are labelled as 'irrational' or even 'stupid'. This hinders discussion of the causes of racism and obscures the systemic racism in which we are all implicated.

Historic responses to disablism are not dissimilar, although equalities legislation for disabled people took considerably longer. In theory, universalism was a key principle of the founding of the National Health Service. As Aneurin Bevan (1952) wrote, 'concern for individual life…is not achieved when limited to people of a certain colour, race, religion, nation of class' (p.177). This theoretical commitment did not, however, result in equality for disabled people. As Peter Townsend wrote in the foreword to Paul Hunt's groundbreaking book about the experience of disability (1966, p.vi):

> inadequacies are not just unwitting gaps in the outer fabric of the Welfare State… They reflect a much deeper problem of a distortion of

the structure and of the value system of society itself. Achievement, productivity, vigour, health and youth are admired to an extreme.

Hunt went on to found the Union of the Physically Impaired Against Segregation in 1972, developing what became known as the 'social model', challenging disabling barriers and previously hegemonic assumptions that disabled people are either to be cured or to be the focus of charity. In a similar way in which racism became seen as taboo, verbal commitment to addressing the barriers faced by disabled people became seen as a sign of 'goodness'. Michael Oliver (2013) describes how, in an effort to validate their existence, many disability charities and professional organisations began to refer to the social model as if they invented it. Again, this is not to suggest that such rhetoric was matched with equal levels of action to uphold disabled people's rights, or that systemic inequalities were ever addressed. However, it became increasingly taboo for racism or disablism to be openly promoted by UK governments of any persuasion.

The theoretical hegemonic commitment to universal human rights was most overtly broken in relation to migrant rights. In contrast to official condemnation of racism and disablism, successive governments of different political persuasions have competed to prove their hostility towards migrants, disabled or not. Since the 1951 Convention on the Status of Refugees, there have been 16 immigration acts, each reducing the rights of migrants, including disabled asylum seekers. The reduction in migrant rights, including those of disabled asylum seekers, has been framed not as 'racist' or 'disablist', but as defending 'our' geographical, material or cultural borders. The result is to promote acceptance that some people deserve human rights, but others do not.

Such undermining of basic principles of universalism has facilitated the normalising of racism and disablism. Recent laws show how rights first denied to migrants have later been denied to a wider population. The Immigration and Asylum Act 1999 removed asylum seekers' access to mainstream benefits, including disability-related benefits. Any acknowledgement of the financial costs associated with disability was thereby removed from the asylum system. People also became subject to forced dispersal to areas of low-cost accommodation around the UK. This can be particularly detrimental for disabled people, for whom support networks may be crucial in addressing access barriers. The 1998 White Paper on which the legislation is based justifies the removal of rights by focusing on the goal of controlling borders. The word 'control' is used 186 times in a

55-page document. The restrictions on the lives of disabled asylum seekers were unreferenced side effects of this goal.

This legislation provoked no organised resistance from disability charities or from disabled people's organisations. The focus of disabled citizens may have been on the more positive goal of the UN Convention on the Rights of Persons with Disabilities (2008). This Convention represented a 'paradigm shift' (Crock, Ernst and McCallum 2012, p.737), in that disabled people became internationally recognised as bearers of rights. However, the UK government added reservations, including one that the Convention should not interfere with the government's ability to carry out immigration policy. Again, such open disregard for the universalism of human rights met with little protest.

The removal of rights from asylum seekers should be seen as the first step in overturning the basic tenet of the welfare state and the post-war antipathy towards racism and disablism. The same year as asylum seekers lost the right to financial support for costs associated with being disabled, then prime minister Tony Blair (1999) devoted the Beveridge lecture to 'rethinking the welfare state'. The 'problem', as he presented it, was not how society should remove barriers (as espoused by the social model), but the dependency encouraged by the welfare state. This challenge to the basis of the welfare state paved the way for austerity politics.

It appears that in 1999 it was politically acceptable to remove rights from asylum seekers; however, before such changes could be brought to citizens, societal responsibility to promoting equal rights had to be replaced by a focus on individual responsibility, distinguishing between deserving and undeserving. For this to be achieved, the social model, with its focus on societal barriers, had to be replaced. With funding from the US insurance company Unum, which would have a major role in UK welfare reform (Jolly 2012), the bio-psychosocial model was developed by Gordon Waddell and Mansel Aylward (2010) at Cardiff University. As they note, 'people with common health problems…bear personal responsibility for their actions' (p.6). Lord Freud, speaking in the House of Lords, stressed the importance of this model in shaping welfare reform, recognising the need for 'personal effort' to 'overcome' (sic) disability (Hansard 2012). This became the basis for cuts to disability services and support.

In 2012, the Welfare Reform Act included the phasing out of Disability Living Allowance and the introduction of restrictions on housing benefits, commonly known as the 'bedroom tax'. This has resulted in people being 'forcibly evicted from their homes' (Koch 2014). Unlike the Immigration and Asylum Act 1999, the Department for Work and Pensions (2010) White Paper, on which the 2012 legislation is based, does not refer to the need for people to be controlled, but the need for people to show individual responsibility. The rationale is ostensibly different, but the results of both laws are similar: removing people's rights to financial support; forcing people to move to low-cost accommodation; distinguishing between the deserving and undeserving.

The 2012 legislation resulted in major protests, emphasising the disproportionate impact of austerity policies on disabled people. This legislation, together with wider cuts to services and support, led an investigation by the UN Committee on the Rights of Disabled People to report the British government's approach as 'grave and systematic violations of the rights' (UN Committee on the Rights of Persons with Disabilities 2016, p.18) of disabled people. Yet similarities with policies imposed on disabled asylum seekers have rarely been mentioned. There has seemed to be hegemonic acceptance that citizens have greater entitlement than asylum seekers. Only as conditions for disabled citizens have become increasingly intolerable has the situation been likened to the hostile environment imposed on asylum seekers (Ryan 2018). I suggest that the wider population pays the price for the failure to respond when rights were first removed from asylum seekers.

Many factors may have contributed to the lack of awareness and response from the disability movement when the rights of disabled asylum seekers were removed. It is difficult for disabled asylum seekers to organise and assert their existence and rights. In addition to the barriers faced by all disabled people, asylum seekers are often restricted by language barriers, lack of knowledge of how the system works, and a struggle for basic survival. One wheelchair user involved in my research explained to me that she is not involved in disabled people's organisations, stating that because 'I'm an asylum seeker it changes everything' (Yeo 2015, p.541). The lack of routine interaction between disabled citizens and asylum seekers reduces awareness of commonalities and hinders the development of joint responses.

The pervasive element of disablism is sometimes used to excuse the denial of rights to asylum seekers. A Home Office policy maker explained to me in an interview that the problem 'permeates through the whole of society' (Yeo 2017a, p.668). Similarly, Parekh (2009, p.16) questions whether there is any place that is 'free of disability oppression or persecution'. Several people who have contributed to my doctoral research have suggested that the problems faced by disabled migrants stem from the stigma associated with disability in their countries of origin. There are undoubtedly parts of the world where disabled people are treated worse than in Britain. However, there are also occasions and places where disabled people are treated better. Kamil explained that despite all the abuses carried out by Sadam Hussein, in some ways, disabled people had more rights in Iraq than he had in Britain.

I suggest that ranking degrees of shame is an unhelpful distraction, which again serves to promote Lacanian forms of 'enjoyment'. 'We' enable ourselves to feel better about injustice if we can convince ourselves that others are no better. Yet, the geographically and historically pervasive nature of disablism and racism does not justify them or make them inevitable. Furthermore, although some aspects of the disadvantages experienced by disabled asylum seekers in Britain are caused by oversight, other aspects are caused by deliberate policy.

The British asylum system is disabling by design. Some people are disabled on arrival in Britain, others become disabled later on. Disabled asylum seekers often describe the system as psychological torture. If someone is tortured, then symptoms are inevitable. The despair one person felt led him to jump off a bridge. This resulted in physical impairment as well as the ongoing mental distress. Another person developed serious back problems after being made destitute and having to sleep on park benches. The Bristol Safeguarding Adults Board Review (2018) into the circumstances of Kamil's murder concluded that the inadequate attention paid to Kamil's needs may, in part, be explained by unconscious discrimination against people whose asylum claims have been refused. This may compound the precarity of people's existence; however, the destitution of refused asylum seekers is not due to individual acts of oversight but to deliberate government policy.

Some Home Office staff are certainly aware of the despair that asylum policies generate. A disabled asylum seeker I interviewed showed me the Home Office letter explaining that their asylum claim had been refused. It included advice that if the news resulted in suicidal thoughts then the Samaritans should be called, or, if the person preferred not to speak to a stranger, then the advice was to talk to a friend. As this person said to me, they 'pretend to be kind, while stoning me to death'; the Home Office 'know what they are doing'.

Many of the disabled asylum seekers I have met as part of my doctoral research describe experiencing disregard for most basic human rights. One person with haemophilia was denied access to medication in detention until they had experienced several days of continuous bleeding. This person was then kept in handcuffs while being treated in hospital. A wheelchair user was dispersed to a new city, far away from family and friends. This person then had to rely on passers-by to get in, or out, of an inaccessible flat. A blind person was released from detention and left on a street corner without assistance. This person was only helped after collapsing and being taken to hospital.

Such experiences cannot be explained as either oversights or the acts of a few deliberately callous people. Fergal Keane (1996, p.226) described how after two years of pondering what kind of person would commit such horrendous brutality as he had witnessed in Rwanda, he realised the answer is:

> anyone, anyone at all. A man [sic] like you or me. Not a psychopath. Not a natural born killer. A man born without prejudice or hatred. But rather a man who was conditioned by the preachings of powerful men. Men who said that the survival of the Hutus depended on the death of small Tutsi children.

The denial of rights was justified by constructing 'them' as a threat to 'us'. Such discourse has been repeated numerous times in history, with variations in the degree, but not the existence, of consequential injustice. Keane (1996, p.229) elaborates that in Rwanda, 'race and identity were used as a means to create and preserve an inherently unjust power structure'. The human rights abuses imposed on asylum seekers in Britain may not be of the magnitude of the atrocities of the Rwandan genocide, but the parallels in the justification should not be dismissed. I suggest the most urgent challenge is not the degree of restriction imposed on disabled asylum seekers, but the notion that there is such a thing as 'them' and 'us'.

I have interviewed people with starkly contrasting roles in the asylum sector, but, as yet, have not come across people who describe their own role in negative terms. A high-ranking officer in the Home Office expressed his irritation at the way in which campaigners lobby him, without understanding that his aim is 'to make this world a better place'. Similarly, a person responsible for Syrian resettlement stated that the UK system is the 'best in the world'. Just as the labelling of racists as evil allows 'us' to feel better about ourselves without challenging systemic racism, it is important that the hostility of the asylum system is understood as beyond the actions of a few individuals. This is not to argue that the role of individuals within the system is unimportant.

One of the key barriers to challenging oppressive policies imposed on asylum seekers in Britain is the lack of clarity and consistency in the decision-making process. One person may be provided with care from social services, another with seemingly similar needs may not. One person may get a bus pass, another may not. One person may be granted asylum, another may be refused. Such discrepancy suggests arbitrary decisions as to who is deserving and who is not, who is 'real' and who is 'bogus' or 'illegal'.

When asylum seekers lost the right to access mainstream benefits, the possibility of support for 'additional' needs was introduced under Section 96(2) of the 1999 Act. However, from my research it appeared that few people were aware of, or using, this provision. The Home Office reissued the guidance in 2017. It remains to be seen how it will be used, but any policy with discretionary elements results in fear that challenging injustice may jeopardise wider decisions. Furthermore, any policy promoting different standards from those available to the wider population may reinforce divisions.

Current initiatives

Some initiatives exist, or have been proposed, to improve the experiences of disabled asylum seekers. Perhaps doing something is better than nothing, but focusing on action to reduce immediate symptoms of injustice risks distracting from systemic causes.

Safeguarding vulnerable people

On the rare occasions when disabled asylum seekers are referred to in the asylum system, it is almost exclusively in the context of 'vulnerability'. In theory, the Home Office and other institutions aim to identify 'vulnerable' asylum seekers, who become eligible for 'safeguarding'. Of course, support should be provided to people in crisis, but labelling disabled people as 'vulnerable' takes us back to before the disability movement began. All humans are vulnerable if their needs are not met. Where there are legal entitlements associated with 'vulnerability', then some individuals may benefit from the label. However, focusing on safeguarding 'vulnerable' people places the problem at the level of the individual, distracts from systemic barriers and implies that some people are more worthy than others. In the Home Office, the problematic labelling is compounded by referring to disabled asylum seekers as 'vulnerable customers', as if the asylum system were an optional business transaction.

The UK Visas and Immigration department of the Home Office has developed a matrix of 24 indicators of vulnerability (including disability) to identify those potentially eligible for safeguarding. However, if, after fleeing trauma and persecution, a person's asylum claim is refused, support and housing are withdrawn and there is no knowing if or when the situation may improve, then it may be more reasonable to attribute despair to systemic causes rather than personal 'vulnerability'. To prevent suicide without addressing the causes of despair should not be labelled as safeguarding but as further oppression.

The propensity for labelling disabled people as 'vulnerable' is not unique to the Home Office. The Bristol Safeguarding Adults Board Review (2018), published in response to Kamil's murder, refers to vulnerability 23 times in a 43-page document. Similarly, the multi-agency review into the circumstances resulting in the murder of Bijan Ebrahimi, also a disabled refugee, also in Bristol, includes 21 references to vulnerability in a 38-page document (Safer Bristol Partnership 2014). Yet, any human subjected to Kamil or Bijan's experiences would have met a similarly horrendous fate. They died not because they were more vulnerable than anyone else, but because they were denied protection from people intent on killing them.

The British response to the Syrian conflict is focused on the needs of the most 'vulnerable', including disabled people. An arduous journey to Britain is undoubtedly harder for people with many forms of impairment. Nujeen Mustafa (Mustafa and Lamb 2016) describes many barriers as a wheelchair-user fleeing from Syria to Europe. Perhaps it is therefore positive that disability is among the eligibility criteria for the increased entitlements of the UK's Vulnerable Persons Relocation Scheme. Those arriving on this scheme are immediately entitled to mainstream benefits, including disability benefits, housing, and local authority support.

Enabling any individual to lead a better life must be positive. However, reinforcing distinctions in human worth exacerbates a hierarchy of entitlement which is destructive to the building of solidarity. In her Conservative Party conference speech on 6 October 2015, the then home secretary Theresa May made a distinction between Syrians deemed deserving by their vulnerability and those 'fit enough' to get to Britain. Action which encourages consciences to be appeased, while ignoring the plight of those labelled as undeserving, reinforces systemic inequalities.

The problems with presenting anyone as undeserving may be obvious, but campaigns presenting particular people as exceptionally deserving are similarly problematic. If someone's worth depends on being exceptional, then the implication is that others are less deserving. This applies to campaigns for individuals or categories of people, including Syrian resettlement programmes, children in Calais, or indeed disabled asylum seekers of any origin. This is not to argue that individual campaigns should be rejected, but that possible negative consequences should be considered.

Data

The Syrian resettlement programme provides local authorities with advance notice of who is arriving. Sometimes it is argued that accurate data regarding numbers and arrival of disabled asylum seekers would facilitate provision of support. However, people seek asylum when they need to, rather than when invited to do so, therefore advance notice of arrival is hindered. In addition, people do not necessarily define themselves as disabled, despite experiencing barriers based on physical, psychological or sensory impairments. Therefore the label of disability is not straightforward. Furthermore, as Jeff Crisp (2018) argues, 'protecting people on the move starts not with better data, but with an ability to understand the key threats to their rights and to change the behaviour of those responsible for putting refugee and migrant lives at risk'. If the problems relate to the barriers that are experienced, then the priority should be to identify and address the barriers, rather than deciding who should be labelled as disabled.

More worrying perhaps is that assumed definitions of disability appear to be different for asylum seekers than for citizens. Many people I have interviewed in the asylum sector referred to the low numbers of disabled asylum seekers, but then spoke of mental distress as being normal for asylum seekers. It is not new, or radical, to include mental distress in definitions of disability. And the idea that if something is 'normal' then it is not disabling is particularly problematic.

Inclusion

The issues faced by asylum seekers also challenge wider campaigning goals. There is a widespread assumption that the problem facing disabled citizens or migrants is exclusion, and that the solution is therefore inclusion. However, inclusion in an oppressive system is no solution. As Grech (2009, p.776) puts it, 'the fundamental question of "inclusion into what" is rarely addressed'. A physically accessible detention system would not change the morality of detention. If the scope of political imagination has become limited to the binary options of exclusion or inclusion within the existing system, then reframing the problem becomes fundamentally important. The 'problem' is not a technical issue of including people, but a political issue of changing the system.

Proposed ways forward

If we accept that the problem is systemic then we need to change the system, not choose who is deserving within it, include people, or count people in it. This is not to suggest that reducing immediate suffering is unimportant, but that focusing only on symptoms is like pulling drowning babies out of a river without stopping the person throwing them in. We need to address the causes as well as the symptoms of injustice.

Focusing on the intersectional experiences of disabled asylum seekers can be useful in highlighting commonalities across traditionally distinct sectors. This may help bring people together to build a broader movement, increasing solidarity, challenging assumptions of a hierarchy of human worth and developing alternatives to the current system. Within these broad goals, I have a number of suggestions.

Rights-based criteria

Instead of discretionary support based on identifying people as 'vulnerable', eligibility for services and support should be based on clear rights-based criteria. This would facilitate advice as to people's options, reduce scope for exploitation and reduce fear of losing discretionary support.

Symptoms and causes

There are undoubtedly times when strategic responses to symptoms of injustice are needed. The problem is if such symptomatic relief becomes confused with solutions to the causal problems. The injustice experienced by disabled asylum seekers cannot be understood as a series of unfortunate oversights, but as a systemic problem.

Building solidarity

Proactive measures are needed to build solidarity, such that there is resistance to whoever's rights are attacked. For this purpose, occasions are needed to bring people together, to raise awareness of commonalities and differences, and to build a movement. Access barriers need to be continually addressed in the asylum sector as well as in the disability movement. The injustice imposed on disabled asylum seekers needs to be challenged not out of generous acts of benevolence from 'us' to 'them', but as defence of our common humanity.

After the coup which brought Pinochet to power in Chile, Dorfman (1998, p.136) recounts his desolation as he wandered the streets, not knowing which way to turn:

> It is then, when I am lost…that I see that man…for a split second that no camera could capture, no spy could register, at that instant…that man I have never before seen and would probably not recognise today, that man closes and opens his left eye and then he is gone, he vanishes as if he had never existed.
>
> He winked at me. Just that. No more than that. But that wink said it all… He saw me there in the pit of my sorrow and offered no more than his encouragement, proof that I was not really alone, that he was there even if we never saw each other again, that we could communicate even if the soldiers patrolled the streets and there seemed no place of refuge… forecasting with the closing and opening of his eye, how we would start rebuilding the country…bit by bit, wink by wink, under their very guns and boots. …the unspoken language of solidarity, the gesture of one man who had not lost hope toward another who was on the verge of losing it.

This wink of the 'unspoken language of solidarity' did not, and could not in itself have overturned the fascism engulfing Chile at the time, yet it restored Ariel Dorfman's hope and sense of purpose.

When organising an event to bring together the asylum sector and the disability movement, I was warned against the danger of raising hope. One asylum seeker stated that she did not want to be involved because to do so would result in hope for change, which would then involve opening herself to yet further disappointment. That was a risk she was unable to take. The aim was therefore to build understanding and solidarity, but not to raise hopes that could then be dashed.

It is easy to understand the appeal of action which is achievable, tangible and makes those involved feel good. This may be why there has been greater public interest in welcoming resettled Syrian refugees rather than attempting to challenge oppressive asylum policy and contribute to long-term systemic change. The challenge is to build a movement able to resist divisions and develop alternatives to current systemic problems.

Conclusions

The Home Office labelled Kamil, and others in similar positions, as *failed* asylum seekers. Kamil did not fail. Kamil *was* failed, badly, in the country in which he had hoped he would find sanctuary.

Tony Benn famously said, 'the way a government treats refugees...shows how they would treat the rest of us if they thought they could get away with it' (cited in Paul 2015). In 1999, the government removed rights from disabled asylum seekers. By 2012, the way had been prepared for similar policies to be brought to disabled citizens. The isolation of disabled asylum seekers contributed to the lack of solidarity in 1999, but the core problem has been the lack of challenge to the basic premise that some people are less deserving than others.

If the injustice experienced by disabled asylum seekers is to be addressed, I suggest the focus of action needs to be on systemic change, as well as reducing immediate individual examples of injustice. Increasing understanding, and respect, for the knowledge of those with lived experience is core to building a movement capable of collectively resisting oppressive policies, and developing alternatives based on equality and universalism. The 'language of solidarity', as Dorfman (1998) puts it, may be a more nebulous goal than addressing particular instances of injustice, but it is that on which systemic change depends.

References

Bevan, A. (1952) *In Place of Fear*. New York, NY: Simon and Schuster.

Blair, T. (1999) *Beveridge Revisited: A Welfare State for the 21st Century*. The Beveridge lecture, 18 March 1999. Accessed 28/11/2018 at: www.bristol.ac.uk/poverty/downloads/background/Tony%20Blair%20Child%20Poverty%20Speech.doc.

Bristol Safeguarding Adults Board (BSAB) (2018) *Safeguarding Adults Review using the significant incident learning process of the circumstances concerning Kamil Ahmad and Mr X*. Accessed 28/11/2018 at: https://bristolsafeguarding.org/media/28657/kamil-ahmad-and-mr-x-sar-report-final-for-publication.pdf.

Care Act (2014) Accessed 25/04/2019 at: https://www.legislation.gov.uk/ukpga/2014/23/contents/enacted.

Clifford, E., Steel, M. and Yeo, R. (2018) 'Response to Bristol Safeguarding review into the murder of Kamil Ahmad.' Accessed 28/11/2018 at: https://dpac.uk.net/2018/06/response-to-bristol-safeguarding-review-into-the-murder-of-kamil-ahmad.

Crisp, J. (2018) 'Beware the notion that better data lead to better outcomes for refugees and migrants.' 9 March. Accessed 28/11/2018 at: www.chathamhouse.org/expert/comment/beware-notion-better-data-lead-better-outcomes-refugees-and-migrants.

Crock, M., Ernst, C. and McCallum, R. (2012) 'Where disability and displacement intersect: Asylum seekers and refugees with disabilities.' *International Journal of Refugee Law*, 24, 4, 735–764.

De Cleen, B., Glynos, J. and Mondon, A. (2018) 'Critical research on populism: Nine rules of engagement.' *Organization*, 25, 5, 649–661.

Dorfman, A. (1998) *Heading South, Looking North: A Bilingual Journey*. London: Penguin.

Goldberg, D.T. (2015) *Are We All Postracial Yet?* Cambridge: Polity Press.

Grech, S. (2009) 'Disability, poverty and development: Critical reflections on the majority world debate.' *Disability and Society*, 24, 6, 771–784.

Hansard (2012) Debate on the Welfare Reform Bill. 17 January 2012: Column 496. Accessed 04/10/2017 at: www.publications.parliament.uk/pa/ld201212/ldhansrd/text/120117-0001.htm.

Herlihy, J. and Turner, S. (2007) 'Memory and seeking asylum.' *European Journal of Psychotherapy and Counselling*, 9, 3, 267–276.

Home Office (1998) 'Fairer, Faster and Firmer – A modern approach to immigration and asylum.' *White Paper*. Accessed 25/04/2019 at: https://assets.publishing.service.gov.uk/government/uploads/system/uploads/attachment_data/file/264150/4018.pdf.

Home Office (2017) *Applications for Additional Support*. Accessed 28/11/2018 at: https://assets.publishing.service.gov.uk/government/uploads/system/uploads/attachment_data/file/598944/Applications-for-additional-support-v1_0.pdf.

Home Office (2018) *Asylum Seekers with Care Needs*. Accessed 28/11/2018 at: https://assets.publishing.service.gov.uk/government/uploads/system/uploads/attachment_data/file/731907/Asylum-Seekers-With-Care-Needs-v2.0ext.pdf.

Hunt, P. (ed.) (1966) *Stigma: The Experience of Disability*. London: Geoffrey Chapman.

Immigration and Asylum Act (1999) Accessed 28/11/2018 at: www.legislation.gov.uk/ukpga/1999/33/contents.

International Convention on the Elimination of All Forms of Racial Discrimination (1969) Accessed 25/04/2019 at: https://ohchr.org/EN/ProfessionalInterest/Pages/CERD.aspx.

Jolly, D. (2012) *A Tale of Two Models: Disabled People vs Unum, Atos, Government and Disability Charities*. Accessed 28/11/2018 at: https://disability-studies.leeds.ac.uk/wp-content/uploads/sites/40/library/A-Tale-of-two-Models-Leeds1.pdf.

Keane, F. (1996) *Letter to Daniel: Despatches from the Heart*. London: Penguin.

Koch, I. (2014) '"A policy that kills": The bedroom tax is an affront to basic rights.' 23 September. Accessed 28/11/2018 at: http://blogs.lse.ac.uk/politicsandpolicy/a-policy-that-kills-the-bedroom-tax-is-an-affront-to-basic-rights.

May, T. (2015) 'Theresa May's speech to the Conservative Party Conference – in full'. 6 October. Accessed 28/11/2018 at: www.independent.co.uk/news/uk/politics/theresa-may-s-speech-to-the-conservative-party-conference-in-full-a6681901.html.

Mustafa, N. and Lamb, C. (2016) *Nujeen. Flucht in die Freiheit. Im Rollstuhl von Aleppo nach Deutschland*. Hamburg: Harper Collins.

Oliver, M. (2013) 'The social model of disability: Thirty years on.' *Disability and Society*, 28, 7, 1024–1026.

Parekh, G. (2009) 'Is there refuge for people with disabilities within the 1951 Convention Relating to the Status of Refugees?' Accessed 28/11/2018 at: https://cdd.journals. yorku.ca/index.php/cdd/article/download/23385/21575.

Paul, A. (2015) 'Living Like a Refugee: New York Must Do More to Help Its Homeless.' *Observer*, 9 September 2015. Accessed 21/05/2019 at: https://observer.com/2015/09/ living-like-a-refugee-new-york-must-do-more-to-help-its-homeless.

Ryan, F. (2018) 'The hostile environment? Britain's disabled people live there too.' *The Guardian*, 26 April. Accessed 27/01/2019 at: www.theguardian.com/ commentisfree/2018/apr/26/hostile-environment-britain-disabled-people-windrush-benefits.

Safer Bristol Partnership (2014) *Safer Bristol Partnership Multi-Agency Learning Review Following the Murder of Bijan Ebrahimi*. Accessed 28/11/2018 at: www.bristol.gov. uk/documents/20182/35136/Multi-agency+learning+review+following+the+mur der+of+Bijan+Ebrahimi.

SCIE (Social Care Institute for Excellence) (2014) 'The Care Act: assessment and eligibility.' Accessed 28/11/2018 at: www.scie.org.uk/care-act-2014/assessment-and-eligibility.

Taylor, D. (2018) 'Home Office official tells man facing deportation: "My job is to piss you off".' *The Guardian*, 3 May 2018. Accessed 27/01/2019 at: www.theguardian. com/uk-news/2018/may/03/home-office-official-tells-man-facing-deportation-my-job-is-to-piss-you-off.

Universal Declaration on Human Rights (1948) Accessed 25/04/2019 at: https://www. un.org/en/universal-declaration-human-rights/index.html.

UN Committee on the Rights of Persons with Disabilities (2016) *Inquiry concerning the United Kingdom of Great Britain and Northern Ireland carried out by the Committee under article 6 of the Optional Protocol to the Convention*. Accessed 28/11/2018 at: https://digitallibrary.un.org/record/1311200/files/CRPD_C_15_4-EN.pdf.

UN Convention on the Rights of Persons with Disabilities (2008) Accessed 28/11/2018 at: www.un.org/development/desa/disabilities/convention-on-the-rights-of-persons-with-disabilities.html.

UNHCR (1951) 'The 1951 Refugee Convention.' Accessed 28/11/2018 at: www.unhcr. org/pages/49da0e466.html.

Waddell, G. and Aylward, M. (2010) *Models of Sickness and Disability Applied to Common Health Problems*. Accessed 28/11/2018 at: www.webility.md/praxis/downloads/ Models-of-Sickness-Disability-Waddell-and-Aylward-2010-2.pdf.

Welfare Reform Act (2012) Accessed 28/11/2018 at: www.legislation.gov.uk/ ukpga/2012/5/contents/enacted.

Yeo, R. (2015) '"Disabled asylum seekers?… They don't really exist": The marginalisation of disabled asylum seekers in the UK and why it matters.' *Disability and the Global South*, 2, 1. Accessed 27/01/2019 at: https://disabilityglobalsouth.files.wordpress. com/2012/06/dgs-02-01-07.pdf.

Yeo, R. (2017a) 'The deprivation experienced by disabled asylum seekers in the United Kingdom: Symptoms, causes, and possible solutions.' *Disability and Society*, 32, 5, 657–677.

Yeo, R. (2017b) 'Kamil Ahmad: failed by the Home Office, then murdered in Bristol.' *The Guardian*, 17 October. Accessed 27/01/2019 at: www.theguardian.com/ commentisfree/2017/oct/18/murdered-asylum-seeker-kamil-ahmad-failed-britain.

Chapter 6

Learning from Immigration Controversies

Natalia Farmer

Social work is a profession that works within various contexts and is shaped by contemporary economic, social, political and cultural forces. Subsequently, frontline activity entails implementing assessments and providing service provision with individuals and families often experiencing the worst effects of austerity, inequality and injustice. Such activity often takes place within controversial contexts that are not difficult to identity; from UK Brexit negotiations to the recent #MeToo movement, such events influence society in uncertain ways, sometimes detrimentally and, at other times, challenging outdated ideals. In this chapter, I take inspiration from science and technology (STS) studies in 'controversy analysis' (Venturini 2010) in order to bring the contemporary controversial landscape of immigration into dialogue with social work practice. The aim is to learn from the concept of controversy and interrogate what it means for practitioners, students and service users 'to live, to know, and to practice in the complexities of tension' (Law and Hassard 1999, p.12).

In order to address these concerns, I draw from my experiences conducting ethnographic 'controversy analysis' fieldwork with the Asylum Seeker Housing (ASH) Project in Glasgow. I start by examining a report by the House of Commons Home Affairs Committee on asylum accommodation in the UK (House of Commons 2017). Asylum accommodation is a notoriously controversial issue and the evidence gathered during this year-long inquiry provides detailed learning opportunities for those working with this service user group. Notably, key concerns emerge, such as health and safety issues, reports of overcrowding and the degrading treatment of asylum seekers.

I then delve into further controversy and explore the issue of 'no recourse to public funds' (NRPF), a legal condition imposed on those subject to immigration control.

In this chapter, my aim is to investigate immigration controversies and interrogate how social work operates within this context. There are tensions between the notion of immigration control and social work practice that need to be critically addressed. While pro-immigration slogans and rhetoric such as 'Refugees Welcome' are worthwhile strategies, my intention in this chapter is to zoom in on the complexity of this context, and 'learn from controversy'. What is happening in these moments, who is implicated and what is the impact? Maybe then, it becomes possible to begin to combat a discriminatory immigration environment that is rife with injustice.

Contemporary immigration context

Current western immigration rhetoric is underpinned by anti-immigrant discourses, as seen during President Donald Trump's controversial 'family-separation policy' (*The Guardian* 2018a) or during what was termed the European 'migrant crisis' (BBC 2016b). In turn, these dominant perspectives shape policy, law and practice, creating various tensions for those located in such a charged context. However, what does this mean in practice? Policies and legislation are the frameworks and guidelines that determine the parameters of social work assessments and of who meets criteria for support. For those requiring access to social care, who also have insecure immigration status, this often translates to questions of 'are you here legally, or are you "illegal", and what conditions are there on your leave?' In these instances, and in order to access certain kinds of welfare or social care provision, not having 'status' can be a barrier to access, as outlined in UK legislation. Hence, controversy meets social work practice, and an environment is created rife with inherent tensions that are in direct conflict with the values and ethics of a profession that endeavours to challenge social injustice.

The notion of 'immigration control' has always been a controversial issue as successive governments scapegoat and blame migrants for societal ills, often harnessing anti-immigrant sentiments. The most recent 2014 and 2016 Immigration Acts in the UK can be seen as examples of increased border control in various ways. Critics have argued that this recent legislation has shifted the external borders of international airports and seaports towards the internal borders within civil society such as employment, housing and health and social care (Yuval-Davies, Wemyss and Cassidy 2018). In a similar vein, Jones and colleagues (2017) have explored the controversy in relation to contentious government immigration campaigns such as the notorious 'In the UK illegally? GO HOME OR FACE ARREST' vans. Their research project, 'Mapping Immigration Controversies', demonstrates the damaging consequences local communities encounter when faced with such campaigns that often provoke anger and fear.

So what can controversial events and encounters offer for social work practitioners and students? What can we learn from immigration controversies such as Windrush? When some of the Windrush generation are told by the local authority that they are not eligible for housing support because they cannot prove their immigration status (*The Guardian* 2018b), what is happening within social work practice? Crucially, how is this controversial context creating inherent tensions for practitioners and, importantly, for service users who attempt to access social services support? Despite the international profession vocalising a dedication towards promoting social justice and challenging unjust policies and practices (International Federation of Social Workers 2017), some argue otherwise. For Humphries (2004, p.93), social work has assumed a 'reactionary and uncritical view' towards immigration policy and is complicit in an oppressive system. Let us unravel that, and tease out some current challenges and possibilities facing critical social work practice.

Lessons from controversial inquiries

It is widely recognised that lessons are to be learned from high-profile serious case reviews in social work (Community Care 2013) and consistent concerns such as 'multi-agency working' and 'budget cuts' continue to be highlighted. Public inquires echo this sentiment as evidence is gathered and documents collated, producing detailed reports with important key findings and recommendations. Prominent controversial public inquiries, such as 'The Mid-Staffordshire NHS Foundation Trust Public Inquiry', 'The Hillsborough Stadium Disaster Inquiry Report' and forthcoming 'The Grenfell Tower Inquiry', demonstrate human rights abuses and failures (Sullivan 2017). During my time researching frontline practice with those subject to immigration control at ASH, inquiries became an important resource for this grassroots organisation, and a tool that helped them to hold those in power to account. One such inquiry involved the House of Commons Home Affairs Committee, which examines the daily activities of the Home Office and related public bodies. It explores policy, expenditure and administration and, in March 2016, the Committee launched an inquiry into asylum accommodation in the UK. Media reports in Glasgow raised the issue of alleged illegal evictions as asylum seekers were locked out of their homes (BBC 2016a). Subsequently, Keith Vaz MP visited the area and, having met with asylum seekers, he described the system as in 'crisis' and believed Glasgow to be worse than other areas of the UK (BBC 2016c).

The inquiry into asylum accommodation provides necessary detail in relation to the Commercial and Operational Managers Procuring Asylum Support Services (COMPASS), a contract in operation on behalf of the Home Office. Private multinational companies are responsible for the provision of asylum services, including Serco, G4S and the Clearsprings Group. According to the House of Commons (2017), the COMPASS contract accommodates 38,000 people in a pressurised system, characterised by a backlog of immigration claims. Detailed information of this system is widely misunderstood and often limited within mainstream discussion. The issues that emerged from this inquiry are useful, for a number of reasons, for developing and understanding not only the lived experience of asylum accommodation but the widespread challenges.

Raising awareness through the media

The Asylum Seeker Housing (ASH) Project is a grassroots community project set up to provide support for those in the asylum system who are being accommodated under the Home Office COMPASS contract. It supports asylum seekers by reporting housing issues to the private provider and provides a safe space and weekly drop-in sessions. A key aspect of its work involves the day-to-day issues asylum seekers face in Home Office accommodation. Often, this can mean supporting service users when they experience racial harassment, threats of eviction, challenges accessing services and general housing repairs. For ASH, alongside these daily activities supporting asylum seekers, outreach work and raising awareness is a significant aspect of the project and engaging with the media is a vital element of practice. As highlighted, it was the media reports in Glasgow that initially prompted the calls for an inquiry into asylum accommodation and this illustrates the benefit of media activity and coverage. Considerable awareness-raising documented the degrading treatment asylum seekers were experiencing. For example, there were issues of 'callous behaviour' and 'mistreatment' by private companies (*The Times* 2016). Interestingly, this coincided with national reports of providers painting the front doors of asylum seekers' accommodation red, making them the target for threats and vandalism (*The Independent* 2016). Other examples documented instances where asylum seekers were made to wear 'red wristbands' in order to access food (*The Guardian* 2016).

The controversial moments created by the media were important because they generated calls from other organisations, such as the Scottish Refugee Council (SRC), to take action. They prompted the initial call for a UK-wide Home Affairs Committee Inquiry into asylum accommodation, by framing the issue as a human rights concern that demanded a humane and dignified approach by the Home Office (Scottish Refugee Council 2016). They identified that the Home Office had legal responsibilities towards refugees, and shifted the issue from solely an accommodation issue towards a legal location. In Glasgow, multinational private contractor Serco was awarded the £175 million Home Office contract (*The Times* 2016) and it subcontracted work to the residential property company Orchard & Shipman (O&S). It was at this point that legal concerns dominated, as media reports stated that the legal protocol for asylum accommodation was being ignored (Commonspace 2015), and O&S lost the contract.

An initial lesson learned in this example demonstrates the vital role the media can play in terms of raising awareness when asylum seekers encounter issues of social injustice. For the ASH Project and the SRC, engaging with the media became an important tool that helped to hold the Home Office and the private provider to account from a legal perspective. With this in mind, social workers also have the opportunity and responsibility to enhance their relationship with media outlets in a similar manner, and lend their much-needed voices to national and global conversations that challenge oppression and discrimination. For example, media activism within immigration was evident during the controversy at Brook House Immigration Removal Centre in the UK. This scandal emerged when nine employees of G4S were filmed mocking, abusing and assaulting people in detention and the centre became a 'toxic mix' of incompetence and abuse (BBC 2017). While it is crucial to acknowledge that both the right wing and liberal media are hugely implicated in reproducing stereotyped and hostile stories about migration, media activism is also a vital channel for accountability. For practitioners and students eager to hold power to account, engaging with investigative journalism may tap into creative collaborations in instances of social injustice.

The relationship between social work and the media is a well-documented area of concern and many have emphasised the inherent tensions in coverage of high-profile child abuse cases and inquiries (Franklin and Parton 2014). However, some have argued for an enhanced relationship between social work and the media (Ayre 2001), and highlighted the potential for positive collaboration (Stanfield and Beddoe 2013). Understanding the role that the media plays in shaping immigration controversies is important for social workers, in order to unpick wider government agendas. Arguably, the media in part operationalise anti-immigration rhetoric, as evident in an interview that the then home secretary, Theresa May, gave to *The Telegraph* (2012), outlining her intentions to create a 'hostile environment' for those subject to immigration control. She stated that:

> Work is under way to deny illegal immigrants access to work, housing and services, even bank accounts. What we don't want is a situation where people think that they can come here and overstay because they're able to access everything they need. (ibid.)

Thus, the media is implicated by providing a platform for anti-immigration sentiment, shaping how immigration controversies unfold and maintaining the hostile environment. Alternatively, as seen by ASH and the SRC, they can also be utilised to challenge malpractice and build public and political interest around pertinent issues, such as immigration removal centres. For social work, this means rethinking how we engage with the media as a way to challenge social injustice. As Stanfield and Beddoe (2013) note, with the rise of 'citizen journalism' and an increase in social media activity, an opportunity is apparent for social work to engage with high-profile campaigns as a strategic manoeuvre to raise awareness in relation to discriminatory issues.

Accessing support

During my research at ASH, the Home Affairs Committee Inquiry continued alongside ongoing controversies over asylum accommodation and the nearby Dungavel Immigration Removal Centre. For me, observing caseworkers at ASH and being actively involved as a volunteer and a researcher provided a close proximity to the issues facing service users. Additionally, by following the evidence submissions throughout the inquiry, I was able to keep up to speed in relation to this fast-changing landscape and both activities developed the necessary skills needed to fully comprehend a very complicated system. This attention to detail is a must for any practitioner, or student, because of the substantial barriers and challenges that those in the immigration system encounter. Accessing asylum accommodation is extremely challenging due to the various complex stages that are tied to immigration status. Therefore, understanding how the process of claiming asylum actually works on the frontlines of practice is vital. Not knowing specific rights and entitlements can have significant consequences, such as giving incorrect advice that places a service user at risk of deportation or detention. In addition, the Office of the Immigration Services Commissioner (OISC) regulates immigration advisors, and it is important to note that it is illegal to provide immigration advice unless registered. Due to the complexity involved with the context of immigration, a detailed understanding of how the system operates is vital in order to challenge and potentially change degrading living conditions.

An important source of knowledge for any frontline practitioner or student is the Asylum Support Appeals Project (ASAP), which helps to reduce destitution by increasing awareness on specific issues when accessing support such as legal rights to food and shelter. Its website[1] is extremely accessible and has a wealth of key information that documents the three types of work the project provides – crucial for anyone working with asylum seekers. Its work entails: free, high-quality legal advice and representation; support, advice and training to frontline organisations (with an advice line); policy, lobbying and litigation.

ASAP is a key organisation to signpost any service user, practitioner or student to and it outlines vital information in a series of factsheets that provide invaluable and correct information (ASAP 2017a). This includes the technicalities of accessing initial emergency support, securing ongoing support during the asylum application assessment process and, in the case of refused applications, detail in relation to last resort support. In summary, the organisation provides the necessary information when applying for Section 98 (temporary emergency support if destitute), Section 95 (ongoing support) and Section 4 (refused asylum, appeal rights exhausted).

In theory, this process appears straightforward but the practicalities are messy and complicated, abusive at best and discriminatory at worst. For instance, in the case of Section 4 support, an application must meet 'the destitution test' and prove an individual or family is either destitute or about to become destitute, alongside meeting other regulations. One of these states

1   www.asaproject.org

that applicants must show that they are 'taking all reasonable steps to leave the UK or place her/himself in a position in which s/he is able to leave the UK' (ASAP 2017b, p.2). Practitioners and students need to be aware that this is not a simple matter because there are often numerous obstacles to families returning to their country of origin. Additionally, further barriers exist, such as receiving financial support that is as low as £37.75 per week, and having to survive in some cases on a cashless payment card system. ASAP is essential as it provides useful reports, bulletins, videos and signposts to other organisations that help support asylum seekers. Such detail helps to build a firm knowledge base for practitioners and students regarding the necessary and correct steps needed to access Home Office support.

Close proximity to the 'issues'

For practitioners and students, engaging with service user-led organisations such as ASH is vital because they remain in close proximity with the issues facing those subject to immigration control. At ASH, I witnessed appalling standards of asylum accommodation, and welfare concerns were a key issue as O&S continued to receive media attention amidst allegations of 'bullying and racism' (*The National* 2016) and ill-treatment breaching human rights (Commonspace 2015). According to the British Association of Social Workers (BASW 2012, p.14), social workers 'should be prepared to challenge discriminatory, ineffective and unjust policies, procedures and practices'. The code of ethics for social work makes clear that challenging the abuse of human rights is a core component of the profession and much can be learned from community projects such as ASH, dedicated to supporting those within the immigration system. Service user-led organisations such as these are crucial because they provide a rich source of information that brings us closer to the myriad ways in which the immigration system affects people. With this in mind, practitioners and students should be mindful to seek out such knowledge from third-sector organisations, which is indispensable because they have listened to the experiences of services users and offer a person-centred perspective that provides reliable expertise in this area.

Waverley Care, Scotland's leading HIV (human immunodeficiency virus) and hepatitis C charity, is an example of this and provided evidence of 'illegal evictions' via 'lock changes' in relation to African asylum seekers living with HIV in Glasgow. It focuses on the particular challenges faced by asylum seekers with HIV who need to access a daily regime of antiretroviral (ARV) medication. It argued that ARVs should be taken on a daily basis because gaps in medication can risk damaging the immune system, creating the 'opportunity for onward transmission' (Waverley Care 2017). The major concern involves the dangerous conditions occurring when the Home Office refuses asylum claims and withdraws support, increasing the risk of destitution. Case study evidence outlines the health and safety consequences of this concerning situation:

> We have worked with many service users who, once their support has been terminated, have returned to their flats to discover that the locks have been changed. In many cases this means HIV-positive service users are locked away from their ARVs too, meaning that they cannot take their medication as planned. (Waverley Care 2017)

In this sense, we can begin to envisage the social work profession encountering service users affected by this hostile context, as the well-being of asylum seekers becomes highly compromised as they are subject to lock changes and potentially illegal evictions. Such actions by private providers have a dangerous and harmful effect on the lives of service users. They are incompatible with the ethical principles underpinning social work practice, and the profession has a duty to challenge this form of social injustice.

Migrant Voice (2017) is another organisation that ensures the voices of those within the immigration system are heard. As a migrant-led organisation, it provides a platform that aims to strengthen migrant voices in order to develop accurate representation. Within the inquiry, its testimony illustrated the gendered impact of practices such as unannounced visits, entering flats without notice and lock changes. In one case, women described feeling 'watched' and experienced 'rude' and 'unprofessional' behaviour that compromised their dignity and privacy. As another report documented, evidence suggested that women did not feel safe or respected. One woman recalled that 'three members of G4S's staff barged into my room and other girls' rooms while we were inside; none of them had badges on, so they could be anyone really' (Migrant Voice 2017).

Furthermore, amidst reports that a pregnant woman in Glasgow was ordered to 'pack up her belongings' (*Evening Times* 2014), the gendered impact becomes more visible. The Refugee Council (2017) expressed its concerns regarding such treatment and took issue with the lack of support pregnant women receive. It argued the additional £3 provided through asylum support fails to support women sufficiently, resulting in the danger of an inadequate diet that could have a serious impact during pregnancy (Refugee Council 2017). Consequently, it maintained that such conditions disproportionately affect pregnant women. It recommended that independent experts implement 'spot check' visits in order to determine whether the food and support available in accommodation remains adequate for pregnant women and new mothers.

What we see from such testimonies is that many within the immigration system are placed in vulnerable positions and experience discriminatory and abusive treatment. The inquiry highlighted that inhumane treatment is prevalent within Home Office asylum accommodation. Moreover, it was suggested that the behaviour of private contractors 'fell far short of the duty to treat people with dignity and respect' (House of Commons 2017, p.40). Human rights abuses were rife during this controversy, and illustrated by testimonies documenting instances such as racial harassment, intimidation and illegal evictions. The overarching lesson to keep in mind clearly highlights that practitioners and students within social work should remain attentive to the discrimination that is occurring within this service user group, because we have a duty to pursue social justice. Failing to challenge these examples will result in the continued violation of human rights, and those in power will not be held accountable for such unacceptable behaviour.

Key points for practice

Since the Immigration and Asylum Act 1999, social work has become increasingly involved with those subject to immigration control. During my time at ASH, the implications of this for social work practice were evident, with the profession conducting social services assessments with refugees, asylum seekers, unaccompanied children and those with insecure immigration status. In an ever-changing landscape, it remains crucial that we have a fundamental understanding and awareness of the challenges that those within the asylum system encounter in relation to Home Office accommodation in the UK. The weekly service user drop-in sessions at ASH were a vital source of information to help me understand the issues asylum seekers were experiencing in Home Office accommodation. The key points generated from the ASH Project (2016) highlight important rights and entitlements that are essential when conducting advocacy work and are helpful for practitioners and students. Essential accommodation rights to keep in mind are to:

- be treated with respect and courtesy
- have safe and good-quality accommodation

- have good-quality furniture

- have any repairs needed to your house

- be able to complain and have representation.

Crucially, it needs to be acknowledged that practitioners are implicated in the provision of necessary support and a more nuanced grasp of the asylum process will allow us to meet the needs of this often vulnerable group, and in turn ensure better outcomes for those needing support services.

In this section, I highlighted the lessons that can be learned from immigration controversies and suggested that inquiries offer the opportunity to delve into the detail of this context. They provide us with resource-rich evidence such as testimonies and reports from community organisations working on the frontlines of asylum advocacy. The profession remains within close proximity to this group of service users and encounters may occur in a variety of different social work settings, such as adult social care, children and families safeguarding teams, mental health teams or criminal justice. To summarise, the key points when learning from immigration controversies are that:

- inquiries are a rich source of knowledge

- media contacts are essential for raising awareness

- accessing asylum support is challenging – there is a need to signpost to relevant organisations

- there is a need to understand the human rights 'issues' asylum seekers encounter.

The practice of 'learning from controversy' is useful in helping us understand the complexity of this context. Immigration legislation, policy and practice create a fast-moving environment, and focusing in on inquires allows us to explore important details such as who the private providers are within asylum accommodation, what their role is and how they impact on the lived experience for those in the immigration system. I suggest that paying attention to controversies, and utilising data within government and independent inquires, helps us develop our expertise and knowledge in order to comprehend the barriers that this context creates. The examples discussed in this section focused on third-sector organisations providing advocacy support for asylum seekers. Statutory social work has not been discussed thus far, and the next section will tackle some issues and tensions within local authority children and family teams.

Social work and 'no recourse to public funds' (NRPF)

I now turn towards the final point and one extremely pertinent for current UK social work practice. This is the issue of 'no recourse to public funds' (NRPF), a legal condition imposed on those subject to immigration control. Uncovering the problematic area of NRPF as an issue demonstrates how 'learning from controversy' is a useful tool to expose concerns that remain concealed. As stated, the previous section explored issues within the immigration system in relation to the Home Office, and the advocacy work of third-sector organisations. So, where does statutory social work sit within the immigration system and what is its role? In this section, I will look at the contemporary role of local authority children and family teams, and their interactions with families who have insecure immigration status.

Although the inquiry into asylum accommodation investigates areas of concern within the immigration system, it does so within the realms of Home Office accountability towards those within the asylum system. While this is an understandable endeavour in relation to exploring Home Office responsibilities surrounding accommodation and financial subsistence, it remains a narrow and rigid examination. It relies on assumptions that those within the immigration system fit a neat box in terms of status, rights and entitlements. However, this is simply not the case as the complexity of the immigration system is substantial. My research conducting controversy analysis with the ASH Project revealed the complexity and uncertainty involved when working with service users who have a condition tied to their immigration status known as 'no recourse to public funds' (NRPF). This issue emerged as a significantly misunderstood area and numerous tensions involving social work practice in relation to NRPF became visible.

During the inquiry, an unlikely actor alluded to this issue within the report on asylum accommodation. In the following statement Serco chief executive, Rupert Soames OBE, refers to tensions involving local authority support for those subject to immigration control:

> In practice, in cases of both positive and negative decisions, service users sometimes find themselves stranded. Local Authorities are sometimes slow and reluctant to take on the financial burden of providing for them, and service users, who may have children at school, be disabled

or elderly or being treated for medical conditions, are often tied to their accommodation. (Soames 2016)

What does this statement mean? As discussed, the duty to accommodate and provide support to those within the asylum system falls to the Home Office under the COMPASS contract. With this in mind, why would Soames mention the local authority? In the complex realms of being 'subject to immigration control', this remains a challenging area to navigate.

Furthermore, immigration status determines rights and entitlements, and this affects what avenues of support are available. For example, it can be easy to assume that social services have limited duties due to restrictions under Schedule 3 of the Nationality, Immigration and Asylum Act 2002. Nevertheless, as the No Recourse to Public Funds Network (NRPF Network 2015, p.1) emphasises, 'exclusion does not apply if the exercise of a duty or power is necessary for the purpose of avoiding a breach of a person's rights under the ECHR or European Community Treaties'.

This detail remains important to keep in mind in terms of statutory community care and children's legislation. As Humphries (2004) warned over a decade ago, social work has become increasingly entangled within a degrading, inherently racist immigration system, adopting a 'reactionary' and 'uncritical' role within policy.

A second inquiry by the Scottish Parliament's Equalities and Human Rights Committee explored this issue. The subsequent report, *Hidden Lives – New Beginnings: Destitution, Asylum and Insecure Immigration Status in Scotland* (Scottish Parliament 2017), addresses the complexity involved. For example, defined by Section 115 of the Immigration and Asylum Act 1999, any 'person subject to immigration control will have No Recourse to Public Funds (NRPF)' (Scottish Parliament 2017, p.7). NRPF involves exclusion from accessing 'public funds' such as welfare benefits, social housing, and homelessness assistance. Moreover, the report outlines key examples of those potentially affected, including: status dependent on a partner, spouse or other family member; people with limited stay in the UK; the undocumented; people with no legal right to be in the UK, but who may secure their legal status if supported to do so. In addition, the report highlights concerns that local authorities are failing to implement NRPF guidance and best practice accordingly.

I contributed written and oral evidence during the inquiry from research with ASH, and this demonstrated the challenges NRPF destitute families encounter when accessing social services support. All the families requiring

ASH advocacy had an NRPF condition and insecure immigration status, and could not access Home Office support. Thus, support from the local authority became a last resort and a final safety net. However, significant tensions emerged in relation to the issue of NRPF and social work practice. Specifically, significant tensions between immigration legislation and social services duty to safeguard and promote the welfare of NRPF families were evident (Farmer 2017).

For instance, the practice of 'gatekeeping' emerged as a consistent theme when NRPF families attempted to secure support from social services. The NRPF Network (2017) emphasises that support from a local authority under community care and children's legislation is *not* considered a public fund. However, my research documented that support is often denied. Examples of this included 'refusal to provide accommodation and financial support' and threats to 'accommodate the child but not the parent', alongside inconsistent child-in-need assessments and 'inadequate levels of support' (Farmer 2017, pp.362–4). Interestingly, despite evidence submitted by Glasgow City Council Social Work Services (GCC SWS 2012) that demonstrated a critical stance regarding Home Office asylum support, its own provision for NRPF families contradicted this position. For example, GCC SWS (2012, p.2) advocates '£89 per week' for a first child in order to meet 'basic necessities' and 'essential needs' to 'fully participate in society'. However, evidence gathered when advocating for NRPF families found that in reality, families were surviving on as little as £25 per week (Farmer 2017). This demonstrates how the profession can become complicit in the constriction and punishment of those subject to immigration controls. Circumventing this would call for social workers to actively refuse to comply with the discriminatory policy of NRPF and the role of an immigration 'border guard'.

At the same time, media reports documented significant frustrations that the UK immigration system is leaving many children destitute (*The Ferret* 2017), and NRPF families are being threatened with having their children removed (*The Guardian* 2017). Alongside this, wider campaign groups began dedicating considerable energy towards raising awareness of discriminatory social services practices with NRPF families. Project 17 is an organisation which aims to address the systemic problems NRPF families encounter through strategic litigation, supporting families, raising awareness and engaging with local authorities. For example, it raised concerns with Mayor Philip Glanville of Hackney in relation to numerous issues pertinent to NRPF families. It also highlights bad practice, such as refusals to conduct child-in-need assessments, inadequate accommodation, low financial subsistence, unlawful advice and intimidating behaviour from council staff (Project 17 2017).

Additionally, the campaigning group North East London Migrant Action (NELMA 2017) created an accompanying scheme in order to support NRPF families approaching social services for support. As a member of NELMA'S forum remarks:

> You can't go there on your own. I went [to children's services] alone and called them from downstairs, asking to see someone. I was seven months pregnant and crying down the phone. They refused to come down to see me for the whole day. (NELMA 2017)

From this, notions of the 'everyday border' (Yuval-Davies *et al.* 2018, p.229) become evident for social work as immigration status, rights and entitlements dominate assessments. Problematically, social work practitioners are assuming the role of internal statutory border guard and implementing exclusionary immigration policies. In the case of NRPF destitute families, what we see is a 'dysfunctional system in which children are the ultimate losers' (Price and Spencer 2015, p.57) and are often pushed into dangerous and exploitative conditions.

In this section 'learning from controversy' entailed uncovering the hidden issue of NRPF within social work practice. So, how do we address the complexities present within the current landscape as practitioners and students committed to challenging social injustice and oppression? Crucially, there are intrinsic tensions that the profession must recognise, such as the relationship between immigration control and welfare provision. Interrogating this environment, one that is characterised by conflict and complexity, remains fundamental in order to comprehend an inherently racialised and gendered immigration system. Therefore, substantial knowledge of the issues that those within the immigration system are encountering becomes necessary. This involves a constant reassessment, to examine how the role of social work operates within a controversial immigration context that is experiencing consistent moments of conflict. When working with destitute NRPF families, The Children's Society (2015) offers some key points: support from social services *is not* a public fund; social services can offer accommodation and financial support; child-in-need assessments should be conducted (seek legal advice if refused); social services *do not* have the power to remove children because of NRPF; and social services can support homeless families while an assessment is being conducted.

Conclusion

In this chapter, lessons from immigration controversies have been explored and I have drawn from high-profile inquires and my own engagement with a grassroots community organisation in order to interrogate this context. As mentioned in the introduction, widespread criticism has rightly focused on the Trump administration's 'family separation' policy. However, as practitioners and students we should not remain complacent about what is occurring in our own profession. We must recognise that the profession is implicated within this context, and assuming the role of an immigration border guard flies in the face of our ethics and values.

Humphries (2004, p.105) argued that social work 'needs to stop pretending that what it calls "anti-oppressive practice" is anything but a gloss to help it feel better about what it is required to do'. I echo these sentiments regarding the treatment of those within the immigration system, from asylum seekers to NRPF families and individuals – and from witnessing the devastating treatment of families by social services during my research. NRPF is state violence and unless the experiences of individuals and families within the immigration system are recognised and valued, and action is taken, many will be further pushed into dangerous and exploitative conditions in order to survive.

References

ASAP (Asylum Support Appeals Project) (2017a) 'Factsheets: Easy-to-Use Resources for Anyone with Questions about Asylum Support.' Accessed 15/11/2018 at: www.asaproject.org/resources/factsheets.

ASAP (Asylum Support Appeals Project) (2017b) *Section 4 Support*. Accessed 15/11/2018 at: www.asaproject.org/uploads/Factsheet-2-section-4-support.pdf.

Asylum Seeker Housing Project (2016) *Written Evidence Submitted by Asylum Seeker Housing Project* and *Support Services in Scotland Asylum Accommodation*. Accessed 15/11/2018 at: http://data.parliament.uk/WrittenEvidence/CommitteeEvidence.svc/EvidenceDocument/Home%20Affairs/Asylum%20accommodation/written/40157.html.

Ayre, P. (2001) 'Child protection and the media: Lessons from the last three decades.' *British Journal of Social Work*, 31, 6, 887–901.

BASW (British Association of Social Workers) (2012) *The Code of Ethics for Social Work: Statement of Principles*. Accessed 15/11/2018 at: http://cdn.basw.co.uk/upload/basw_95243-9.pdf.

BBC (2016a) 'Asylum seekers allegedly locked out of homes.' 1 March. Accessed 15/11/2018 at: www.bbc.co.uk/news/uk-scotland-35639585.

BBC (2016b) 'Migrant crisis: Migration to Europe explained in seven charts.' 4 March. Accessed 15/11/2018 at: www.bbc.co.uk/news/world-europe-34131911.

BBC (2016c) 'MPs to probe claims of asylum seekers locked out of homes.' 18 March. Accessed 15/11/2018 at: www.bbc.co.uk/news/uk-scotland-35848080.

BBC (2017) 'Detainees "mocked and abused" at immigration centre.' 1 September. Accessed 15/11/2018 at: www.bbc.co.uk/news/uk-41121692.

The Children's Society (2015) *Your Rights and Entitlements: A Guide to Social Services Assistance for Destitute Migrant Families.* Accessed 29/01/2019 at: www. childrenssociety.org.uk/sites/default/files/cfd097_family-voice-17-leaflet_v7_low-res_web.pdf.

CommonSpace (2015) 'Evictions, bullying, racism: The horror faced by Scotland's asylum seekers revealed.' 5 March. Accessed 15/11/2018 at: www.commonspace. scot/articles/604/evictions-bullying-racism-the-horror-faced-by-scotland-s-asylum-seekers-revealed.

Community Care (2013) 'The lessons to be learnt from three recent high profile serious case reviews.' 9 October. Accessed 15/11/2018 at www.communitycare. co.uk/2013/10/09/the-lessons-to-be-learnt-from-three-recent-high-profile-serious-case-reviews.

Evening Times (2014) 'Pregnancy won't halt eviction.' 23 October. Accessed 18/04/2019 at: https://www.eveningtimes.co.uk/news/13294713.pregnancy-wont-halt-eviction.

Farmer, N.J. (2017) '"No Recourse to Public Funds", insecure immigration status and destitution: The role of social work.' *Critical and Radical Social Work,* 5, 3, 357–367.

Ferret, The (2017) 'The children left destitute on Scotland's streets.' Accessed 15/11/2018 at: https://theferret.scot/destitution-children-scotland.

Franklin, B. and Parton, N. (2014) *Social Work, the Media and Public Relations* (Routledge Revivals). Abingdon: Routledge.

GCC SWS (Glasgow City Council Social Work Services) (2012) *Glasgow City Council Social Work Services Response to the Parliamentary Inquiry into Asylum Support.* Accessed 15/11/2018 at: www.childrenssociety.org.uk/what-we-do/resources-and-publications/publications-library/glasgow-city-council-social-work-services.

Guardian, The (2016) 'Asylum seekers made to wear coloured wristbands in Cardiff.' 23 September. Accessed 15/11/2018 at: www.theguardian.com/uk-news/2016/jan/24/asylum-seekers-made-to-wear-coloured-wristbands-cardiff.

Guardian, The (2017) 'Destitute immigrants in UK are threatened with having children removed.' 13 June. Accessed 15/11/2018 at: www.theguardian.com/uk-news/2017/jun/13/destitute-immigrants-uk-threatened-with-having-children-removed.

Guardian, The (2018a) 'Trump policy of detaining children "may amount to torture", UN says – as it happened.' 22 June. Accessed 15/11/2018 at: www.theguardian.com/us-news/live/2018/jun/22/trump-family-separation-crisis-immigration-border.

Guardian, The (2018b) 'The children of Windrush: "I'm here legally, but they're asking me to prove I'm British."' 15 September. Accessed 15/11/2018 at: www. theguardian.com/uk-news/2018/apr/15/why-the-children-of-windrush-demand-an-immigration-amnesty.

House of Commons (2017) *The House of Commons Home Affairs Committee Report on Asylum Accommodation.* London: House of Commons.

Humphries, B. (2004) 'An unacceptable role for social work: Implementing immigration policy.' *British Journal of Social Work,* 34, 1, 93–107.

Immigration and Asylum Act (1999) Accessed 28/11/2018 at: www.legislation.gov.uk/ukpga/1999/33/contents.

Independent, The (2016) 'Red doors of asylum seeker housing in Middlesbrough repainted "range of colours" after vandalism and abuse.' 26 January. Accessed 15/11/2018 at: www.independent.co.uk/news/uk/home-news/red-doors-of-asylum-seeker-housing-in-middlesbrough-repainted-range-of-colours-after-vandalism-and-a6834391.html.

International Federation of Social Workers (2017) 'Global Social Work Statement of Ethical Principles.' Accessed 15/11/2018 at: www.ifsw.org/global-social-work-statement-of-ethical-principles.

Jones, H., Gunaratnam, Y., Bhattacharyya, G., Davies, W. *et al.* (2017) *Go Home?: The Politics of Immigration Controversies.* Manchester: Manchester University Press.

Law, J. and Hassard, J. (1999) *Actor Network Theory and After.* Oxford: Blackwell.

Migrant Voice (2017) 'Emerging findings from Migrant Voice research into the living conditions of asylum seekers in Birmingham and the West Midlands.' *The House of Commons Home Affairs Committee Report on Asylum Accommodation.* Accessed 15/11/2018 at: http://data.parliament.uk/WrittenEvidence/CommitteeEvidence.svc/EvidenceDocument/Home%20Affairs/Asylum%20accommodation/written/40119.html.

Nationality, Immigration and Asylum Act (2002) Accessed on 13/05/2019 at: http://www.legislation.gov.uk/ukpga/2002/41/schedule/3.

National, The (2015) 'Bullying and racism: The life of an asylum seeker in Scotland.' 6 March. Accessed 15/11/2018 at: www.thenational.scot/news/14897052.Bullying_and_racism__The_life_of_an_asylum_seeker_in_Scotland.

NELMA (North East London Migrant Action) (2017) *Testimonies.* Accessed 15/11/2018 at: https://novaramedia.com/2017/01/15/surviving-hostile-environments-migrant-families-with-no-recourse-to-public-funds.

NRPF (No Recourse to Public Funds) Network (2015) *Schedule 3 of the Nationality Immigration and Asylum Act 2002 and the Care Act 2014.* Accessed 15/11/2018 at: www.nrpfnetwork.org.uk/Documents/Care-Act-Schedule-3.pdf.

NRPF (No Recourse to Public Funds) Network (2017) 'About us.' Accessed 15/11/2018 at: http://www.nrpfnetwork.org.uk/aboutus/Pages/default.aspx.

Price, J. and Spencer, S. (2015) *Safeguarding Children from Destitution: Local Authority Responses to Families with 'No Recourse to Public Funds'.* Oxford: University of Oxford.

Project 17 (2017) Accessed 15/11/2018 at: www.project17.org.uk.

Refugee Council (2017) *Written Evidence Submitted by the Refugee Council.* Accessed 15/11/2018 at: http://data.parliament.uk/WrittenEvidence/CommitteeEvidence.svc/EvidenceDocument/Home%20Affairs/Asylum%20accommodation/written/40185.html.

Scottish Parliament (2017) *Hidden Lives – New Beginnings: Destitution, Asylum and Insecure Immigration Status in Scotland.* Accessed 15/11/2018 at: www.parliament.scot/S5_Equal_Opps/Reports/EHRiC_3rd_Report_2017.pdf.

Scottish Refugee Council (2016) 'Scottish Refugee Council calls for investigation into housing for people seeking asylum.' Accessed 15/11/2018 at: www.scottishrefugeecouncil.org.uk/news_and_events/news/2819_scottish_refugee_council_calls_for_investigation_into_housing_for_people_seeking_asylum.

Soames, R. (2016) *Letter from Rupert Soames OBE, Chief Executive, Serco Group Plc, to The Chair of the Committee, 6 April 2016.* Accessed 15/11/2018 at: http://data. parliament.uk/writtenevidence/committeeevidence.svc/evidencedocument/home-affairs-committee/asylum-accommodation/written/36673.html.

Stanfield, D. and Beddoe, L. (2013) 'Social work and the media: A collaborative challenge.' *Aotearoa New Zealand Social Work,* 25, 4, 41.

Sullivan, R, (2017) 'What is a public inquiry?' Accessed 15/11/2018 at: https://rightsinfo. org/explainer-public-inquiry.

Telegraph, The (2012) 'Theresa May interview: "We're going to give illegal migrants a really hostile reception."' 25 May. Accessed 15/11/2018 at: www.telegraph.co.uk/ news/uknews/immigration/9291483/Theresa-May-interview-Were-going-to-give-illegal-migrants-a-really-hostile-reception.html.

Times, The (2016) 'Inquiry call over "callous treatment" of refugees.' 18 February. Accessed 15/11/2018 at: www.thetimes.co.uk/article/inquiry-call-over-callous-treatment-of-refugees-7q3c93w7kph.

Venturini, T. (2010) 'Diving in magma: How to explore controversies with actor-network theory.' *Public Understanding of Science,* 19, 3, 258–273.

Waverley Care (2017) *Written evidence submitted by Waverley Care.* Accessed 15/11/2018 at: http://data.parliament.uk/WrittenEvidence/CommitteeEvidence.svc/ EvidenceDocument/Home%20Affairs/Asylum%20accommodation/written/40145. html.

Yuval-Davis, N., Wemyss, G. and Cassidy, K. (2018) 'Everyday bordering, belonging and the reorientation of British immigration legislation.' *Sociology,* 52, 2, 228–244. Doi: 10.1177/0038038517702599.

Narrative 4
Learning from Jan

We went to social services to tell them that my brother was not well. I had to be there to look after him 24 hours a day. He needed a support worker, or accommodation. He was living with me. Social services said they could not help him, he had to go to mental health services. Mental health services said we needed to go to social services. We then went to a refugee advocacy service in my city who called mental health services for us, to ask them to help him. They spent two hours on the phone, it was at Christmas time. In the end, mental health services provided him with some money but there was no support worker. Eventually he went to hospital for one year because of his mental health. After he came out of hospital they gave him some accommodation and now he is getting the support he needs.

It was hard to get the service he needed as we don't have a background here, we couldn't explain what we need. We don't come from here. It was easy for them to say no. In the end, services accepted he needed help, but by then he had to go to hospital. Social services weren't available for us at the right time, in the right place.

At that time, he didn't have a claim or any status, but now he has five years' leave to remain. It was a very hard issue for me, and for him and the whole family. It was hard at first because he didn't have any documents; once he got them they could help him. Eventually, once mental health services accepted that they needed to help him and give him some medication, it got better. It has got better, step by step.

In the end, social services were not there for supporting him or talking about what was going on. They didn't ask anything about what was going on, we had to keep chasing him to ask for food bank vouchers. But now he's okay. And he has me.

Now my brother mostly uses the GP to get medication. They are okay. They try to help him. He can't eat good food, he only gets £30 a week. So he has been to hospital many times as his diabetes has been very bad.

It has been a very tough situation. I had to care for him 24 hours a day, I couldn't have a social life like other young people. I was seeing on the news that no one was supporting these people, the government isn't helping. If I wasn't there, nothing would have happened. I couldn't work as I had to look after him. I couldn't leave him alone in the house with the other people who lived there as they didn't want me to leave him there with them. When people help you, you don't forget them. It was a lot of pressure and I was very young. I wanted to do my own thing and be independent. I couldn't because my brother was there; he was homeless before and he would be distressed if I left him.

I want to write something about social services, so that they can look at the difficulties people have and see that many people need help. They think we don't know the law, that we don't know how to get the service. Then we ask the refugee advocacy service to ask for us and they know the law, they speak good English, and then they can get the service. They couldn't deny them. For other people, it is easy for them to say what they want, to say their opinion. But for the refugee it is harder.

We asked the solicitor if he could help us but he said go to the refugee services. He couldn't just go and live anywhere, he needed me, or someone around to support him. Now he is living in shared accommodation with 24-hour care. Now I can work and do my own thing. I go and help him with food and some small things. He doesn't see the social worker very much; they don't try to call me. The social worker is getting paid, but wasn't helping as much as they could do. The social worker has changed three times, and now I think there will be a fourth one. He didn't mind the first time but…the good social worker, they made appointments with him, they asked how he was and how far he had come. It was the small things that became big things. This gave my brother comfort.

Chapter 7

Working with Separated Children and Young People Seeking International Protection

What Social Workers Need to Know

Jen Ang

My happiest memory...is to get permission to live in the UK. And to live my life happy. With no worries, no fear. To get my freedom.

'Zahra', age 16, who arrived in the UK travelling alone, from Somalia

Introduction

Forced migration is a reality for many of the world's children. In June 2018, there were an unprecedented 68.3 million forcibly displaced people worldwide, according to the UN High Commissioner for Refugees (UNHCR). Of these, over 25.4 million were refugees, over half of whom were children under the age of 18 (UNHCR 2018). A small proportion of these refugee children make it to Europe and the UK. For example, in 2017, there were 209,756 applications for international protection in Europe made by children, of which only 7455, or 3.6 per cent, were made in the UK. Of these, only 3382 (or 1.6%) were made by unaccompanied asylum-seeking children (UNICEF UK 2018a). The media has, in recent years, documented the current refugee crisis in Europe and highlighted how journeys across borders and seas have become increasingly dangerous. There are currently more child refugees in Europe than at any time since the end of the Second World War (UNICEF UK 2018b).

Against this backdrop, it is becoming increasingly likely that social workers currently in practice, and students about to enter practice, may, at some stage in their careers, find themselves responsible for safeguarding, and supporting, separated children and young people seeking international protection in the UK.[1] Similarly, this chapter is of value to all social services staff, such as residential care staff, and not just social workers undertaking assessments in fieldwork settings. This chapter attempts to set out, in a modest number of pages, some practical advice to those social workers and social care professionals and is drawn from my practice experience as a specialist immigration and asylum lawyer working with children and young people.

Child first, migrant second

Should you manage to read no further, this chapter carries one key message: *children seeking international protection are children first, migrants second.* Although migration status (and legal processes associated with migration status) is a significant feature in casework with a child or young person you may be working with, your starting point, in terms of best practice and your obligation to be guided by the principle of best interests, should be the same for a migrant child as for any other, non-migrant, young person. For the same reason, even a social worker who has never worked with a migrant child or young person before should still feel entitled to some confidence that bringing best practice social work skills to bear – even in this novel and unfamiliar context – is the right starting point. It is worth noting, however, that the advice 'children first, migrants second' is not always the general perception of how rights and entitlements of these children and young people are determined in society. There are several reasons for this. Some you will be familiar with or will be able to guess. Others can be traced to historical decisions of the UK government, of which you may not yet be aware.

---

1   'Seeking international protection' is the term used throughout the chapter to refer to individuals who have made an application to remain in the UK either because they are a refugee, or because they face some other feared harm on return to their home country. This is commonly referred to as 'seeking asylum' and the terms have broadly the same meaning; however, the term 'asylum' has become increasingly associated with negative perceptions of asylum seekers in recent years, and so some practitioners have shifted to the term 'international protection', which more clearly situates these processes and relationships within an international human rights framework.

To help you place this advice in a legal and historical context, this chapter will start with a brief overview of how children's rights are protected in international and domestic law. It will then go on to highlight some of the significant differences in the process that apply to children and young people claiming international protection, as compared to adult claimants. The chapter will then highlight some particular challenges and barriers that arise for children and young people, and close with some practical advice on how social workers and other social care staff can effectively support children and young people seeking international protection.

Children's rights in international and domestic law

Children's rights are robustly articulated and protected in international law, and these protections are directly expressed in our UK domestic law. This section seeks to briefly explain the key instruments of international law that guarantee rights to children and young people seeking international protection, and to illustrate how these principles are enshrined in domestic law, policy and statutory and non-statutory guidance.

UN Convention on the Rights of the Child (UNCRC) 1989

The 1989 UNCRC is the most widely ratified international human rights treaty in the world. It grants rights to all children and young people up to age 18 and sets out in a list of more than 40 substantive rights what every child needs to have a safe, happy and fulfilled childhood, on equal terms, and without discrimination on any basis.

If jointly considered, Articles 1, 2 and 3 of the UNCRC clarify why the chapter opens by saying *children seeking international protection are children first, migrants second*. Article 1 of the UNCRC defines children as anyone under the age of 18. Technically, the UNCRC defines a child as anyone under the age of 18, or such earlier age as children are deemed to reach the age of majority in any particular country. So, for example, legal arguments have been framed in Scotland to suggest that children attain the age of majority at 16, for some purposes (see Age of Legal Capacity (Scotland) Act 1991; Hill *et al.* 2017). However, using a lower age of majority is widely considered to be an indefensible position when considering aspects of legislation which are intended to protect the rights of children and safeguard them from harm. For these purposes, there is widespread international agreement that the protections should extend to children up to the age of 18.

Article 2 of the UNCRC is the anti-discrimination clause: it establishes that all children are protected equally by the rights enshrined in the UNCRC, regardless of race, ethnicity, nationality or migration status. Finally, Article 3 of the UNCRC articulates the 'best interests' principle. This is the principle that in all matters in which a government takes a decision concerning a child, 'the best interests of the child should be a primary consideration'. This applies to social work decision making, as well as other administrative bodies (such as decisions of UK Visas and Immigration (UKVI)), to our tribunals and to decisions of our courts.

If it is true that the UK is wholly compliant with the UNCRC, then no government agency should ever treat a migrant child in need of help or support – even a child who is clearly unlawfully resident – differently from any other child in the UK, even a native-born indigenous British child. However, frontline practitioners know that this is not always the experience in practice. Children in families who have irregular migration status or limited leave to remain, and separated children[2] are often told that they are not 'eligible' for certain forms of government support, or they face other significant barriers to accessing support. 'Irregular migration status' means an individual does not have lawful leave to remain in the UK. This may be because the individual overstayed the expiration of lawful leave to remain, or has breached a condition of leave to remain, or formerly claimed international protection and was unsuccessful, but has not yet left the country (The Migration Observatory 2011).

Why might this be the case? One key reason is that we do discriminate in access to accommodation and financial support when it comes to adults. Adults who have irregular immigration status or limited leave to remain, and adult asylum seekers are lawfully restricted in their access to support. For example, adult asylum seekers are not eligible for mainstream housing or homelessness assistance, or for most welfare benefits, and are instead financially supported and accommodated in a separate and parallel system called Home Office asylum support.

Another reason might be the way in which rules on eligibility impose residence requirements to access certain types of benefits. For example, if a young person requires to be ordinarily resident in an area for at least

---

2   'Separated children' refers to children under 18 years of age who are outside their country of origin and separated from both parents or from their previous legal or customary primary caregiver. Some children are totally alone, while others may be living with extended family members (Separated Children in Europe Programme 2009).

three years in order to obtain funding for further or higher education, this requirement may work to the disadvantage of a recently arrived child seeking international protection, even though the requirement is not phrased in terms of discrimination on the basis of nationality or migration status.

You might also pragmatically note that, sometimes, practitioners simply misunderstand the law. Or, where there are resource constraints, a government department might choose to follow an interpretation of the law that is very narrow – and might not allocate enough resources to meet the needs of these children and young people. Finally, it is important to acknowledge that some social workers and social care staff work in settings where there is a culture of racism that reflects the wider popular support for anti-immigration policies and the 'hostile environment'.

However, there is one more, historical, reason for this, and it is an important one. When countries ratify international treaties, they have the right to enter into reservations at the time of ratification. This means that they agree to abide by the terms of the treaty, subject to certain exceptions. The UK entered into a reservation at the time it signed the UNCRC in 1991, in relation to Article 22. Article 22 stipulates that states should take appropriate measures to ensure that refugee children receive the protection they need in the UK. The effect of the UK's reservation was to disapply the protections of the UNCRC to the entry, stay in and departure from the UK of children subject to immigration control. The UN Committee on the Rights of the Child (2005) General Comment No. 6 is a useful document setting out how Article 22 UNCRC should apply.

And so it was the case – astonishingly – that for many years, the UK guaranteed it would respect the rights of all children in the UK, except migrant children. Of course, this does not mean that migrant children had no rights in the UK during this time – they were still protected in other ways – but this was a powerful public message projected by the UK government. During this time, several generations of frontline practitioners, managers and policy makers were educated and entered the workforce in a political context which explicitly denied the idea of equal rights and protection against discrimination for children and young people seeking international protection. Fortunately, after years of lobbying, the UK agreed to drop this reservation in November 2008 (Department for Children, Schools and Families 2008). To make the new position absolutely clear, Section 55 of the Borders, Citizenship and Immigration Act 2009 was later enacted to create a statutory duty on the Home Office to take into account the best interests of children in all its decision making, as discussed further below.

Refugee Convention 1951

Article 1A of the Refugee Convention (also referred to as the Geneva Convention) establishes the definition of a refugee in international law and articulates the principle of *non-refoulment*. This means that someone who has established that they are a refugee cannot be forcibly returned to the country in which they fear they will be persecuted or harmed. The Refugee Convention does not contain a specific provision for the protection of children; however, it applies equally to child claimants as to adults, and therefore is an important source of protection for them in advancing their claims in the UK. Furthermore, children are recognised in international law as deserving of special protection because of their vulnerability by virtue of their young age. The UNHCR has, accordingly, issued guidance on the protection and care of refugee children (UNHCR 1994) and also on how Article 1 of the Refugee Convention should be interpreted and applied to the claims of refugee children (UNHCR 2009).

European Convention on Human Rights (ECHR) 1950

The ECHR is the key source of international human rights law which applies in the UK. As with the Refugee Convention, there are not specific provisions that relate to children, but rather broad provisions that protect the human rights of all people, regardless of age. The most important of these for individuals seeking international protection are: Article 2 (right to life), Article 3 (freedom from torture, inhumane and degrading treatment or punishment), Article 4 (freedom from slavery and forced labour) and Article 8 (right to private and family life). In brief, the ECHR protects people against decisions of our government that might breach these basic rights that we all possess. Most often, these rights are raised in the context of an individual seeking international protection when the UK government proposes to remove someone to a country in which the individual alleges that they may suffer breach of any of the above rights.

For example, if a child is a survivor of trafficking, they are many times more likely to suffer re-trafficking if they are returned to the country from which they were trafficked (International Organisation for Migration (IOM) 2009). Therefore, if the UK government proposes to return them to that country, they can raise a claim that the government's decision might breach their right to freedom from slavery because they may be re-trafficked on return, and this would be a direct consequence of the UK government's decision and failure to protect them.

European Union Common European Asylum System

The EU, of which the UK has been a member state since 1973, has entered into a series of agreements that have created what is known as a 'common European asylum system' (CEAS) (European Commission 2014). These establish minimum standards for registering asylum claims, and for accommodating and supporting individuals while their claims are pending. The UK has opted into the so-called 'first phase' asylum directive of CEAS, but not to join the 'second phase' of reforms. In light of Brexit, the UK is not likely to advance further towards adoption of CEAS and may, in fact, choose to withdraw from the agreements. The directives to which the UK has opted in are:

- the Minimum Standards for the Reception of Asylum Seekers Directive 2003/9/EC (the Reception Conditions Directive)

- the Refugee and Subsidiary Protection Directive 2004/83/EC (the Qualification Directive)

- the Minimum Standards on Procedures in Member States for Granting and Withdrawing Refugee Status Directive 2005/85/EC (the Procedures Directive) (Council of Europe 2003, 2004, 2005).

The EU has also established a system for determining which country is responsible for examining an asylum claim, where an individual has passed through more than one country, as set out in a regulation commonly called the Dublin Regulation, or Dublin III (European Parliament and Council of Europe 2013). There are some special protections for children and young people contained in these EU directives and regulations. For example, key parts of the CEAS contain provisions recognising the particular vulnerability of children and their heightened need for protection. Article 20 of the Qualification Directive (Council of Europe 2004) requires states to take into account the specific situation of vulnerable persons such as minors and unaccompanied minors. The same Article also states 'the best interests of the child shall be the primary consideration for Member States when implementing the provisions...that involve minors' (ibid.). Article 30 of the Qualification Directive goes on to set out specific safeguards for the legal guardianship, care and accommodation of unaccompanied minors.

Furthermore, Article 8 of Dublin III provides that the claim of a separated child should be examined in the state in which they present themselves to the authorities, or another EU state in which they have family, but only if transferring them to another state is in their best interests. This is a change to the general rule under Dublin III that a claim should be examined in the first country in which a claimant has been recorded – and a provision specifically designed to recognise the special position and heightened vulnerability of children seeking international protection.

Children's rights in UK domestic law

As mentioned previously, the international legal obligations set out above flow through our domestic legislation and, in fact, become enforceable in our UK courts through this legislation. This section briefly highlights some key pieces of domestic legislation relevant to social workers who are supporting young people in this context.

Child welfare legislation

The obligations of local authorities to accommodate and support children in need in their area are set out variously in The Children Act 1989, the Children (Scotland) Act 1995, the Social Services and Well-Being (Wales) Act 2014, and the Children (Northern Ireland) Order 1995. These pieces of legislation require local authorities to ensure that all decisions taken in respect of children are taken following a balanced assessment as to what is in their best interests.

The obligations on statutory authorities arising under these pieces of legislation are widely accepted to be read in light of the UK's obligations under the UNCRC,[3] and therefore the principles of non-discrimination and the primacy of best interests determinations in decision making clearly apply here. In addition, these obligations imply that assessments conducted in carrying out these duties must be progressed in a manner that is child-centred and sensitive to different cultural, religious and ethnic backgrounds and practices. Social workers required to conduct such assessments should therefore have access to support and information that will help inform

---

3   Although the UNCRC has been ratified by the UK, it has not been incorporated into domestic law, which means that individuals cannot obtain remedies for breach of UNCRC in UK domestic courts. However, Wales became the first country in the UK to incorporate the UNCRC through the Rights of Children and Young Persons (Wales) Measure 2011, and the First Minister for Scotland announced an intention to incorporate the UNCRC into Scotland in her Programme for Government 2018– 19 (Scottish Government 2018b)

them on such matters. In brief, migrant children and young people seeking international protection can – and should – expect to receive the same level of care and support under these Acts from local authorities as their indigenous British peers.

Similarly, migrant children and young people are, generally speaking, entitled to the same access to leaving care and aftercare support, provided they were accommodated as looked-after children for the requisite period of time before leaving care. This can be true even if the young person subsequently becomes 'appeal rights exhausted' or 'unlawfully resident', or is granted a form of immigration status with a 'no recourse to public funds' restriction. This is because assistance under children's welfare legislation, including leaving care and aftercare provision, is not a 'public fund' for purposes of immigration legislation. It is worth noting that, in some circumstances, Schedule 3 of the Nationality, Immigration and Asylum Act 2002 purports to break this link with respect to young people leaving care (Department for Education 2017; for a further reflection on the interaction of immigration legislation with devolved welfare legislation see Craig and Ang 2016).

Human Rights Act (HRA) 1998

The Human Rights Act 1998 incorporates certain key provisions of the ECHR and makes it easier for individuals to assert their ECHR rights in UK domestic courts. Of importance, in this context, is that the HRA 1998 makes it unlawful for a public authority (such as a local authority or a government department like the Home Office) to breach an individual's ECHR rights. Technically, therefore, when an individual raises a claim against a public authority for breach of the individual's human rights, the claim is raised under the Human Rights Act 1998.

Section 55 of the Borders, Citizenship and Immigration Act 2009 ('Section 55', BCIA)

As mentioned above, when the UK withdrew its reservation to Article 22 of the UNCRC, Section 55 of the BCIA was passed in order to place a statutory duty on the Home Office to ensure that *all its functions* are discharged 'having regard to the need to safeguard and promote the welfare of children who are in the United Kingdom'. The best interests duty applies equally to the substance of decisions made by the Home Office (for example, to grant permission to remain in the UK, or to provide accommodation and support to a family) as to the process by which the Home Office arrives at decisions (for example, how interviews of children are conducted, and whether or not correspondence is expressed in a child-friendly manner).

Challenges and barriers facing children and young people seeking international protection

Children and young people claiming asylum in their own right struggle to navigate these complex systems alone. They may be less confident in putting forward their accounts, and also struggle to understand why our bureaucracy requires the volume and detail of information they are asked to provide. In addition, children and young people who arrive alone and need to be looked after by the local authority often engage with multiple additional legal processes, further complicating the experience of seeking protection.

Case study: Mariam

Let's explore some of these issues, by considering a case study.

Seeking asylum: Mariam's journey

Mariam is a 16-year-old from Eritrea. Police find her at the city bus station. She is wet and cold. She is alone, and does not speak any English. She will not make any eye contact, she flinches when approached, and rocks and mutters to herself continuously.

– What are your concerns?

– What do you think happens next?

You may have thought about a number of immediate concerns that need to be addressed. Mariam may be hungry and tired. She appears to be traumatised. She needs warmth and dry clothes. She may be injured, or very unwell, and require urgent medical attention. She needs to be moved from the bus station to a safer place, and someone will need to assess what type of place that might be. You need an interpreter, but there will be a period of time during which you will initially have to support Mariam without an interpreter. How would you approach that challenge? What are some of the other challenges that come with working with an interpreter?

You may have moved on to longer-term issues, also relevant to your assessment. She requires at least temporary accommodation. You need to ascertain whether she is lost or abandoned, or whether there is anyone she can be safely reunited with. She may have been trafficked and in current danger of being re-trafficked or exploited. She may be pregnant. She could require mental health and sexual health assessments. You, and the other professionals working alongside you, will, over the following two weeks, subject Mariam to a number of different types of assessment. She will be interviewed multiple times, for different purposes.

Mariam will have contact with many organisations in the coming two weeks. She will be interviewed multiple times, for different purposes.

Figure 7.1: *Mariam's journey*

Imagine you are working with Mariam and supporting her to attend these assessments. It is your role to explain to her the purposes of these meetings and what she might be asked, and why. Are these professionals acting in her best interests? Looking at this process as a whole, would you say it is working in her best interests? Why or why not? You might have observed that each of the professionals is fulfilling an important role – safeguarding Mariam, ensuring she has access to health services and education, securing appropriate accommodation for her and so on – which collectively aim to protect her and promote her best interests.

However, you may also have noticed that Mariam has very quickly been put at the centre of a series of processes, which taken together may not be in her best interests. Information is taken from her by a variety of individuals, for a variety of purposes, in very different contexts. It may be recorded inconsistently. Mariam may trust some professionals more than others. She may be confused about the purpose of certain assessments. All these professionals will need to use interpreters, and the use of interpreters can pose additional barriers and risks to working with her, securing her trust in these processes, and ensuring her disclosure is accurately recorded. Furthermore, these professionals – even if they work together in multi-agency assessments – do not all share a central system for recording information. Therefore, information sharing between professionals can be inconsistent, leading to further complexity.

Mariam's situation is not exceptional. Looked-after children are known to require formal interactions with a wider range of professionals from statutory agencies than most other individuals in our society. Children and young people seeking international protection who are also in care need to navigate all these processes, as well as the Home Offices processes for claiming asylum.

Trafficking

There is a high correlation between arriving in the UK as a separated child and identification as a potential survivor of trafficking (Crawley and Kohli 2013). The current system for identifying survivors of trafficking in the UK, the National Referral Mechanism (NRM), is an entirely separate process that a separated child will need to navigate – it requires additional interviews and separate fact-finding determinations by the Home Office. A child survivor of trafficking is also more likely to be referred for a policy interview and may be asked to assist the police in investigations of trafficking rings, or as a witness in a prosecution. Finally, special considerations apply in safeguarding children who may have been trafficked and exploited, particularly in identifying appropriate accommodation and support options (see Department for Education 2017; London Safeguarding Children Board 2017).

Age dispute and age assessment

It would be remiss to discuss barriers to international protection for children and young people without briefly discussing the issue of age disputes and age assessments. As of 2013, there are 230 million children in the world for whom there is no formal record of birth (*The Independent* 2017), and whose legal age is therefore unknown, or only identifiable within a range of possible dates. When children seeking international protection arrive in the UK, they are required to give a certain date – our bureaucratic processes are incapable of registering an asylum claim or taking responsibility for the care and protection of a young person without a fixed date, even a fictitious or approximate one. It is for this reason that many separated children who can only estimate their age within a year will have their date of birth recorded as 01/01/20xx.

If the date of birth a young person has given appears plausible to the statutory authorities, current law and policy requires that the young person be given 'the benefit of the doubt' and the given date be recorded and accepted as likely to be true (Home Office 2018a). However, there are times when either the Home Office or the local authority will consider a child to be 'significantly over' or under the age a young person has given, and in such cases, it is open to the statutory authority to formally dispute the young person's age.

A young person who is 'age disputed' may be subject to a 'Merton-compliant age assessment' by the local authority (Association of Directors of Children's Services 2017; Scottish Government 2018a). It is worth highlighting that although this is generally accepted practice, many social workers believe that it is unethical for social workers to be required to conduct age assessments for this type of administrative purpose, and this view is supported by some organisations that represent social workers and social care professionals as employees (BASW 2015; UNISON and the Scottish Association of Social Workers 2017).

If the conclusion of the age assessment is that the young person is, in fact, an adult, they will thereafter be treated as an adult. For some young people who are wrongly age disputed and are, in fact, still children, the experience of being treated as an adult, and therefore being accommodated in adult asylum support – rather than local authority – accommodation can be itself traumatic. Such young people also miss out on educational opportunities, as well as the guidance and support they would otherwise have received if they had been treated as looked-after children.

In addition, a child who is 'age disputed' and found not to be their claimed age faces an immediate challenge to their credibility when their claim for international protection is examined by UKVI. This is because identity (which includes age) is considered to be a core issue in examining an individual's account. It is often the case that such claims are refused, on the basis that as a young person was dishonest about a fact as central as their age, their credibility is called into question, and the decision maker concludes that they are likely to have been dishonest about the rest of their claim as well.

Summary

Children and young people face multiple and overlapping challenges while seeking international protection embedded in overlapping legal processes (see the boxes below). This necessarily leads to uneven disclosure, with some agencies holding information that others do not, and creates, by its nature, inconsistency between written records. Young people are also given little to no choice whether or not to engage in these processes, which are put in place largely for their own protection, yet they are also aware that they are being constantly 'judged' and given no assurances that they will actually achieve protection.

Summary of multiple and overlapping challenges and barriers facing children and young people seeking international protection

- Fear and mistrust of authority

- Separation and loss

- Language barriers and cultural barriers

- Limited education or lack of education

- Lack of confidence in communicating with adults

- Physical injury or disability

- Trauma (due to war, poverty, displacement, exploitation, physical, emotional or sexual abuse)

- Poor mental health

- Shame

- Loneliness

- Experience of discrimination, harassment or bullying in the UK

> ### Summary of challenges faced by children and young people seeking international protection during overlapping legal processes
>
> – Multiple interviews, with multiple agencies, for different purposes
>
> – Repetitive and overlapping questioning
>
> – Use of different interpreters
>
> – Questioning about sensitive and personal matters, including past experiences of trauma, separation, injury and abuse

The asylum process for children and young people seeking international protection

There are some key differences in how children under the age of 18 seeking international protection in the UK are treated within the asylum process, compared with adults. These are largely set out in Immigration Rules 350 to 352ZB (Home Office 2018c) and the guidance *Children's Asylum Claims* (Home Office 2018b) and are required by Section 55 of the Borders, Citizenship and Immigration Act 2009, which establishes – as previously mentioned – that in all actions concerning children, the best interests of the child are a primary consideration.

Processing of child asylum claims

The guidance noted above sets out in some detail how Home Office asylum case owners are required to process child asylum claims. Key differences are summarised in the remaining part of this section.

Responsible adult

Child asylum claimants can only be interviewed by UKVI in the presence of a responsible adult. This is a procedural safeguard, to ensure that an independent adult attends to provide appropriate support to the child, monitors their welfare and makes sure that the conduct of the interview and associated processes are carried out in line with 'best interests' principles. Although social workers often attend as 'responsible adults' for child asylum claimants, this is not a statutory requirement. Technically, it is for the child to choose their 'responsible adult' and this can include a foster carer, an independent advocate (such as a guardian from the Scottish Guardianship Service or an advocate from The Children's Society) or a residential care unit keyworker. If a young person requires help in choosing an appropriate 'responsible adult', they might be asked whom they feel most comfortable speaking about their asylum claim with. It is also worth considering the experience and confidence of the 'responsible adult' in supporting young people in this environment.

Welfare interview

Whereas adults who have not claimed asylum immediately on entry at port are required to travel to Croydon in order to initiate an asylum claim and undergo a screening interview, children are permitted to make a claim for asylum anywhere in the UK and can attend their initial interview at a regional UKVI office, rather than at Croydon. The initial interview for a child is called a 'welfare interview' and is conducted in a different form entirely. It has been tailored for use with child applicants, with the aim of identifying key welfare and protection needs so that UKVI can appropriately signpost child claimants, where necessary, to services that can meet those needs.

Statement of Evidence Form

At the welfare interview, child claimants are issued with a 'Statement of Evidence Form' (SEF), which is required to be completed and returned to UKVI within 60 working days of issue. The young person should complete this form with the aid of a legal representative, because the evidence they provide is of crucial importance to the consideration of their claim, and they require legal advice in deciding what they should disclose. The SEF form has been revised by UKVI in order to assist child claimants to provide detailed, relevant information for a UKVI case owner to review before conducting the 'substantive asylum interview'. Best practice in working with child asylum claimants is not to restrict the narrative of the young person to the boxes provided on the SEF form, but for the legal representative to take a separate witness statement, expressing as closely as possible, in the young person's own words, the background and context to their fear of return to their own country. There are a number of reasons why a witness statement is best practice, and these apply whether working with child or adult asylum claimants.

First, provision of a narrative in witness statement form is arguably a more natural and authentic form of evidence for UKVI decision making, as well as a better expression of the 'voice' of the young person, in terms of Article 12 of the UNCRC. Second, the process of giving and revising a witness statement with the aid of a legal representative can be helpful to prepare the young person for the type of questioning they are likely to encounter in the substantive asylum interview which follows. UKVI caseworkers, in their interviewing technique and assessment of asylum claims, tend to adopt a linear chronological approach, and also favour certain types of reasoning in response to questioning. These paradigms are not prevalent in other cultural contexts, or in different socio-economic strata, which means that young people may not have any prior experience of this type of questioning to draw on, to understand what kind of answer might be expected (Given-Wilson, Herlihy and Hodes 2016). Therefore, preparing a witness statement with a legal representative can give young people a framework for understanding why they are being asked these questions, and how they might frame their answers so as to be better understood.

Finally, furnishing a detailed witness statement to UKVI in advance of a substantive asylum interview should result in a briefer, and more focused, interview. UKVI policy requires caseworkers to review any evidence submitted in advance, and to restrict their questioning to areas that require clarification. Therefore, a detailed witness statement should assist both the caseworker and the client in conducting a briefer – and hence more tolerable – interview.

Substantive asylum interview

A child claimant should be interviewed by a UKVI case owner who has been specially trained to interview minors, and accompanied by a responsible adult. The *Immigration Rules* (Home Office 2018c, para 351) direct that 'close attention should be given to the welfare of the child at all time'. During the interview, 'the child shall be allowed to express themselves in their own way and at their own speed' and, furthermore, 'if they appear tired or distressed, the interview will be suspended' (ibid., para 352). In some UKVI offices, it is possible to ask that the interview be conducted in a child-friendly interview suite. This may be, for example, a room that is painted and furnished in a more welcoming manner than the usual interview suites.

In exceptional cases, a request can be made to UKVI to interview a child claimant elsewhere, other than in UKVI offices, on the basis that a 'best interests' approach requires this. For example, if the child has an overwhelming fear of UKVI offices because of some previous traumatic experience, and is likely to be in a better position to provide accurate and detailed disclosure by being interviewed in their legal representative's offices, or in their independent advocate's offices, UKVI should seriously entertain a request to interview in an alternate venue, and grant it in appropriate circumstances. A request of this type has to be framed in terms of the UKVI's Section 55 duties, and should be supported by appropriate evidence.

Service of decision

The decision in a child's asylum claim is normally served on the legal representative, and the social worker responsible for the child, not on the child themselves. If the decision constitutes a refusal of asylum there is a limited period of 14 days in which to lodge an appeal, and it is therefore imperative that the social worker promptly arranges for the child to receive legal advice from the legal representative on the decision, and their right to lodge any appeal.

Determination of child asylum claims

As mentioned above, the UKVI guidance also sets out in some detail how asylum case owners are required to adjudicate child asylum claims.

Shift in burden of proof

In adult asylum claims, the burden of proving that an individual meets all the elements of the Refugee Convention rests on the claimant, who must meet this burden by proving 'on the balance of probabilities' that they are a refugee. Requiring a child claimant to prove all the parts of their claim, without assistance, would, however, be an insurmountable barrier. For this reason, the burden is shifted in child asylum claims. It is therefore not the responsibility of the child alone to prove all parts of the claim, but rather a responsibility held jointly by the UKVI case owner to conduct investigations to identify evidence indicating whether or not the child is a refugee (Home Office 2018b). Specifically, case owners are directed that 'account should be taken of the applicant's maturity and in assessing the claim of a child more weight should be given to objective indications of risk than to the child's state of mind and understanding of their situation' (Home Office 2018c, para 351).

Child-specific persecution

When considering the application of the Refugee Convention to the claims made by children for international protection, it is important to bear in mind that there are some forms of persecution that children are more likely to suffer than adults. These are called child-specific forms of persecution,[4] and are often missed by professionals who are not specialist in working with children and young people. They include situations when children might be street homeless (street children), subjected to forced marriage, subjected to female genital mutilation (FGM), trafficked or exploited (for example, in domestic servitude, forced labour, forced begging, or some other form of modern slavery), or forcibly conscribed (as a child soldier).

Child-specific assessment of the claim

When considering a child's asylum claim, the asylum case owner must take care to consider the credibility and plausibility of the child's account from the perspective of a child of similar age and experience, not from the perspective of an adult. Recent research has shown, however, that many children's asylum claims fail because of poor interview techniques (Warren and York 2014) or incorrect assumptions (Given-Wilson, Hodes and Herlihy 2017) by case owners that do not meet the appropriate legal standard.

Case study: Ahmad's case, where UKVI failed to apply the correct standards

Ahmad's case is summarised in the box on the next page. What is your view of UKVI's reasoning in this case? Why is it arguably flawed?

---

4   For further discussion of child-specific forms of persecution, and how to sensitively apply Article 1A of the Refugee Convention 1951 to child asylum claims, see UNHCR (2009).

Ahmad's case

Ahmad is a 13-year-old child from Afghanistan. His father was arrested by the authorities and disappeared. Shortly afterwards, Ahmad was arrested, held by the police, and interrogated for a number of days. A neighbour who recognised Ahmad helped him to escape from the police station, and Ahmad immediately ran home, to his mother.

UKVI refused Ahmad's claim for asylum, writing in the reasons for refusal letter:

'I do not find it plausible that, knowing that your home was the one place the police were likely to look for you, you would run there, instead of hiding elsewhere... I therefore find your claim that you were arrested, interrogated by the police, and helped to escape by a neighbour not credible...'

You may have considered the reasoning challengeable because it failed to take sufficient account of Ahmad's age and experience. Although it may be true that an adult would not necessarily run home after escaping from a police station, it is more likely that a child would have thought immediately of running home as the best possible option. Indeed, if evidence could be brought to demonstrate that from the perspective of an expert in child development, a child is more likely than not in this circumstance to run home rather than elsewhere, Ahmad's behaviour arguably strengthens – rather than weakens – the plausibility of his actions and hence the credibility of his claim. In fact, UKVI's reasoning in the above case is demonstrably flawed, and the relevant law and guidance supports this conclusion (Home Office 2018b). See the box below for a summary of the relevant sections of the guidance.

Assessing credibility in children's claims (Home Office 2018b, p.50)

Decision makers must take account of what it is reasonable to expect a child to know in their given set of circumstances and in doing so taking account of their age, maturity, education and other relevant factors.

Decision makers must demonstrate as part of the decision-making process consideration of any distinct factors taken into account during the assessment of credibility in a child's claim. This will also apply to behaviours that fall within Section 8 of the Asylum and Immigration (Treatment of Claimants, etc.) Act 2004, including:

- the child's age and maturity at the time of the event and at the time of the interview

- mental or emotional trauma experienced by the child

- educational level

- fear or mistrust of authorities

- feelings of shame

- painful memories, particularly those of a sexual nature.

A case-by-case approach will be required and if there is doubt, decision makers must discuss the case with a senior caseworker.

Finally, consider the case study of Ahmed above, and bear in mind that while the child-trained UKVI case owner may have received some guidance in relation to adjudicating the claims of children and young people, they are not an expert in child development, and certainly not as expert as a trained and practising social work professional. What evidence can you furnish to improve decision making for young people like Ahmad? How can you support the production of other evidence that might assist?

Social workers are expert at working with children and young people, and also expert report writers, in other contexts. It may be the case that you can assist a young person you are working with by providing a letter of evidence, and, if so, you should discuss this with the young person and their legal representative. Alternatively, you may have a useful role to play in helping the young person and their legal representative think about the other professionals in the young person's life who might be able to furnish letters and other forms of evidence to support the case.

The asylum decision

There are a range of possible outcomes for a child or young person seeking international protection: refugee status (five years); humanitarian protection (five years); refusal, with a grant of limited leave under Section 67 of the Immigration Act 2016 (Dubs amendment[5] leave under Immigration Rule 352ZH) (five years); refusal, with a grant of limited leave to age 17.5, on the

---

5   www.gov.uk/government/news/changes-to-the-immigration-rules--2

basis that there are no adequate reception arrangements in the child's home country (under Immigration Rule 352ZC, Home Office 2018c); refusal, with no grant of leave to remain. It is important to understand that anything other than a grant of refugee status or humanitarian protection is, in effect, a refusal of the asylum claim. This refusal can – and often should – be challenged by way of an appeal to the First-tier Tribunal, an administrative tribunal with the power to review and overturn UKVI asylum and immigration decisions.

Further, as mentioned above, there is a limited period of 14 days after service of a negative decision to lodge an appeal. Therefore, it is particularly important that a young person who has been granted any form of leave other than refugee status or humanitarian protection be promptly advised by their legal representative of the type of status they have been granted, and on their right to appeal. Specifically, the young person should be given the information they require in order to make a timely and informed decision about whether or not to exercise the right of appeal in these circumstances. Social workers can help to prepare children and young people for receiving their asylum decisions by informing themselves about the possible outcomes and helping children and young people think through the consequences. Best practice in this area suggests that it can be useful to engage in 'triple pathway planning' – planning for each of three possible eventualities: (1) a young person is granted leave to remain, (2) a young person is refused leave but is not returned to their country of origin, and (3) a young person is returned to their country of origin.

Conclusion

The previous section highlighted a number of differences between how an asylum claim for a child is processed by UKVI, as compared with that of an adult. In addition, it has pointed out that UKVI policy requires that child asylum claims are adjudicated differently from adult claims. However, in practice, these standards are not always met. Therefore, a social worker supporting a separated child through the asylum process can greatly assist by familiarising themselves with these procedural and substantive differences and using this as a guide to ensure that the young person receives the benefit of fair process and good legal representation throughout their journey. This chapter concludes with some brief advice on the ways in which social workers can effectively support children and young people seeking international protection (see box on the next page).

Practical advice on how social workers can effectively support children and young people seeking international protection

- Be mindful of the multiple barriers that separated children and young people face, and the trauma and fear that may have marked their journey to the UK.

- Engage with young people like Mariam with sensitivity, remembering to consider how they might perceive you when you first meet them.

- Ensure young people have early access to specialist legal representation.

- Critically examine your own practice and the processes of other agencies and consider whether they are operating in the 'best interests' of the young person.

- Challenge cultures in workplaces that work against good practice, with the help and support of colleagues, trade unions and professional associations.

- Familiarise yourself with relevant legal processes, in order to better support young people and ensure that they are fairly treated and supported to produce the best possible evidence for their claim.

- Expand your networks and share best practice with peers and other professionals who are more experienced in working with separated and trafficked children. Don't be afraid to ask questions.

- Remember that *children seeking international protection are children first, migrants second.*

- Trust your professional instincts. Embrace the challenges of working in a new and unfamiliar area, with young people who might help you re-examine your own beliefs and practices. Engage in your work with compassion and honesty, but also with humour.

References

Age of Legal Capacity (Scotland) Act (1991) Accessed 16/11/2018 at: www.legislation.gov.uk/ukpga/1991/50.

Association of Directors of Children's Services (2017) 'Age Assessment Guidance and Information Sharing Guidance for UASC.' Accessed 23/10/2018 at: http://adcs.org.uk/safeguarding/article/age-assessment-information-sharing-for-unaccompanied-asylum-seeking-children.

BASW (British Association of Social Workers) (2015) *BASW Response to the Age Assessment Guidance Document.* Accessed 23/10/2018 at: www.basw.co.uk/system/files/resources/basw_115208-6_0.pdf.

Borders, Citizenship and Immigration Act (2009) Accessed 16/11/2018 at: www.legislation.gov.uk/ukpga/2009/11/contents.

Children Act (1989) Accessed 16/11/2018 at: www.legislation.gov.uk/ukpga/1989/41/contents.

Children (Northern Ireland) Order (1995) Accessed 16/11/2018 at: www.legislation.gov.uk/nisi/1995/755/contents/made.

Children (Scotland) Act (1995) Accessed 16/11/2018 at: www.legislation.gov.uk/ukpga/1995/36/contents.

Council of Europe (2003) *Council Directive 2003/9/EC of 27 January 2003 Laying Down Minimum Standards for the Reception of Asylum Seekers.* Accessed 16/11/2018 at: https://eur-lex.europa.eu/legal-content/EN/TXT/?qid=1542462961236&uri=CELEX:32003L0009.

Council of Europe (2004) *Council Directive 2004/83/EC of 29 April 2004 on Minimum Standards for the Qualification and Status of Third Country Nationals or Stateless Persons as Refugees or as Persons Who Otherwise Need International Protection and the Content of the Protection Granted.* Accessed 16/11/2018 at: https://eur-lex.europa.eu/legal-content/EN/TXT/?uri=celex%3A32004L0083.

Council of Europe (2005) *Council Directive 2005/85/EC of 1 December 2005 on Minimum Standards on Procedures in Member States for Granting and Withdrawing Refugee Status.* Accessed 16/11/2018 at: https://eur-lex.europa.eu/legal-content/EN/ALL/?uri=CELEX%3A32005L0085.

Craig, S. and Ang, J. (2016) 'Hostility enacted.' *Journal of the Law Society of Scotland.* July. Accessed 16/11/2018 at: www.journalonline.co.uk/Magazine/61-7/1021987.aspx.

Crawley, H. and Kohli, R. (2013) *'She Endures with Me' An Evaluation of the Scottish Guardianship Service Pilot.* Accessed 16/11/2018 at: www.scottishrefugeecouncil.org.uk/assets/6798/Final_Report_2108.pdf.

Department for Children, Schools and Families (2008) *United Nations Convention on the Rights of the Child: Priorities for Action.* Accessed 23/10/2018 at: http://webarchive.nationalarchives.gov.uk/20130409131533/https://www.education.gov.uk/publications/eOrderingDownload/01099-2009BKT-EN.pdf.

Department for Education (2017) *Care of Unaccompanied Migrant Children and Victims of Modern Slavery: Statutory Guidance for Local Authorities.* November. Accessed 23/10/2018 at: https://assets.publishing.service.gov.uk/government/uploads/system/uploads/attachment_data/file/656429/UASC_Statutory_Guidance_2017.pdf.

European Commission (2014) *A Common European Asylum System.* Accessed 23/10/2018 at: https://ec.europa.eu/home-affairs/sites/homeaffairs/files/e-library/docs/ceas-fact-sheets/ceas_factsheet_en.pdf.

European Convention on Human Rights (1950) Accessed 16/11/2018 at: www.echr.coe.int/Documents/Convention_ENG.pdf.

European Parliament and Council of Europe (2013) *EU Regulation 604/2013: Establishing the Criteria and Mechanisms for Determining the Member State Responsible for Examining an Application for International Protection Lodged in One of the Member States by a Third-Country National or a Stateless Person.* 26 June. Accessed 16/11/2018 at: https://eur-lex.europa.eu/legal-content/EN/TXT/?uri=CELEX%3A32013R0604.

Given-Wilson, Z., Herlihy, J. and Hodes, M. (2016) *Telling the Story: A Psychological Review on Assessing Adolescents' Asylum Claims.* Accessed 23/10/2018 at: http://csel. org.uk/assets/images/resources/telling-the-story/Given-WilsonHerlihy-Hodes-Nov.pdf.

Given-Wilson, Z., Hodes, M. and Herlihy, J. (2017) 'A review of adolescent autobiographical memory and the implications for assessment of unaccompanied minors' refugee determinations.' *Child Psychology and Psychiatry.* Doi: doi. org/10.1177/1359104517748697.

Hill, M., Lockyer, A., Head, G. and McDonald, C.A. (2017) 'Voting at 16 – lessons for the future from the Scottish Referendum.' *Scottish Affairs,* 26, 1, 48–68.

Home Office (2018a) *Assessing Age: Version 2.0.* Accessed 23/10/2018 at: https://assets. publishing.service.gov.uk/government/uploads/system/uploads/attachment_data/ file/746532/assessing-age-v2.0ext.pdf.

Home Office (2018b) *Children's Asylum Claims: Version 2.0.* Accessed 16/11/2018 at: https://assets.publishing.service.gov.uk/government/uploads/system/uploads/ attachment_data/file/650514/children_s-asylum-claims-v2_0.pdf.

Home Office (2018c) *Immigration Rules Part 11: Asylum.* Accessed 16/11/2018 at: www. gov.uk/guidance/immigration-rules/immigration-rules-part-11-asylum.

Human Rights Act (1998) Accessed 16/11/2018 at: www.legislation.gov.uk/ ukpga/1998/42/contents.

Immigration Act (2016) Accessed 16/11/2018 at: www.legislation.gov.uk/ ukpga/2016/19/contents/enacted.

Independent, The (2017) 'Hundreds of millions of children "lack any record of birth".' 16 September. Accessed 23/10/2018 at: www.independent.co.uk/news/world/africa/ invisible-children-unicef-birth-registration-campaign-india-uganda-somalia-birth-certificate-a7950056.html.

IOM (International Organisation for Migration) (2009) *The Causes and Consequences of Re-trafficking: Evidence from the IOM Human Trafficking Database.* Geneva: IOM. Accessed 23/10/2018 at: https://publications.iom.int/books/causes-and-consequences-re-trafficking-evidence-iom-human-trafficking-database.

London Safeguarding Children Board (2017) 'Safeguarding Trafficked and Exploited Children.' Accessed 23/10/2018 at: www.londoncp.co.uk/chapters/sg_trafficked_ ch.html.

Migration Observatory, The (2011) 'Irregular Migration in the UK: Definitions, Pathways and Scale.' Accessed 15/11/2018 at: https://migrationobservatory.ox.ac.uk/ resources/briefings/irregular-migration-in-the-uk-definitions-pathways-and-scale.

Nationality, Immigration and Asylum Act (2002) Accessed 16/11/2018 at: www. legislation.gov.uk/ukpga/2002/41/contents.

Refugee Convention (1951) Accessed 16/11/2018 at: www.unhcr.org/uk/1951-refugee-convention.html.

Rights of Children and Young Persons (Wales) Measure (2011) Accessed 18/11/2018 at: www.legislation.gov.uk/mwa/2011/2/contents.

Scottish Government (2018a) *Age Assessment: Practice Guidance.* Accessed 23/10/2018 at: https://beta.gov.scot/publications/age-assessment-practice-guidance-scotland-good-practice-guidance-support-social.

Scottish Government (2018b) *Delivering for Today, Investing for Tomorrow: The Government's Programme for Scotland 2018–2019.* Accessed 18/11/2018 at: www.gov.scot/publications/delivering-today-investing-tomorrow-governments-programme-scotland-2018-19.

Separated Children in Europe Programme (2009) *Statement of Good Practice.* Accessed 15/11/2018 at: www.scepnetwork.org/p/1/69/statement-of-good-practice.

Social Services and Well-Being (Wales) Act (2014) Accessed 16/11/2018 at: www.legislation.gov.uk/anaw/2014/4/contents.

UN Committee on the Rights of the Child (2005) *General Comment No 6: Treatment of Unaccompanied and Separated Children Outside Their Country of Origin.* Accessed 23/10/2018 at: www.refworld.org/docid/42dd174b4.html.

UNCRC (United Nations Convention on the Rights of the Child) (1989) Accessed 23/10/2018 at: www.unicef.org.uk/what-we-do/un-convention-child-rights.

UNHCR (1994) *Refugee Children: Guidelines on Protection and Care.* Accessed 16/11/2018 at: www.unhcr.org/protect/PROTECTION/3b84c6c67.pdf.

UNHCR (2009) *Guidelines on International Protection: Child Asylum Claims under Articles 1(A)2 and 1(F) of the 1951 Convention and/or 1967 Protocol Relating to the Status of Refugees.* Accessed 23/10/2018 at: www.unhcr.org/uk/publications/legal/50ae46309/guidelines-international-protection-8-child-asylum-claims-under-articles.html.

UNHCR (2018) 'Figures at a Glance.' Accessed 23/10/2018 at: www.unhcr.org/uk/figures-at-a-glance.html.

UNICEF UK (2018a) 'Latest Statistics and Graphics on Refugee and Migrant Children.' Accessed 23/10/2018 at: www.unicef.org/eca/what-we-do/emergencies/latest-statistics-and-graphics-refugee-and-migrant-children.

UNICEF UK (2018b) 'What's Happening to Child Refugees in Europe?' Accessed 23/10/2018 at: www.unicef.org.uk/child-refugees-europe.

UNISON and the Scottish Association of Social Workers (2017) *Refugee and Asylum in Scotland: Social Work Support a Human Right Not an Administrative Burden.* Accessed 23/10/2018 at: www.unison-scotland.org/library/refugee-and-asylum-seeker-good-practice-guide-webversion-final.pdf.

Warren, R. and York, S. (2014) *How Children Become Failed Asylum-Seekers: Research Report on the Experiences of Young Unaccompanied Asylum-Seekers in Kent from 2006 to 2013, and how 'corrective remedies' have failed them.* Accessed 23/10/2018 at: https://Kar.kent.ac.uk/44608.

Chapter 8

Asylum-Seeking Children In and Leaving Care

Practice and Policy Issues

Anna Gupta

> I arrived alone in the UK when I was 14, fleeing persecution. I built a life for myself here, going to school and college, learning English and now I am studying for an IT qualification. I have made friends and a future for myself in London, but I am facing having all of that taken away from me.
>
> 'J' Clayton (2016)

Each year over a thousand children arrive in the UK separated from their families and seeking asylum. Separated and unaccompanied children seeking asylum face significant uncertainty and harm not just during their journeys from their countries of origin, but in their experiences within the care and immigration systems in the UK, and in their everyday lives, especially when making the transition to adulthood. The United Nations Convention on the Rights of the Child (UNCRC) and domestic child welfare legislation, such as the Children Act 1989 in England and Wales, provide a framework for the provision of state services; however, children's experiences of care and support services vary greatly (Humphris and Sigona 2016; Kohli and Mitchell 2007; Matthews 2014). Once the young people turn 18, their legal protection is reduced and most face possible forced return to their countries of origin.

In this chapter, policy and practice issues in relation to unaccompanied asylum-seeking children are explored, concluding with key messages for social workers working within a human rights and social justice framework. The terms 'children' and 'young people' are used interchangeably to refer to people under the age of 18. Various different terms are used in literature and policy documents to describe children travelling across national boundaries, without family, in order to seek asylum elsewhere. Sometimes the term 'separated' is used as the child, possibly trafficked or smuggled, does not necessarily travel alone, but is separated from close family members. The Department for Education (DfE) terminology and definition is:

> an unaccompanied asylum-seeking child (UASC) is an individual, who is under 18, who has applied for asylum in his/her own right, is separated from both parents and is not being cared for by an adult who by law or custom has responsibility to do so. (DfE 2017a)

Unaccompanied children seeking asylum in the UK

Unaccompanied asylum-seeking children come from various parts of the world, most making hazardous journeys before reaching the UK. All will have experienced forced family separation. Some will have been trafficked and others smuggled, with many having experienced violence, abuse, destitution and hunger on their journeys. Some will arrive via clandestine routes, such as in the back of lorries, while others will come as part of government programmes. Some who are trafficked for illegal activities are found by police during raids, such as Vietnamese boys trafficked to work in cannabis factories.

According to Home Office statistics there were 3175 asylum applications from unaccompanied asylum-seeking children in 2016, a 2 per cent decrease compared to 2015 (3253). The nationalities that lodged the highest numbers of UASC applications in the UK were Afghani (740), Albanian (407) and Eritrean (405). These three countries contributed half (49%) of the total UASC applications (Home Office 2017). Although Iran, Iraq and Sudan are not in the top three countries where unaccompanied asylum-seeking children originate from, the Refugee Council (2017) statistical data noted significant increases in the number of applications from these countries in 2016. In 2016, the age distribution was: 16–17 years, 61 per cent; 14–15 years, 27 per cent; under 14 years, 7 per cent; age unknown, 5 per cent. In relation to age-disputed cases, there was a large increase in 2015 (148%) and a further increase in 2016 (18%) (Refugee Council 2017).

As discussed in sections below, local authority children's services departments have responsibility for unaccompanied asylum-seeking children, the majority of whom become 'looked-after children'. Department for Education (2017b) statistics indicate that the number of looked-after children at 31 March 2017 who were unaccompanied asylum-seeking children increased by 6 per cent compared to the previous year, up to 4560 from 4300 in 2016, and up 134 per cent from 1950 in 2013. Although recently there has been an increase in unaccompanied asylum-seeking girls, females accounted for only 8 per cent of unaccompanied asylum-seeking children looked after. In relation to age, 78 per cent of unaccompanied asylum-seeking children looked after at 31 March 2017 were aged 16 years of age and over, and 22 per cent were aged under 16 years (ibid.).

Policy and legal contexts

The UK is a signatory to the UN Convention on the Rights of the Child (UNCRC) 1989. Until 2008, the UK government opted out of applying the UNCRC to immigration issues. However, in 2008 the then Labour government removed the opt-out. Now, wherever the children come from and however they arrive in the UK, all are entitled to the same rights enshrined in the UNCRC as children born in Britain. From November 2009, Section 55 of the Borders, Citizenship and Immigration Act (BICA) 2009 requires that immigration, asylum and nationality functions are discharged 'having regard to the need to safeguard and promote the welfare of children'. In the case of ZH (Tanzania) v Secretary of State for the Home Department,[1] the UK's Supreme Court recognised that Article 3 of the NCRC, which requires that the best interests of children must be the primary concern in making decisions that may affect them, was a binding obligation in international law. The 'best interests' principle is described as 'a holistic concept, embracing the child's physical, mental, spiritual, moral, psychological and social development' (DfE 2017a, p.8). However, as is discussed in this chapter, the experiences of many of the children are a far cry from the ideals of the UNCRC.

The Home Office is responsible for deciding on whether unaccompanied asylum-seeking children are entitled to leave to remain in the UK. In practice, relatively few unaccompanied children are granted asylum or humanitarian protection when they first make their application. The majority are granted

---

1   ZH Tanzania v SSHD [2011] UKSC 4.

'UASC leave', which is a temporary status granted only on the basis that the person is still under 18 and there are no adequate reception arrangements in their home country. At 17½ they have to reapply for leave to remain in the UK. It is often very difficult for young people to again prove their case for refugee status after the passing of time. Also, the Home Office now considers UASC leave to be 'precarious', thereby lessening their chances of arguing a right to remain based on the right to private life under Article 8 of the European Convention on Human Rights (ECHR) (Warren 2016). The process fails to address children's needs for a 'durable solution', a concept developed by UNICEF and required by the UNCRC, which Gregg and Williams (2015, p.5) define as being:

> A long-term and sustainable solution which ensures that the separated child is able to develop into adulthood in an environment which will meet his or her needs as well as fulfil his or her rights, not putting the child at risk of persecution or harm while also taking into account their views in accordance with their capacity.

Depending on the country in the UK in which an unaccompanied asylum-seeking child arrives, domestic childcare legislation applies in terms of their status, entitlements and rights to protection and support. In England, the Children Act 1989 and the Children (Leaving Care) Act 2000 are the key pieces of legislation, which have been amended over the years and are supported by regulations and statutory guidance, including the *Care of Unaccompanied Migrant Children and Child Victims of Modern Slavery: Statutory Guidance for Local Authorities* (DfE 2017a).

In principle, unaccompanied asylum-seeking children are entitled to the same care and support from local authority children's services teams as any other child in the UK. The vast majority of separated children in England are given support under Section 20 of the Children Act 1989 and will become 'looked after' in the care of the local authority. Some older young people only receive services under Section 17 of the Children Act 1989 and do not become looked-after children, reducing their entitlement to a range of services, including access to education and therapeutic services. A 2003 court judgement following a judicial review of the London Borough of Hillingdon, known commonly as the 'Hillingdon judgement',[2] made explicit the level of support that was expected of local authorities for unaccompanied children, including that all unaccompanied children should,

---

2   *R (Behre) v London Borough of Hillingdon* (2003) EWHC 2075.

on arrival, be supported under Section 20 of the Children Act 1989 until an assessment has been completed, and that Section 17 should only be used in exceptional circumstances. There is significant variation in the number of unaccompanied asylum-seeking children across the country, with most concentrated in a few areas in the South East of England (e.g. Kent, Croydon, Hillingdon). In 2016, a National Transfer Scheme was introduced, resulting in some of the children being moved across to other local authorities.

Many unaccompanied asylum-seeking young people arrive in the UK without documentation, or with documentation deemed to be forged or counterfeit, and the age of some claiming to be under 18 years is disputed by the Home Office. Unless the physical appearance of the individual very strongly suggests that they are significantly over 18 years of age, they should be given the benefit of the doubt and treated as a child until a more holistic assessment is completed by local authority social workers (Dorling, MacLachlan and Trevena 2017). Guidance for local authorities also suggests that age assessments should only be carried out where there is reason to doubt that the individual is the age they claim. Age assessments should not be a routine part of a local authority's assessment of unaccompanied children (DfE 2017a).

The Association of Directors of Children's Services (ADCS 2015) has produced best practice guidance for social workers on conducting age assessments that is compliant with previous case law. This includes the important 2003 judgement *B v London Borough of Merton* (known as the 'Merton judgement'),[3] that detailed a number of basic principles to be considered in order to make assessments lawful, for example that two qualified and properly trained social workers should conduct the age assessment. The requirement that the age assessment is to be a single agency social work and not a multidisciplinary assessment has been criticised, especially as these assessments are complex and there is currently no available method that can accurately assess the age of young asylum seekers (British Association of Social Workers 2015).

Research studies exploring age assessments highlight the influences on social workers' analyses, such as anti-immigration discourses and a pervasive 'culture of disbelief', as well as the pressures of working in organisations under severe financial constraints and the implications of any decision having financial consequences (Cemlyn and Nye 2012; Crawley 2007). Cemlyn and Nye (2012, p.685) argue that the age-assessment process

---

3   *R (B) v London Borough of Merton* [2003] EWHC 1689.

can be seen 'as paradigmatic for the tensions facing social work with asylum seekers between a focus on the rights of service users and the demands of conformity to the restrictions of immigration law'.

For young people, the age that they are assessed as being will have huge implications, with far greater access to support and protection if they are deemed a child. Clarke's (2011) study importantly highlights how the process and outcome, if they are wrongly assessed as adults, can be extremely distressing for the young people, with mental health implications for their sense of identity; sense of self and trust in others; education development and safety (especially the risk of absconding). Even if assessed as under 18, the determined age also has implications for the level of support and section of the Children Act 1989 under which they receive this support (e.g. Section 20 or Section 17). The section of the Children Act 1989 under which the child is supported also determines the level of leaving care support they are entitled to once they turn 18.

General legislation in relation to children leaving care, including the Care Leavers (England) Regulations 2010 amended in 2014, is relevant for unaccompanied asylum-seeking children. The majority of young people should be entitled to leaving care support when they turn 18, which should be based on pathway plans that include accommodation and financial help and are facilitated through the involvement of personal advisors. However, young people who arrive, or start receiving support, within 13 weeks of their 18th birthday will not qualify for full leaving care services, even if they have been provided with support under Section 20 of the Children Act 1989 for the weeks leading up to their 18th birthday. Local authorities can provide accommodation and financial support for a care leaver who is 'appeals rights exhausted' (ARE) in relation to their asylum claim, if a human rights assessment concludes that withdrawing such support would be in breach of their human rights. However, the Immigration Act 2016 reduces entitlements to leaving care support for young people who are ARE and no longer have a legal basis to remain in the UK. At the time of writing, in early 2019, these changes are not in force and guidance has not as yet been published (Coram Children's Legal Centre 2017).

Care and protection for unaccompanied asylum-seeking children

Over the past two decades, research has been undertaken that explores the needs of unaccompanied asylum-seeking young people and this knowledge, combined with the wider literature on looked-after children, provides useful frameworks for meeting the needs and promoting the rights of unaccompanied asylum-seeking children. The literature also provides an exploration of children's experiences and the barriers faced by professionals. Work with unaccompanied asylum-seeking children is particularly challenging for practitioners seeking to work within a social justice and human rights framework. Central is the tension between child welfare and immigration control, with the influence of political and mainstream media discourses, including the culture of disbelief and suspicion towards unaccompanied migrant children permeating organisational cultures and professional practice. This is compounded by increasingly harsh immigration law and the impact of stringent cuts to local authority budgets and services under 'austerity' (Cemlyn and Nye 2012; Connolly and Pinter 2015; Humphries 2004; Kvittingen 2010).

In England and Wales under the Children Act 1989, local authorities have a duty to safeguard and promote the welfare of unaccompanied asylum-seeking children. These children and young people are entitled to the same local authority provision as any other looked-after child, which includes appropriate accommodation, education provision and therapeutic support. Broadly speaking, the promotion of unaccompanied asylum-seeking children's well-being has been seen as needing to encompass safety, good physical and mental health, education and opportunities to build futures, enduring relationships and friendships in the UK and transnationally, and a sense of belonging and identity (Chase 2013, 2017; Kohli 2006; Wade et al. 2012). Kohli (2011) provides a framework comprising the dimensions of safety, belonging and success, to act as the foundations of a stable life for all vulnerable children. He describes a process for unaccompanied children starting with acclimatisation and adaptation, and moving through participation and absorption into the society where they are living, to a place of reciprocation, which marks 'the mature stages of finally slipping away from places where they were once visible and scrutinised to a life where house and "home" coexist once again' (ibid., p.314). However, for most unaccompanied asylum-seeking children who only have temporary leave to remain, their stability and safety are contingent and conditional, and their subjective well-being, which is linked to their notions of future and being able to imagine and work towards future goals, is compromised (Chase 2013). Although within the immigration and care systems young people's autonomy, identity and agency are often very constrained, there is much professionals can do to promote their safety, well-being and rights.

In terms of well-being and safety, unaccompanied asylum-seeking children when first identified by authorities will need somewhere to stay. Generally, children assessed to be under 16 are placed in a foster placement or sometimes a residential children's home, where they will receive higher levels of support than in hostel accommodation. Many children assessed as over 16 are placed in hostel accommodation. For some unaccompanied children, foster care can provide a secure base, somewhere they feel valued and cared about (Wade *et al.* 2012). In foster placements that worked well in Wade and colleagues' (2012) study, an initial offer of 'hospitality' to a stranger paved the way for the development of more intimate family-like relationships over time. Familiar foods, with their smells, tastes and reminders of home, could act as a marker of inclusion and belonging. However, food could also act as a marker of difference and exclusion within the household (e.g. meals cooked entirely separately and locked kitchen cupboards to regulate access to food (ibid.)). Some unaccompanied asylum-seeking children who experienced foster care have spoken of feeling that they were treated differently, were uncared for and isolated, with any growing sense of 'becoming settled' negligible (Chase, Knight and Statham 2008).

In reviewing the different types of placements, Wade and colleagues (2012) identified three broad categorisations:

- *Family-like relationships*, where the adaptation and adjustment of structure, relationships and practices had resulted in a sense of settlement that was expected to provide a source of enduring, meaningful support after the placement had ended.

- *Temporary home bases*, where the foster carer and young person had made adjustments that enabled the placement to work well, but where a sense of emotional distance was present that resulted in there being a limited form of family life that would be unlikely to continue after the young person left.

- *Lodgings*, where the basics of daily living were usually available but where boundaries were firmly drawn in ways that indicated this was a functional arrangement with no real prospect of settlement.

Research studies have shown that the care offered to unaccompanied asylum-seeking children varies considerably across local authorities in the UK (Kohli and Mitchell 2007; Matthews 2014; Wade, Mitchell and Baylis 2005). Local authorities interpret their duties to unaccompanied and former unaccompanied asylum-seeking children differently, and stringent cuts to budgets have further polarised such experiences, with some wealthier areas being able to maintain services no longer available or only partially available elsewhere (Connolly and Pinter 2015). Humphris and Sigona (2016) found that increasingly children were placed outside the local authority with statutory responsibility to support them, with receiving local authorities being rarely informed. Money-saving concerns are also affecting the care local authorities are able to provide to young people seeking asylum in their care, with services for older children particularly affected (Sigona, Chase and Humphris 2017a). The Becoming Adult research project also noted a loss of specialist teams for unaccompanied asylum-seeking children and their incorporation into general children services teams, leading to a loss of critical expertise and 'a risk that the best interests of "foreign" children in care become deprioritised and that they experience a decline, qualitatively and quantitatively, in services and support' (Sigona *et al.* 2017a, p.3).

Some unaccompanied asylum-seeking children will have been trafficked to the UK for the purposes of exploitation, or may be at risk of in-country trafficking due to their vulnerabilities, including possible debt bondage (O'Connell Davidson 2013). If this is identified or suspected there needs to be a multi-agency response, involving the police as well, and accommodation provided that addresses these safety needs (DfE 2017a). A study by ECPAT (Every Child Protected Against Trafficking) UK and Missing People (2016) found that, from September 2014 to September 2015, 760 trafficked or unaccompanied children went missing from care, of whom 207 had not been found at the time of the study. Various factors impact on the reasons for going missing, including: control/influence of traffickers; lack of trust in adults who are there to keep them safe; feeling socially isolated; lack of engagement with school and social networks; and, crucially, uncertain immigration status and stressful procedures (ECPAT UK and Missing People 2016; Humphris and Sigona 2016). Attentive and engaged adults who are 'on their side' are crucial to the protection of children from further significant harm, but the study by Humphris and Sigona (2016) identified a lack of consistency in the way in which local authorities identify risk of going missing, and the 'invisibility' of many of these children.

Despite the turmoil and often traumatic experiences leading to and during their journeys to the UK, the young people in a number of studies typically described a process through which they began to re-establish structure, routine and predictability in their lives through education, learning and other activities that generate routine and social connections (such as attending community and religious groups) (Chase 2013;

Hek 2005; Ni Raghallaigh and Gilligan 2010). The academic, emotional and social value of school or college can be enormous in the lives of many unaccompanied children. Being able to communicate in English is a crucial step to acclimatising and adapting and being able to access other educational opportunities. Young people in Chase's (2013) study repeatedly mentioned 'college', 'school' and 'learning' as being among the most positive dimensions of their current lives. Zemar, one of the young people in the study, explains that:

> College was like a haven for me, you know? A safe haven where I could go and hide. I'd be in the college morning to evening every day. Education provided a smokescreen in a way –that's how I sort of coped with it…until I stood on my feet. That's my way of looking at it…that's my analysis. (Chase 2013, p.864)

In Scotland, the Scottish government and charitable organisations established a pilot independent guardianship system for unaccompanied asylum-seeking children, which was positively evaluated by Crawley and Kohli (2013). Although similar guardianship services do not exist across the UK, the work of the Scottish Guardians provides helpful ways of thinking about professional practice with unaccompanied asylum-seeking children. It is crucial for all professionals to work together to help children engage with positive educational experiences, and to understand what may be going on for the young person or the resource provision if he/she is not able to engage. One of the case studies in the Crawley and Kohli (2013) report was about Honor, an age-disputed child who was unwilling to enrol for college, because he was intimidated by being with young people a lot older than him. His guardian made a referral to a life skills class and attended the first one with him. He was also supported to become involved in a local football team, a dance class and a boxing club. After four months of encouragement, Honor was able to develop the confidence to enrol in a mainstream college. Although it was far from a uniform experience, Meloni and Chase (2017) found that some young people had enjoyed excellent support from social workers. Their educational development had been encouraged and resourced, and they spoke positively of social workers who went out of their way to do everything they could to provide emotional as well as practical support.

Unaccompanied asylum-seeking children need to be linked in with appropriate health services, in relation to both their physical and mental health needs, and be supported by good-quality interpreters. The negative effects of forced migration on the physical, psychological and emotional well-being of separated children prior to and on their journeys to Europe is well documented (Bean *et al.* 2007; Bronstein and Montgomery 2011; Hodes *et al.* 2008). These difficulties can, however, be compounded by their experiences once in the UK, in an environment often hostile to asylum seekers and in which they experience discrimination and stigmatisation, as well as the uncertainties of not knowing what their final immigration status (or lack of it) will be. Feelings of connectedness were central to young people's sense of health and well-being, and friendships can provide important emotional support (Meloni and Chase 2017). Devising care plans and support packages able to nurture consistency and predictability and promote resilience are crucial, but also challenging in the current context, especially as related to asylum and immigration policy.

In Chase's (2013) study, young people talked of experiencing a wide spectrum of emotional health difficulties, including anxiety, depression, attempted suicide in some cases, and periodic mental illness requiring hospitalisation. She concluded that:

> while the roots of such difficulties lay in earlier trauma and upheaval, there was little doubt from the analysis of young people's accounts that other uncertainties, most crucially with respect to their immigration status, exacerbated these mental health problems. (ibid., p.862)

Chase and Allsop (2013) argue that young people's subjective well-being is linked to their notions of future, and being able to imagine and work towards future goals. However, precarious legal status impacts adversely on all aspects of young people's lives, including their sense of identity and belonging, access to resources, learning and education pathways and their potential to construct viable futures.

While specialist therapeutic services are likely to be necessary for some unaccompanied asylum-seeking children, all will require care and support that promotes resilience and emotional well-being, which is very dependent on having some sense of security about the future. When evaluating the Scottish Guardianship Service, Crawley and Kohli (2013) highlighted the importance of the 'asylum domain', within which guardians support young people with their claims for asylum, including helping them understand their rights and the process, ensuring they have legal representation, and attending meetings and court hearings.

Social workers working for local authorities with unaccompanied asylum-seeking children who are looked after are in effect *in loco parentis*, responsible for safeguarding and promoting the welfare of the children. The centrality of their immigration status to the children's emotional and physical well-being requires that concerted attention needs to be paid to supporting and advocating for children through often very confusing and intimidating processes. The only secure legal status for an unaccompanied child who is seeking asylum is indefinite leave to remain. The alternative is an increasingly abrupt transition at 18 to the 'hostile environment' of the adult asylum system. When a child's initial application is refused and they are granted UASC leave, it is essential that they obtain legal advice about immediately appealing the asylum and humanitarian protection refusal. Good-quality legal representation is crucial in securing favourable outcomes in asylum cases, and cases can be appealed successfully.

It is important that a young person on UASC leave applies for further leave to remain before it expires. If they apply within the currency of their existing leave, the conditions of their leave remain the same while the application is pending, including throughout any appeals. However, it is often very difficult to make a successful 'new claim' and there is no longer legal aid to support young people's arguments about their Article 8 ECHR rights to family and private life in the UK. As is discussed in the next section, once the child is 18, no 'best interests' considerations apply to them and many face very precarious futures.

Turning 18

For many children, leaving care at 18 can be a very anxiety-provoking time. Criticisms about the abrupt nature of the ending of support for children in care when they end their legal minority have led to changes and extensions to local authority duties over the past two decades. Legal residency is fundamental to determining whether young people have access to the services offered to other care leavers. For unaccompanied asylum-seeking children who have not received leave to remain, the difficulties making the transition to adulthood are exacerbated by their uncertain immigration status, combined with some ambiguity and inconsistency in terms of their entitlement to care and support on turning 18 (Meloni and Chase 2017). Precarious legal status is associated with feelings of stigma, discrimination, alienation and isolation, leading to physical and mental health problems, as they await a Home Office decision that could lead to forced removal from their established networks in the UK and to countries where they face dangers and may have few or no connections.

Prior to turning 18, all young people in care are required to have a pathway plan, based on an assessment of their needs and covering areas such as accommodation, practical life skills, education and training, employment, financial support, specific support needs, and contingency plans (DfE 2015). For unaccompanied asylum-seeking children, their pathway plan needs to cover these areas, as well as any additional needs arising from their immigration status and the action required to resolve these. Due to the uncertainty of many young people's asylum application, social workers are expected to plan for various possible outcomes for those turning 18, which is often referred to as 'triple planning'. Dorling *et al.* (2017) explain that the three options under consideration are:

- assisting the young person to create a future for themselves in the UK if they receive some form of leave to remain past their 18th birthday

- helping the young person to prepare for return to their country of origin either if they are refused an extension to remain in the UK and are going to be returned, or if they are returning voluntarily

- supporting the young person who has been refused leave to remain in the UK and who has exhausted all appeal rights but are not removed. This may be for a number of reasons, such as difficulties in returning them to their country of origin or place from which they fled.

However, this can be a difficult and emotionally demanding process for the young person and professionals working with them.

Young people involved in the Becoming Adult research project spoke of very varied experiences of care and support after turning 18. Some spoke of how they maintained relationships with foster carers after they had moved to other forms of accommodation and of the important role foster carers had in providing continuity of support (Meloni and Chase 2017). However, for many of the young people the quality of support and service provision sharply declined once they turned 18, and they spoke of having no choice or control over the process and experiencing high levels of stress, loneliness and social isolation. Young people who were ARE often described abrupt and violent transitions, 'including immediate homelessness; enforced relocation far from their social networks and friendship groups and reduced models and packages of care' (Sigona *et al.* 2017a, p.3).

A number of young people in the Becoming Adult project described intentionally disengaging from social care and going missing when they received or anticipated a negative outcome from their asylum application

(Meloni and Chase 2017). The young people who the researchers met in this situation typically experienced destitution, homelessness, poor physical and mental health and increased vulnerability to exploitation. They feared seeking professional help for mental or physical health problems and lived precarious lives relying on the good will of others or working in exploitative conditions in continuous fear of being reported or apprehended by the police because of their undocumented status (Sigona, Chase and Humphris 2017b).

Very limited information is available about the outcomes for young people who have been returned voluntarily or forcibly, or indeed those that go 'missing'. Gladwell and colleagues (2016) undertook a study of 25 care leavers returned to Afghanistan and found that, without exception, the young people reported experiencing a range of interconnected difficulties on return, with the majority finding their networks had disappeared, weakened or become fractured. The majority faced significant barriers to accessing help, education and employment, and remained either without support or dependent on unsustainable and ad hoc assistance from people in the UK. Mental health difficulties and a protracted deterioration in emotional well-being were noted to be clear and significant outcomes for them. Many spoke of plans to leave Afghanistan and at the end of the project, six had already left the country and the whereabouts of 11 more were unknown (Gladwell *et al.* 2016).

The Becoming Adult project also explored the experiences of former unaccompanied asylum-seeking children and noted fundamentally different pathways through the asylum and immigration system depending on nationality. Albanian young people were the most likely to be refused a right to remain in the UK; a large proportion of young people from Afghanistan were either returned to Afghanistan or went missing to avoid deportation. Eritrean young people were most likely to have their claims to asylum accepted (Sigona *et al.* 2017b). Of the 30 young people from Afghanistan included in the study, eight young people were deported to Afghanistan, and of these, seven re-migrated, with the remaining young person still dependent for survival on networks of support in the UK. Aware that they were unlikely to secure leave to remain, young people from Albania often avoided removal through disengaging from statutory services and going 'missing' (ibid.).

Sigona and colleagues argue that the health and well-being consequences of forced or threatened removals of young people, for whom local authorities previously had a duty of care, require much closer monitoring. There is an urgent need to reconsider the impact of removal as a 'durable solution' and promote alternative pathways to regularise the status of young people who have had their asylum claims rejected but who have established relationships, networks and a life in the UK (ibid.). In a similar way, Gladwell and Elwyn (2012) concluded that local authorities have a moral if not legal duty to young people as former children in care to monitor those who are returned and provide support, both pre- and post-return, to give them the best possible chances of success.

Practice issues

The contradictions social workers face in relation to adhering to their professional values, alongside the social work task increasingly having become embedded in restrictive immigration control, makes work with unaccompanied asylum-seeking children particularly challenging for workers striving to promote social justice and human rights (Cemlyn and Nye 2012; Humphries 2004). For the young person, understanding the role of the social worker as someone responsible for their care and protection but with links to the Home Office can be confusing and make developing effective relationships based on trust more difficult.

While these have been challenges workers have been grappling with for years, the current context has exacerbated difficulties. In 2013, the then home secretary, Theresa May, promised to introduce a 'hostile environment' for irregular migrants (*The Guardian* 2013), a pledge made good by the implementation of the Immigration Act 2016. As discussed above, a 'culture of disbelief' often permeates professional responses to age assessments and other aspects of practice with unaccompanied asylum-seeking children, influenced at least in part by dominant anti-immigrations discourse in some parts of the media and among many politicians. The Becoming Adult project concluded that the principle of the 'best interests of the child' that underpins child protection processes is being transformed by the related pressures from budget cuts, expanding market logics in the asylum system and widespread anti-immigration attitudes that find expression in the policy goal of producing a "hostile environment" for foreigners' (Sigona *et al.* 2017a, p.2).

As with other social work assessments and interventions, the process and decisions will be impacted on by the individual professional's values and assumptions, as well as organisational cultures and resources. Despite the considerable constraints faced by practitioners and managers, it is important for individual workers to recognise their agency and what can be done to ensure that care and support services help young people to promote their voices, rights and well-being.

A human rights perspective provides a robust framing for contemporary social work, with private troubles seen as public issues and the acceptance of political dimension to problems (Ife 2012). Banks (2016) discusses 'ethics work', a concept that highlights the work practitioners do to see the wider political (macro) context of their practice and take responsibility for being ethical and acting ethically. This needs to be a starting point for all practitioners and managers. Recognising and challenging institutional harm caused by immigration and asylum processes, and addressing the consequential risks to mental and physical health of young people, is essential. However, it is also important for social workers to have an awareness of prejudices, assumptions and 'othering' affecting asylum-seeking young people, and ways in which they and their colleagues' practices may perpetuate these exclusionary processes that frame so much of young asylum-seekers' lives. Important in the development of workers' capabilities to practice in this way is the opportunity for space in teams and organisations for critical reflection, whether this is through supervision or in groups.

The importance of developing supportive relationships with young people, getting to know the individual and their story and working with them to promote their wishes, needs and rights has been highlighted. The positive evaluation of the Scottish Guardianship Service conducted by Crawley and Kohli (2013, pp.89–90) concluded that the service put the young people, 'rather than the processes to which they were subjected – at the centre and that the Guardians provided them with a level of acceptance and support which, for complex reasons, they were unable to secure from other adults in their lives'. Although not independent of the local authority, social workers can and should fulfil many of the roles that the guardians did in order to promote young people's rights and welfare. These include ensuring that young people's voices are heard, and they are provided with good-quality legal advice, safe accommodation that promotes a sense of belonging and connections, and access to coordinated education, health and social supports. Developing practitioners' own and young people's links with voluntary, non-governmental, refugee and anti-deportation organisations is important to ensure that information is provided to young people facing uncertain futures, so they can make informed decisions based on sound legal advice, and contact is maintained if they are in detention or forcibly returned.

Williams and Briskman (2015) draw on the concept of 'moral outrage' to argue that the translation of personal distress into public issues is at the heart of the political project of social work. Social work is not just about work with individual unaccompanied children seeking asylum, but should also involve actions to challenge discriminatory and unlawful practices in organisations, and engage in debate about relationships between Home Office processes and professional values. Social workers need to use their professional voices and experiences to bear witness to injustices and act in solidarity with unaccompanied asylum-seeking young people, others affected by forced migration and controlled borders, and activist groups seeking to promote a more humane and socially just society and world.

Key messages for social workers

- Develop supportive relationships with children and young people; ensure that they understand your role. Get to know the individual and their story, and accept that this may take time.

- Provide emotional and practical support and advocacy, demonstrating that you are someone who cares about them and their well-being and will 'go the extra mile'.

- Ensure that the voices of the children are heard and their involvement in decision making is promoted.

- Be aware of the power of dominant anti-immigration discourses; critically reflect on your own personal values and assumptions that could lead to discriminatory practices.

- Remember that all young people need to be treated with respect and humanity, as individuals and with their human rights upheld. Be prepared to challenge the prejudices, assumptions and discriminatory practices of others.

- Acknowledge the importance of relationships and the promotion of a sense of security, belonging and future through all involvement with unaccompanied children and young people seeking asylum, including educational opportunities and access to good-quality legal representation.

- Where possible be a 'courageous ethnographer' (Briskman 2013) and use your privileged position to bear witness to the lives of unaccompanied asylum-seeking children by exposing unjust policies and challenging dominant discourses together with community and social activist organisations with similar social justice goals.

References

Association of Directors of Children's Services (ADCS) (2015) *Age Assessment Guidance: Guidance to Assist Social Workers and Their Managers in Undertaking Age Assessments in England.* Accessed 23/11/2018 at: http://adcs.org.uk/assets/documentation/Age_Assessment_Guidance_2015_Final.pdf.

Banks, S. (2016) 'Everyday ethics in professional life: Social work as ethics work.' *Ethics and Social Welfare*, 10, 1, 35–52.

Bean, T., Derluyn, I., Eurelings-Bontekoe, E., Broekaert, E. and Spinhoven, P. (2007) 'Comparing psychological distress, traumatic stress reactions, and experiences of unaccompanied refugee minors with experiences of adolescents accompanied by parents.' *Journal of Nervous and Mental Disease*, 195, 4, 288–297.

Borders, Citizenship and Immigration Act (2009) Accessed 16/11/2018 at: www.legislation.gov.uk/ukpga/2009/11/contents.

Briskman, L. (2013) 'Courageous ethnographers or agents of the state: Challenges for social work.' *Critical and Radical Social Work*, 1, 1, 51–66.

British Association of Social Workers (BASW) (2015) *BASW Response to the Age Assessment Guidance Document.* Accessed 23/11/2018 at: http://cdn.basw.co.uk/upload/basw_115208-6.pdf.

Bronstein, I. and Montgomery, P. (2011) 'Psychological distress in refugee children: A systematic review.' *Clinical Child and Family Psychology Review*, 14, 1, 44–56.

Cemlyn, S.J. and Nye, M. (2012) 'Asylum seeker young people: Social work value conflicts in negotiating age assessment in the UK.' *International Social Work*, 55, 5, 675–688.

Chase, E. (2013) 'Security and subjective wellbeing: The experiences of unaccompanied young people seeking asylum in the UK.' *Sociology of Health & Illness*, 35, 6, 858–872.

Chase, E. (2017) *Health and Wellbeing.* Becoming Adult Research Brief no. 5. London: UCL. Accessed 23/11/2018 at: https://becomingadultproject.files.wordpress.com/2017/12/ba-brief-5-low-res.pdf.

Chase, E. and Allsop, J. (2013) *Future Citizens of the World? The Contested Futures of Independent Young Migrants in Europe.* RSC Working Paper Series 97. Oxford: Refugee Studies Centre.

Chase, E., Knight, A. and Statham, J. (2008) *The Emotional Wellbeing of Unaccompanied Young People Seeking Asylum in the UK.* London: British Association for Adoption and Fostering.

Children Act (1989) Accessed on 13/05/2019 at: https://www.legislation.gov.uk/ukpga/1989/41.

Children (Leaving Care) Act (2000) Accessed on 13/05/2019 at: https://www.legislation.gov.uk/ukpga/2000/35/contents.

Clarke, S. (2011) *Young Lives in Limbo: The Protection of Age-Disputed Young People in Wales.* Cardiff: Welsh Refugee Council.

Clayton, S. 'Living in the UK.' (2016) Big Journeys – Untold Stories. Accessed 11/05/2019 at: www.bigjourneys.org/living-in-the-uk.

Connolly, H. and Pinter, I. (2015) *Cut Off from Justice: The Impact of Excluding Separated Migrant Children from Legal Aid.* Children's Society. Accessed 23/11/2018 at: www.childrenssociety.org.uk/sites/default/files/LegalAid_Full_0.pdf.

Coram Children's Legal Centre (2017) 'Recent changes in leaving care support include the introduction of the "local offer" and support for young migrants.' Accessed 23/11/2018 at: www.childrenslegalcentre.com/local-offer-care-leavers/4.

Crawley, H. (2007) *When Is a Child not a Child? Asylum, Age Disputes and the Process of Age Assessment*. London: Immigration Law Practitioners' Assocation.

Crawley, H. and Kohli, R. (2013) *'She Endures With Me': An Evaluation of the Scottish Guardianship Service Pilot*. Accessed 23/11/2018 at: www.scottishrefugeecouncil. org.uk/assets/0000/6798/Final_Report_2108.pdf.

DfE (Department for Education) (2015) *The Children Act 1989 Guidance and Regulations Volume 2: Care Planning, Placement and Case Review*. London: DfE.

DfE (Department for Education) (2017a) *Care of Unaccompanied Migrant Children and Child Victims of Modern Slavery: Statutory Guidance for Local Authorities*. Accessed 23/11/2018 at: https://consult.education.gov.uk/children-in-care/care-of-unaccompanied-and-trafficked-children/supporting_documents/Revised%20 UASC%20Stat%20guidance_final.pdf.

DfE (Department for Education) (2017b) *Children Looked After in England (Including Adoption), Year Ending 31 March 2017*. SFR 50/2017, 28 September. Accessed 23/11/2018 at: www.gov.uk/government/uploads/system/uploads/attachment_data/ file/664995/SFR50_2017-Children_looked_after_in_England.pdf.

Dorling, K., MacLachlan, S. and Trevena, F. (2017) *Seeking Support: A Guide to the Rights and Entitlements of Separated Children*. Accessed 23/11/2018 at: www. childrenslegalcentre.com/wp-content/uploads/2017/05/Seeking-Support-2017.pdf.

ECPAT (Every Child Protected Against Trafficking) UK and Missing People (2016) *Heading Back to Harm: A Study on Trafficked and Unaccompanied Children Going Missing from Care in the UK*. Accessed 23/11/2018 at: www.ecpat.org.uk/Handlers/ Download.ashx?IDMF=875b65b5-08d4-4e9f-a28c-331d1421519f.

Gladwell, C., Bowerman, E., Norman, B. and Dickson, S. with Ghafoor, A. (2016) *After Return: Documenting the Experiences of Young People Forcibly Removed to Afghanistan*. London: Refugee Support Network.

Gladwell, C. and Elwyn, E. (2012) *Broken Futures: Young Afghan Asylum Seekers in the UK and in Their Country of Origin*. Geneva: UNHCR.

Gregg, L. and Williams, N. (2015) *Not Just a Temporary Fix: The Search for Durable Solutions for Separated Migrant Children*. London: Children's Society.

Guardian, The (2013) 'Immigration bill: Theresa May defends plans to create "hostile environment".' 10 October. Accessed 23/11/2018 at: www.theguardian.com/ politics/2013/oct/10/immigration-bill-theresa-may-hostile-environment.

Hek, R. (2005) *The Experiences and Needs of Refugee and Asylum Seeking Children in the UK: A Literature Review*. Accessed 23/11/2018 at: http://dera.ioe.ac.uk/5398/1/ RR635.pdf.

Hodes, M., Jagdev, D., Chandra, N. and Cunniff, A. (2008) 'Risk and resilience for psychological distress amongst unaccompanied asylum seeking adolescents.' *Journal of Child Psychology and Psychiatry*, 49, 7, 723–773.

Home Office (2017) 'National Statistics: Asylum.' 23 February. Accessed 23/11/2018 at: www.gov.uk/government/publications/immigration-statistics-october-to-december-2016/asylum#unaccompanied-asylum-seeking-children.

Humphries, B. (2004) 'An unacceptable role for social work: Implementing immigration policy.' *British Journal of Social Work*, 34, 93–107.

Humphris, R. and Sigona, N. (2016) *Mapping Unaccompanied Asylum Seeking Children in England.* Becoming Adult Research Brief Series, no. 1. Accessed 23/11/2018 at: https://becomingadultproject.files.wordpress.com/2016/07/research-brief-series-01_2016.pdf.

Ife, J. (2012) *Human Rights and Social Work: Towards Rights-Based Practice* (third edition). Port Melbourne: Cambridge University Press.

Immigration Act (2016) Accessed on 13/05/2019 at: http://www.legislation.gov.uk/ukpga/2016/19/contents/enacted.

Kohli, R. (2006) 'The sound of silence: Listening to what unaccompanied children say and do not say.' *The British Journal of Social Work*, 36, 707–721.

Kohli, R. (2011) 'Working to ensure safety, belonging and success for unaccompanied asylum-seeking children.' *Child Abuse Review*, 20, 5, 311–323.

Kohli, R. and Mitchell, F. (eds) (2007) *Working with Unaccompanied Asylum-Seeking Children: Issues for Police and Practice.* Basingstoke: Palgrave Macmillan.

Kvittingen, A. (2010) *Negotiating Childhood: Age Assessment in the UK Asylum System.* Oxford: Refugee Studies Centre.

Matthews, A. (2014) *'What's Going to Happen Tomorrow?' Unaccompanied Children Refused Asylum.* Office of the Children's Commissioner. Accessed 23/11/2018 at: http://dera.ioe.ac.uk/20002/1/ARE_FINAL_for_Web.pdf.

Meloni, F. and Chase, E. (2017) *Transitions into Institutional Adulthood.* Becoming Adult Research Brief no. 4. London: UCL.

Ni Raghallaigh, M. and Gilligan, R. (2010) 'Active survival in the lives of unaccompanied minors: Coping strategies, resilience, and the relevance of religion.' *Child and Family Social Work*, 15, 2, 226–237.

O'Connell Davidson, J. (2013) 'Troubling freedom: Migration, debt, and modern slavery.' *Migration Studies*, 1, 2, 176–195.

Refugee Council (2017) *Children in the Asylum System.* November. Accessed 23/11/2018 at: www.refugeecouncil.org.uk/assets/0004/2380/Children_in_the_Asylum_System_Nov_2017.pdf.

Sigona, N., Chase, E. and Humphris, R. (2017a) *Protecting the 'Best Interests' of the Child in Transition to Adulthood.* Becoming Adult Research Brief no. 3. London: UCL.

Sigona, N., Chase, E. and Humphris, R. (2017b) *Understanding Causes and Consequences of Going 'Missing'.* Becoming Adult Brief no. 6. London: UCL.

The Care Planning and Care Leavers (Amendment) Regulations (2014) Accessed on 13/05/2019 at: https://www.legislation.gov.uk/uksi/2014/1917/contents/made.

UN Convention on the Rights of the Child (1989) Accessed on 13/05/2019 at: https://www.unicef.org.uk/what-we-do/un-convention-child-rights.

Wade, J., Mitchell, F. and Baylis, G. (2005) *Unaccompanied Asylum Seeking Children: The Response of Social Work Services.* London: British Association for Adoption and Fostering.

Wade, J., Sirriyeh, A., Kohli, R. and Simmonds, J. (2012) *Fostering Unaccompanied Asylum-Seeking Young People: A Research Project.* London: BAAF. Accessed 22/05/2019 at: www.york.ac.uk/inst/spru/research/pdf/FosterUAS.pdf.

Warren, R. (2016) 'Private life in the balance: Constructing the precarious migrant.' *Journal of Immigration, Asylum and Nationality Law*, 230, 2, 124–141.

Williams, C. and Briskman, L. (2015) 'Reviving social work through moral outrage.' *Critical and Radical Social Work*, 3, 1, 3–17.

Chapter 9

Social Work with Survivors of Torture

Jude Boyles, Anna Turner and Katy Tolman

The writers of this chapter have worked with refugees both as colleagues and activists for many years. During this time, we have practised within creative and innovative non-governmental organisation (NGO) settings, where social workers have played a key role in the care and rehabilitation of refugee survivors of torture. We share a commitment to human rights and to delivering social work practice from a rights-based framework. As Bashir (2017, p.206) reminds us:

> A human rights standpoint forces practitioners to look beyond survivors' individual needs and take action to support their rights as human beings. Respect for universal human dignity underpins human rights law. A human rights standpoint identifies the 'duty bearers'...[social workers] who hold the responsibility to ensure these rights are honoured.

As human rights practitioners, we believe in the rights of survivors to rehabilitation and justice. Article 14 of the UN Convention against Torture (UNCAT) (1984) places a duty on nation states to ensure effective rehabilitation for survivors. Rehabilitation is an important component of reparation, and the UN Basic Principles on remedies for victims provide that 'rehabilitation should include medical and psychological care as well as legal and social services' (Mendez 2013, p.2).

Katy works as a social worker with separated young people in a statutory service and Anna works within an early intervention in psychosis team. Jude manages a psychological therapy service for Syrian refugees resettled through the UN's High Commissioner for Refugees Vulnerable Person's

Resettlement Scheme. Anna coordinated a social work service in an NGO for refugees with complex needs for ten years and Jude has worked as a psychological therapist with refugees for nearly two decades and established and managed a torture rehabilitation service for 14 years. This chapter outlines our approach to social work with refugees who have been tortured. It is informed by Anna's social work practice with refugees, Katy's work with separated young people and Jude's work in torture rehabilitation. Social workers practising in the third and statutory sector are likely to come across individuals and families at all stages of the asylum process who have experienced torture and other human rights abuses. Working with refugee survivors of torture is an area that all social workers need to be both prepared for and informed about.

People seeking asylum are bound to a legal system that excludes and constrains them, without assigning them a status within that system. As such, they are both within the law and outside it. They are 'literally pending recognition' (Tyler 2006, p.189) in their status as an asylum seeker: 'In effect, they are deprived of life "in the sense that a political animal lives, in community and bound by law"' (Butler 2004, cited in Tyler 2006, p.189). This not only impacts on their access to support, but on how people are viewed and treated by society.

Constructions of people seeking asylum within popular discourse often function to dehumanise through language, such as 'tides', 'waves', or 'floods' of migrants. This water imagery has become ubiquitous in talk about migration: 'such metaphors serve to remove direct reference to human beings as well as reinforce the sense of urgency' (Masocha and Simpson 2011, p.13). A tide, for example, is unstoppable, fast and potentially deadly. This construction of people seeking asylum, it has been suggested, reinforces and legitimises their dehumanising treatment within law. It can also act to restrict access to services when a person is seen as not eligible, or 'illegal'. Crucially, the way we define and construct the 'refugee' and 'asylum seeker' in wider society can also impact on how we practise as professionals: 'social workers are not immune to these discourses' (Masocha and Simpson 2011, p.5).

The imposed label of 'asylum seeker', with all the negative connotations that it has come to imply, can also shape the way that torture survivors come to understand themselves. An awareness of the negative effects that this can have on a torture survivor's sense of identity is particularly relevant here, given that it is often the identity of the torture survivor that is targeted and broken down through the act of torture.

For the purposes of this chapter, we will use the general term 'refugee' to refer to anyone who has left their country of origin to seek protection, whether they have been granted asylum or not. Where relevant, we will use the term 'seeking asylum' to refer to those still within the asylum process.

Background

Article 1.1 of the United Nations Convention against Torture (UNCAT), The Convention against Torture and Other Cruel, Inhuman or Degrading Treatment or Punishment (UN 1984, p.1), defines torture as:

> Any act by which severe pain or suffering, whether physical or mental, is intentionally inflicted on a person for such purposes as obtaining from him, or a third person, information or a confession, punishing him for an act he or a third person has committed or is suspected of having committed, or intimidating or coercing him or a third person, or for any reason based on discrimination of any kind, when such pain or suffering is inflicted by or at the instigation of or with the consent or acquiescence of a public official or other person acting in an official capacity.

Women's experiences of torture and abuse and of seeking asylum are different from men's, and fewer women claim asylum than men. In 2015, 21 per cent of people applying for asylum in the UK were women (Refugee Council 2012).

Rape is now classified as a war crime and a crime against humanity, but international law still does not adequately protect women from the range of gender-specific abuses that they flee from, such as rape, female genital mutilation, forced marriage, child marriage, trafficking and 'honour' killing. Girma *et al.* (2014, p.11) remind us that although many women are tortured within the definition above, many are survivors of gender-based abuse which 'is more likely to take place in the private sphere, such as from pimps and family members, in a situation where she feels that she cannot seek protection from her own state'.

Seeking safety

It feels almost impossible to define the torture survivor's experience, given the huge diversity within the refugee population, but it feels important to try.

> The aim of torture is not always to make the victim confess and give information. The primary aim is more to break down the identity of the

victim. The pain consists in particular in this breaking down and in the destruction of the personality. (Elsass 1997, p.10)

Survivors may have been imprisoned by the state or by organised rebel or opposition groups such as the Taliban, who operate in Afghanistan and Pakistan. The torture can last days, weeks or years, and involves not just physical and/or sexual torture, but psychological humiliation and mental abuse. Most survivors are held in appalling conditions and live in fear of being executed. All the survivors we have worked with have described a feeling of powerlessness and dread that continues into exile and can last for many years, long after they have been granted asylum.

Survivors are held in camps or prison and are repeatedly raped and assaulted. Others are imprisoned in houses, containers, caves or underground. Men, women, young people and children are beaten, whipped, electrocuted or burnt, suspended, have nails or limbs removed or are forced to watch or partake in the torture of others. People are held in overcrowded, hot and stinking cells, where there may be sexual violence between prisoners or repeated rape by guards. Some are held in solitary confinement for many years or are kept naked and unable to wash and must urinate and defecate in the cell. Survivors describe mock executions and being given contaminated food and/or water or being forced to drink their own/others' urine. People are threatened with death or the violent killing of family members. They are mocked and humiliated and deprived of their dignity. They are forced into painful positions and kept awake by noises, or water being repeatedly thrown into the cell.

After escape or release, many face traumatic journeys to the UK having made the heart-breaking decision to leave family members behind. Others manage to come to the UK with their immediate family, but leave behind relatives, friends, colleagues and their community. Many have left stable and relatively secure lives, others are fleeing war and conflict, and countries where access to education, healthcare and food/water are limited for many. The losses are almost impossible to comprehend for those of us who are not from a refugee background.

The asylum system is often experienced as re-traumatising and dehumanising, and the process itself can last many years. Seeking asylum in the UK is fraught with crises and delays. The system is poorly administrated and punitive, and poor decision making (Amnesty International 2004) generates high levels of stress and anxiety. Survivors describe living in constant fear of immigration detention and/or removal to their own or a transit country. This stress is exacerbated by the requirement to report 'like a criminal' to the immigration or police authorities on a regular basis.

The current climate of xenophobia is deeply felt by the refugees we work with, and the micro assaults that are part of the experience of living in a hostile and racist context impact on survivors' mental health. Malloch and Stanley (2005, p.53) describe how 'Media and political representations of asylum seekers and refugees have been infused with language denoting images of "danger", "criminality" and "risk". Alongside this, it is important to remember that survivors also describe welcoming communities, supportive organisations and local families/faith groups that are helpful and compassionate.

The combination of pre-flight and flight experiences, as well as the stressors and threats within the UK and its asylum system, can create complex layers of difficulties for a survivor and their family.

Survivors describe living with nightmares, flashbacks, sleeplessness, intrusive thoughts, anxiety and panic. Social workers may observe that survivors are easily startled, hypervigilant, irritable and avoid talking about past events. In the West, someone describing these responses is likely to be given a diagnosis of post-traumatic stress disorder (PTSD). As human rights practitioners, we may be anxious that we are pathologising a survivor's responses to torture by adopting a diagnostic framework that invalidates the refugee experience: PTSD 'does not recognise the shattered individual, familial and communal lives of torture victims – a shattering that goes far beyond the specific clinical syndrome of a single individual' (Laub 2001, p.xix). Summerfield (1996, p.4) argues that using a diagnostic approach 'risks creating inappropriate sick roles and side-lines a proper incorporation of people's own choices, traditions and skills into strategies for their creative survival.'

However we choose to describe a survivor's responses to torture, social workers are required to understand trauma in order to undertake culturally congruent psycho-education and ensure that traumatised survivors access psychological help: 'Early psychosocial support is a decisive factor in the development and severity of PTSD symptoms' (Drozdek and Wilson 2004, p.245).

What follows is an outline of the holistic model of therapeutic social work that Anna developed in conjunction with refugee clients, and an example of her work with a family affected by torture. Katy then reflects on her work with separated young people, and grapples with the tricky concept of empowerment-based practice in a setting where the social worker's time is limited and survivors are overwhelmed, disempowered and speak little English. The case studies are fictionalised and anonymised examples of Anna and Katy's work.

Creating a framework

In our experience, survivors are often referred to social workers at times of crises, particularly when they become destitute after their claim for protection has failed and their access to financial support and accommodation in the UK is withdrawn by the Home Office.

The holistic social work approach combines the use of theoretical knowledge of trauma recovery, assessment skills, psycho-educational work and solution-focused practice. Within this model, there is an emphasis on the quality of the therapeutic relationship, which serves to instil hope and trust. The primary focus of this framework aims to honour the identity of a survivor and their family. We achieve this through a process that we have termed 'journey mapping', where the social worker explores the client's life before, during and after the traumatic events. This process can facilitate the survivor to identify their personal strengths as well as recognise their resilience. Fluidity between each of the stages is important and it is not a tool to apply in a rigid assessment format.

The enquiry into life before the traumatic events includes an exploration of childhood experiences and development, as well as conversations about a survivor's cultural beliefs and systems, family life, social networks, faith, work status and educational achievements. The process aims to engage survivors in their own self-assessment by exploring their well-being and levels of functioning before torture, and asks them to measure where they are now. The outcome of the self-assessment should inform the setting of personal goals. Consider asking about what led to the torture, and the subsequent migration process. The latter may include other traumatic experiences such as being trafficked or witnessing the death of friends on the journey.

Social workers need to be sensitive to the fact that discussing traumatic experiences may be emotionally overwhelming or shaming for many survivors and, in some cases, survivors may not remember details of their experiences. Herman (1992, p.160) describes how 'survivors feel unsafe in their bodies. Their emotions and their thinking feel out of control. They also feel unsafe in relation to other people.' At such times, offering safety and containment within the relationship, rather than pursuing a history of imprisonment and torture, may be more beneficial in stabilising a survivor's mental health.

When engaging children in conversation, be creative by using objects or games. Consider exploring their likes, dislikes, fears and wishes. Genograms, which are a pictorial display of a person's family relationships, can be a useful tool in the framework.

Crisis intervention is a central component in this area of work, particularly when assessing risk to self and others, or risk of homelessness and immigration detention and/or removal. Risk of self-harm is usually heightened in response to a crisis in the asylum claim, and the threat of removal of financial and housing support can lead to a rapid deterioration in a survivor's mental health. Social workers are required to assess the nature of the suicide risk and apply appropriate interventions, such as ensuring a place of safety for those at immediate risk of serious self-harm.

Strengths and protective factors are explored, and preventative measures put into place through a crisis management plan. Usually this is a coordinated approach involving multi-agency professionals and the survivor. If approached effectively, survivors may experience a sense of containment and support, and acknowledge that services are working in their best interests. Demonstrating that we have verifiably understood their situation and looking at potential solutions may help to restore faith in others and encourage survivors to care for themselves and seek support in times of stress. This may involve:

- use of visual mapping tools to look at the needs of survivors and their families to ensure a holistic approach beyond the crisis that brought them into your care

- exploration of any barriers to accessing support and the formulation of plans to overcome them together; these plans should be reviewed and evaluated regularly and new goals set as the suvivor's situation stabilises

- defining and agreeing tasks for completion in a participative way, being sure to incorporate individual language or communication preferences in the action plan; this could include people writing in their own language or using diagrams or colour-coded tools.

A communication style that encourages openness through the application of active listening and enquiry can be helpful. The Exchange Model

(Smale, Tuson and Statham 2000) is useful for building a therapeutic alliance and defining actions. It is based on the sharing of information between the service user and social worker. It recognises and draws on the expertise of the individual, in conjunction with the expertise of professionals and wider networks.

The concepts of 'connection' and 'reconnection' are central to theoretical frameworks of working with refugees and trauma recovery. Judith Herman (1992) similarly establishes safety as the essential first stage of recovery, alongside the stages of 'remembrance and mourning', and 'reconnection'. Kohli (2007) in his social work practice with separated young people identifies the stages of recovery as: cohesion (bringing order to the outside world), connection (resettlement of inner worlds) and coherence (resettlement as feeling reconstructed). Both models are relevant to social work practice as they focus on the interplay between the internal and external context. Supporting a survivor to access good-quality legal advice, advocating and enabling access to appropriate housing and linking in to educational, medical and community-based activities are highly beneficial to the recovery process.

Social workers are advised to access training on working with interpreters and should ensure that qualified interpreters where possible are used in meetings with survivors to avoid what Van Parijs (2004) refers to as linguistic injustice – the denial of a non-English-speaking individual's right to understand and influence.

Social workers have a pivotal role in the provision of emotional support and offering psycho-education. Undertake a positive-traits exercise that identifies a survivor's strengths and resilience. Encourage survivors to look at how their strengths can be applied to the present; for many destitute survivors, this may be a focus on basic survival skills.

Social workers also need to be aware of the intersectional layers of power and oppression that torture survivors in exile face. From the political arena to public and private life, survivors frequently face multiple oppressions in relation to their ethnicity, language, gender, disability, immigration status, culture, sexual orientation, class and caste, employment status and health. Social workers need to reflect on their structural position of power in the racialised context of exile, and examine how their own assumptions and prejudices inform their decision making and interventions:

> a reflective practitioner is one who uses careful mental reflection to
> consider their practice. A reflexive practitioner, on the other hand,
> is one who considers from moment to moment how his/her own

interests, position, standpoint, reactions and assumptions influence what is happening at any given point in his/her practice, and uses this to improve practice in the moment and afterwards. (Bashir 2017, p.206)

Regular supervision and peer/managerial support in a trauma-informed work setting are vital for social workers supporting refugees to avoid vicarious trauma: 'the expectation that we can be immersed in suffering and loss daily and not be touched by it is as unrealistic as expecting to walk through water without getting wet' (Remen 1996, p.52).

Social workers are often constrained by a lack of resources, high caseloads and punitive legislative frameworks that they are expected to apply to those seeking asylum. This can create conflict for them within statutory settings, and restrict the approaches used as well as create ethical dilemmas. In our experience, it is not uncommon for social workers to become entwined in a bureaucratic system of resource management and, in the process, discount the needs and rights of a survivor at risk of homelessness/immigration detention and/or removal.

Central to all social work practice is a process of continuous assessment, which requires an open mind and a commitment to not knowing. Curiosity can assist and empower the practitioner to understand and honour the identity of those who we work with. Ortega (2011) reflects that in practising a rights-based approach, practitioners need to be grounded in cultural humility, rather than cultural knowing.

Social workers can advocate at an individual level and from a broader organisational and political level. Often people seeking asylum have little or no knowledge of their national and international rights; practitioners can inform and empower clients, so they can exercise and advocate for their rights. We must also recognise that survivors are experts in their own experience and bring an essential voice to awareness raising and local and national campaigning.

Examples from practice
Francois and Alvine - Democratic Republic of the Congo

Francois and Alvine are from a rural region of the Democratic Republic of the Congo (DRC). They live with their two children, Frank (12) and Jonathan (14). Francois was active in opposition politics and the children witnessed him being beaten and arrested. Alvine was badly beaten during his arrest. Francois was imprisoned for four months and tortured.

Alvine was the main carer in the home. She had raised concerns about Francois's psychological well-being and said his memory and concentration were poor. He was often irritable and withdrawn and he screamed in the night. Jonathan was anxious and depressed. Both Francois and Jonathan had frequent thoughts about suicide. Frank often accompanied his parents to medical and legal appointments and spoke on behalf of the family, who had limited English. Their asylum claim had been refused and their appeal rights were exhausted. They were frightened of removal and there were high levels of anxiety and high expressed emotion within the home.

Anna conducted her initial assessment over several visits, meeting with the parents, then the children and with the family together. Anna asked to see a copy of their immigration documentation, which provided a wealth of information about their circumstances prior to fleeing to the UK. With the family's consent, she contacted their legal representative to establish the status of their asylum claim and was informed that their case had been closed. She referred the family to a legal aid solicitor to consider preparing a fresh claim for asylum. The solicitor provided the family with information on the legal processes of removal for families and reassured them that this was not imminent.

Using a systemic approach,[1] Anna considered the functioning of the family as a whole and individually, and how this presented externally, as well as external stressors such as their fear of removal. Anna asked about support networks and whether any other services were involved. Jonathan was being supported by a child and adolescent mental health service (CAMHS) and Francois was in regular contact with his GP.

Along with paying attention to the safeguarding concerns about the children, Anna assessed how they were achieving against the Every Child Matters outcomes. Every Child Matters (Department for Education and Skills 2003) sets out the five key outcomes for a child: being healthy; staying safe; enjoying and achieving; making a positive contribution; and achieving economic well-being. She used stones as a therapeutic aid to work with the children: one stone represented a bad memory, the other a current concern, the third a positive thought and wish. From this, they spoke about what they had witnessed in the DRC and explored the changes to the roles within the family home. The children were very worried about their father and expressed anxiety about the family being removed to the DRC. Both children presented with a heightened state of anxiety and were hypervigilant.

---

1   www.cfssw.org

They were distrustful of others and frightened they would be taken away and harmed. The children enjoyed school because it was a place to escape and they both wished to study and work in the future. Both said they would like to have more activity outside school.

Following the assessment, Anna formulated a plan with the family to respond to the immediate needs, sought consent to liaise with CAMHS and suggested the GP refer Francois to a community mental health team. She also contacted the school's safeguarding and well-being team. With the family's involvement, Anna initiated a multi-agency meeting, under the Common Assessment Framework (CAF) guidelines. A CAF is a recognised national standard framework, promoting a collaborative approach of assessing children and young people's additional needs and working together to implement interventions. Some local authorities have since developed this tool and use alternative names for the assessment, such as Team Around the Child (TAC), Team Around the Family (TAF) or Early Help.

Collaboratively, a list of actions and desired outcomes were listed, and a referral was made to Children and Families Social Services, under Section 17 of the Children Act 1989. A request was made for short-term intervention, due to the impact on the children of the family's situation. Anna gathered information for their asylum case, including medical letters, social work reports, risk assessments and recommendations for services and the family. These reports were provided to the solicitor, who subsequently requested further detailed reports from the treating psychiatrists for Jonathan and later for Francois.

Through these actions, Anna was building a therapeutic alliance with the family. Anna worked with Francois and Alvine to harness their strengths to cope with their current circumstances. She completed pre-/post-migration mapping sheets (see Figure 9.1) and explored their experiences. Francois was convinced he was no longer a good father and Alvine was exasperated, tired of trying to hold the family together on her own. Anna agreed to hold six sessions with the couple to identify their strengths and skills and examine how they could apply these at home and in supporting the children.

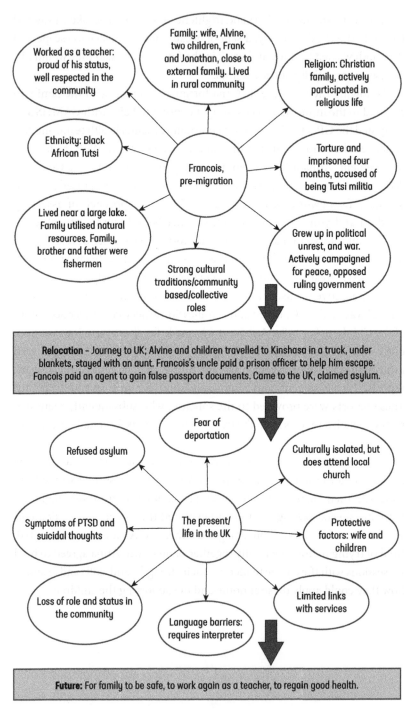

Figure 9.1: *Francois's pre-/post-migration mapping sheet*

Anna completed a genogram with both parents to gain an understanding of their family life before and after they fled the DRC. She asked them to think about the personal strengths used to leave their country and travel to the UK. Anna asked how they made decisions in the past and what their roles were. She asked how they liked to spend time with the children and what they enjoyed doing as a family. Anna explored how they might manage the change in roles that had occurred since they fled to the UK, and the meaning of these changes for them.

Both Francois and Alvine expressed concerns about the children absorbing their fear of removal, and Anna asked them to consider ways of reducing the anxiety in the home. She asked them to think about how they spent their time and what tasks they thought they did well. Francois reported that when he was having flashbacks, he was not aware of his surroundings. Anna talked about trauma with him and encouraged him to explore his grief at what he had lost. She worked with him to identify the triggers that led to his flashbacks and encouraged him to plan strategies around this. Francois identified that going out for walks, attending the local church to pray and listening to music were helpful distractions at times of stress. Alvine felt isolated and said she missed the man her husband used to be. She described feeling exhausted and said she did not have any time to relax on her own. Anna explored her interests and referred her to English classes and volunteering opportunities.

Anna encouraged Francois and Alvine to think of activities they could do with the children, and reassured Francois that he could have a positive relationship with his children despite his PTSD. She asked him to consider what he could do on a good day and the couple suggested activities they could undertake as a family and report back. The children were referred to a young carers' project and to activities outside the home, and both reported feeling more settled.

Once their solicitor agreed to prepare a fresh claim for asylum, the family felt safer and more protected, which impacted on the level of anxiety in the family home. The family are still waiting on the outcome of their fresh claim for asylum and have been in the UK for six years.

Hassan - Afghanistan

In Katy's case studies, we use the term 'separated young person'. The Immigration Law Practitioners' Association (Crawley 2012, p.10) defines separated young people as: 'children who are outside their country of origin and separated from their parents or legal or customary primary carer…in each case, separated children are, by definition, children who have been deprived of their family environment.'

In statutory children's services in the UK, the term 'unaccompanied asylum-seeking children' or 'UASC' is often used. It refers to children under 18 who have applied for asylum in the UK and for whom the local authority has a duty of care. We use the term 'young people' to refer to anyone between the ages of 14 and the early to mid-20s given that development continues up to the age of 25 (Montgomery 2013).

Within statutory provision, there is invariably limited time with service users. Social workers carry heavy caseloads and have large volumes of paperwork to complete for each service user. In Katy's work, the support can be limited to six-weekly statutory visits, in which care and pathway plans are set out. Much of the relationship building occurs in the time spent driving to appointments, doing an activity together or completing a casework task that enhances well-being or meets a basic need. It is the task of the social worker to make each interaction matter with a service user in order to, in some way, counter the organisational and socio-political contexts of our workplaces.

Hassan was a separated young person and a survivor of torture, human trafficking and modern slavery. Hassan was diagnosed with PTSD and experienced vivid auditory and visual hallucinations, flashbacks and dissociative episodes. He was frequently suicidal. Hassan was age assessed by social services as over 18. The age assessment is arguably a highly inaccurate process (Community Care 2015) fraught with discrimination, for example on cultural and racial grounds (Crawley 2006). This had a significant impact on the support that was available to Hassan. Without an allocated local authority social worker, a pathway plan and support workers to develop his skills and prepare him for adulthood, he was left at risk of homelessness, poverty and social exclusion.

Developing a trusting relationship with Hassan was made more complex given his experiences of interrogation from the Taliban, and his treatment at the hands of traffickers who had manipulated and lied to him during his journey, and in the UK, where they forced him to work on arrival. An assessment process that involved asking him lots of questions would have been inappropriate and may have caused him to withdraw or feel threatened, and it had the potential to destabilise his fragile mental health.

In their first session, Katy and Hassan developed an understanding of Katy's role and their joint responsibilities. Some young people will not have heard of a social worker before and have little understanding of the role. Using pictures or photographs to explain this can be helpful, including other support staff such as housing providers, or family support practitioners, explaining when and how they could contact each person in a given situation, and how often they might expect to see them. Katy's role was to support Hassan to find housing and benefits as part of his transition from a person seeking asylum, to a person with refugee status. The agreement was to have an ongoing dialogue about the tasks, considering other issues as they arose.

In one of their early meetings together, Katy and Hassan travelled to his local crisis housing team. They got lost trying to find the building, and when she admitted this they laughed together and eventually Hassan was the one to direct them to the housing office. Katy felt that this had broken down the perception he may have had of her as an 'expert' or someone who 'knew better' than him.

Part of the development of the social work profession has been the acknowledgment of social work as an expertise that is legitimate and professional (Birkenmaier, Berg-Weger and Dewees 2014; Healy and Meagher 2004), while also looking at the service user as an expert and the importance of this for empowerment (Wilson *et al.* 2011). A collaborative stance might be realised through the idea of sharing power (Birkenmaier *et al.* 2014; Smith 2008), while also challenging normalised exploitative behaviour (Smith 2008).

Hassan seemed to grow in confidence and was more forthcoming with conversation following the journey to the housing office. In the waiting area, however, a fight broke out and the experience shook him. Katy was aware that such an event was likely to cause distress or trigger a flashback, as she knew of Hassan's history. Here, she used her 'expert' power. Katy and Hassan had spoken about using grounding techniques, which she employed by doing some drawing with Hassan in the waiting room.

Katy reflected, at that time, that preparation and consultation with other professionals was an important aspect of beginning to develop a relationship with Hassan, but that it was important not to make assumptions about him from this information. Hassan drew his family home and a picture of his mother. Through this vehicle, he told Katy some of his experiences of conflict, loss and torture. In later sessions, Hassan would ask if he could draw, and this became one of the ways in which he felt comfortable to speak and allow Katy to get to know him in a way that was not based on a 'question and answer' assessment process.

Filling in forms for welfare benefits, or applying for social housing, often involves questions aimed at highlighting problems or defining vulnerability, and as such, suitability for a service. This culture of assessment means that, in some instances, using 'language that is pathologising and alienating' (Maclean and Harrison 2008, p.124) can aid people in getting a service when there are resource deficits and high demands. When first advocating for Hassan to get into temporary accommodation, Katy explained that emphasising what he found difficult may help him to be prioritised – showing them himself 'on a bad day'. The mismatch between the strengths perspective, and the climate it functions in, can make it at times a difficult approach to maintain while seeking to put in place the necessary services for service users. It can be easy for social workers to uncritically take on this narrative, victimising those we work with in order to understand them ourselves as 'legitimate' or entitled to services. One of the impacts of this victimising construction of the refugee is that it 'sticks' (Ahmed 2004, cited in Tyler 2006). Furthermore, there are consequences when someone who has been described as such does not demonstrate appropriate passivity. Arguably there is a 'turn from sympathy into antipathy when victims defy the expected victim role' (van Dijk 2009, p.3).

Constructing someone solely as having agency, or as a victim, misses the complexity of a person's subjectivity. A positive of using the strengths perspective with survivors is that it challenges this idea of a person as only 'victim': it 'denies that all people who face trauma and pain in their lives inevitably are wounded or incapacitated' (Saleebey 1996, p.297) and draws on a person's resources. Seeing people as 'survivors' rather than 'victims' of torture reflects this idea of a more complex understanding of people; it neither denies their vulnerabilities, nor defines the person by them. It is important for the social work profession to recognise the power of the language we use, and how it can shape the way we work with people, as well as how service users see themselves. Practitioners should be encouraged to reflect on their practice in a way that challenges these 'common-sense' notions of victimhood that function as a perceived prerequisite to services.

In addressing risk with Hassan, Katy took a strengths perspective. In his high-rise temporary accommodation, where he lived on the eighth floor, he told Katy that a voice had told him to 'fly out of the window'. She asked Hassan what he thought his therapist would say if he told her that, and he responded that she would say not to do it, that he would die if he did. Together they recognised the internalised voice of his therapist as a resource he could use when he was hearing negative voices. Hassan was able to come to a decision himself about his reaction to the voice, and was therefore left with a sense of his own abilities in managing the voices. The housing team decided that Hassan should be moved to a ground floor flat to minimise the risk of him jumping from the window. They did not consult him on his needs, but reacted to what Hassan said without knowing his situation, his strengths or his vulnerabilities.

In reflecting on risk and resilience with Hassan from a strengths perspective, Katy observed that he had demonstrated resilience factors: an ability to check in with others regarding his voices, and to seek help from his therapist when he felt he needed it. Hassan had also developed a good friendship with another young person. Hassan was able to remain in his accommodation after sharing the risk assessment with the housing team. In addition to seeing how important a strengths perspective can be in combating risk-adverse practice and ideas of the 'victim' in work with torture survivors, we can also see the benefit of multi-agency working, and how sharing information between professionals can create a joined-up approach, where we enhance and build on each other's work to the benefit of the survivor.

Amrine – Cameroon

Amrine was a separated young person from Cameroon, who was a survivor of torture. She experienced hallucinations and would often dissociate, as well as having low confidence and feelings of fear in working with officials.

Acknowledging when service users may be in a position of powerlessness, and questioning when we can 'empower' people to undertake self-advocacy are important aspects to reflect on in our work with torture survivors. Although self-advocacy is clearly important in building confidence and autonomy, in some circumstances this can be unhelpful. An example from Katy's practice is where she was supporting Amrine to apply for housing. Amrine had auditory and visual hallucinations, as well as an aversion to questioning following her experience of interrogation. Katy realised that answering some of the questions on Amrine's behalf was in her best interests at that time and they negotiated this together. Amrine was intimidated by the environment, as well as struggling to stay present, and this sharing of the questions at interview was reassuring. Empowerment is at the heart of social work practice, but the ability of a person to change their circumstances is moulded by social power and assumes that all service users 'already possess the personal, economic and social resources by which to take power for themselves' (Tew 2006, p.36).

One of the stepping stones towards autonomy is the capacity to recognise oneself as a bearer of rights, and to have the ability to make demands on others, especially those in positions of power. This can be particularly difficult for survivors of torture because the experience of torture itself can erode and undermine the identity of the survivor, and their capacity to trust people, particularly those in positions of power. The Social Care Institute for Excellence (2015) notes that the disempowering nature of these systems for refugees results in a denial of a person's human rights. While supporting Amrine to claim welfare benefits, Katy reflected that given the urgency of her situation, and the barriers she was facing at the agency due to language, her poor mental health and aversion to questioning, expecting Amrine to apply for welfare benefits without support was inappropriate. More important, perhaps, was empowering her to see that she was entitled to benefits and had a right to be treated as any other citizen in her contact with the agency.

Actively challenging other agencies that have little understanding of the refugee context is also essential to the social work role. When working with Amrine, the housing officer asked if she could explain what torture she had experienced in Cameroon. The question was intrusive and irrelevant. Amrine asked Katy to answer the question for her, as recounting her experiences in this setting with a man had the potential to be overwhelming. Katy challenged the advisor, explaining why the question was unnecessary. Amrine witnessed this and they could reflect together after the meeting on her right to privacy in relation to her own information, as well as her right to ask for a female housing officer.

Conclusion

This chapter has explored the potential experiences, discrimination and challenges that torture survivors face in their countries of origin and in navigating the asylum, welfare and support systems in the UK. It has sought to outline and reflect on what an effective practice might look like for social workers engaging with this group. Crucially, this involves pushing for an approach that addresses the complex issues and challenges surrounding the identity of refugees. This approach should seek to help rebuild and strengthen the identities that have been broken down through torture and challenge the negative constructions that impact on the treatment and experience of refugees.

Social workers should remain critically reflective of the negative discourses around people seeking asylum and narratives that label service users as victims or as 'underserving' of essential services. Social workers may otherwise be involved in restricting, for example, a person's eligibility for services based on their immigration status, or victimising a person in order to claim them as 'legitimate'. We must learn to read between the lines of others' and our own discourses in respect of the more subtle manifestations of discrimination and racism aimed at torture survivors, and at people seeking asylum in general.

We may not be able to simply 'remove' racism or discrimination against this group from language, but we can engage in bringing forward 'subjugated knowledges' (Foucault 1980, p.81) and challenge our assumptions and practices with this group (Turney 1996). So, for social workers, there perhaps needs to be an acknowledgement and an embracing of this contradiction: continued advocacy and solidarity with refugees within the current context and legislative framework they must work within, but equally questioning the very assumptions or prejudices these policies and practices are based on.

It may be pertinent for social workers to form alliances with refugee groups and activists who look to question and resist current punitive policies. This is already happening at the border in Calais, and in refugee camps in Greece (King and Grant 2016). Social work skills are being used on the ground and at the level of policy, standing in solidarity with, and advocating for and alongside, people who are affected by borders. Social workers are speaking out about the appalling conditions in camps and the dehumanising nature of border controls. Using our assessment and relationship-building skills, as well as our ability to be reflexive, we can evidence and inform a practice that is more human-rights led and that gives space to the voice of the survivor.

References

Amnesty International (2004) *Get It Right: How Home Office Decision Making Fails Refugees*. London: Amnesty International.

Bashir, C. (2017) 'The Application of Cognitive Behavioural Therapies with Survivors of Torture.' In J. Boyles (ed.) *Psychological Therapies for Survivors of Torture: A Human Rights Approach with People Seeking Asylum*, pp.187–222. Monmouth: PCCS Books.

Birkenmaier, J., Berg-Weger, M. and Dewees, M. (2014) *The Practice of Generalist Social Work*. New York, NY: Routledge.

Community Care (2015) 'Tools used for age assessments very inaccurate, study finds.' 7 March. Accessed 03/09/2017 at: www.communitycare.co.uk/2015/07/03/tools-used-age-assessments-inaccurate-study-finds/?cmpid=NLC|SCSC|SCNEW-2015-0708.

Crawley, H. (2006) *Child First, Migrant Second: Ensuring that* Every *Child Matters.* Accessed 03/09/2017 at: www.childmigration.net/files/child_first_migrant_second.pdf.

Crawley, H. (2012) *Working with Children and Young People Subject to Immigration Control: Guidelines for Best Practice.* London: Immigration Law Practitioners' Association.

Department for Education and Skills (2003) *Every Child Matters: Presented to Parliament by the Chief Secretary to the Treasury by Command of Her Majesty, September 2003.* London: The Stationery Office.

Drozdek, B. and Wilson, J.P. (2004) 'Uncovering: Trauma-Focused Treatment Techniques with Asylum Seekers.' In J.P. Wilson and B. Drozdek (eds) *Broken Spirits: The Treatment of Traumatized Asylum Seekers, Refugees, War and Torture Victims,* pp.243–276. Hove and New York, NY: Brunner-Routledge.

Elsass, P. (1997) *Treating Victims of Torture and Violence: Theoretical, Cross-Cultural and Clinical Implications.* New York, NY and London: New York University Press.

Foucault, M. (1980) *Power/Knowledge: Selected Interviews and Other Writings, 1972– 1977.* New York, NY: Pantheon Books.

Girma, M., Radice, S., Tsangarides, N. and Walter, N. (2014) *Detained: Women Asylum Seekers Locked Up in the UK.* Accessed 10/07/2017 at: https://www.refugeewomen.co.uk/wp-content/uploads/2019/01/women-for-refugee-women-reports-detained.pdf.

Healy, K. and Meagher, G. (2004) 'The reprofessionalization of social work: Collaborative approaches for achieving professional recognition.' *British Journal of Social Work,* 34, 2, 243–260.

Herman, J.L. (1992) *Trauma and Recovery: The Aftermath of Violence – From Domestic Abuse to Political Terror.* New York, NY: Basic Books.

King, L. and Grant, K. (2016) 'Meet the social workers supporting refugees in Calais.' Accessed 03/09/2017 at: www.communitycare.co.uk/2016/08/24/meet-social-workers-supporting-refugees-calais.

Kohli, R. (2007) *Social Work with Unaccompanied Asylum-Seeking Children.* Basingstoke: Palgrave Macmillan.

Laub, D. (2001) 'Survivors' Silence and the Difficulty of Knowing.' In M.D. Graessner, N. Guris and C. Pross (eds) *At the Side of Torture Survivors: Treating a Terrible Assault on Human Dignity,* pp.xxvi–xxii. Baltimore, MD: John Hopkins University Press.

Maclean, S. and Harrison, R. (2008) *Social Work Theory: A Straightforward Guide for Practice Assessors and Placement Supervisors.* Lichfield: Kirwin Maclean Associates Ltd.

Malloch, M.S. and Stanley, E. (2005) 'The detention of asylum seekers in the UK: Representing risk, managing the dangerous.' *Punishment and Society,* 7, 1, 53–71.

Masocha, S. and Simpson, M.K. (2011) 'Xenoracism: Towards a critical understanding of the construction of asylum seekers and its implication for social work practice.' *Practice: Social Work in Action,* 23, 1, 5–18.

Mendez, J.E. (2013) 'Foreword.' In J. Pettitt (ed.) *The Poverty Barrier: The Right to Rehabilitation for Survivors of Torture in the UK,* pp.2–95. London: Freedom from Torture.

Montgomery, A. (2013) *Neurobiology Essentials for Clinicians: What Every Clinician Needs to Know.* New York, NY and London: Norton.

Ortega, R.M. (2011) 'Training child welfare workers from an intersectional cultural humility perspective: A paradigm shift.' *Child Welfare*, 90, 5, 27–39.

Refugee Council (2012) *The Experience of Refugee Women in the UK*. Accessed 30/04/2019 at: https://www.bl.uk/collection-items/experiences-of-refugee-women-in-the-uk.

Remen, R.N. (1996) *Kitchen Table Wisdom: Stories That Heal*. New York, NY: Penguin Group.

Saleebey, D. (1996) 'The strengths perspective in social work practice: Extensions and cautions.' *Social Work*, 41, 3, 296–305.

Smale, G., Tuson, G. and Statham, D. (2000) *Social Work and Social Problems: Working Towards Social Inclusion and Social Change*. London: Palgrave.

Smith, R. (2008) *Social Work and Power: Reshaping Social Work*. London: Macmillan.

Social Care Institute for Excellence (2015) 'Good practice in social care for refugees and asylum seekers.' Accessed 27/11/2018 at: www.scie.org.uk/publications/guides/guide37-good-practice-in-social-care-with-refugees-and-asylum-seekers.

Summerfield, D. (1996) *The Impact of War and Atrocity on Civilian Populations: Basic Principles for NGO Interventions and a Critique of Psychosocial Trauma Projects*. London: Overseas Development Institute. Accessed 01/07/2017 at: www.files.ethz.ch/isn/97846/networkpaper014.pdf.

Tew, J. (2006) 'Understanding power and powerlessness: Towards a framework for emancipatory practice in social work.' *Journal of Social Work*, 6, 1, 33–51.

Turney, D. (1996) *The Language of Anti-Racism in Social Work: Towards a Deconstructive Reading*. Accessed 03/09/2017 at: www.gold.ac.uk/media/documents-by-section/departments/research-centres-and-units/research-centres/centre-for-urban-and-comm/turney.pdf.

Tyler, I. (2006) '"Welcome to Britain": The cultural politics of asylum.' *European Journal of Cultural Studies*, 9, 2, 185–202.

United Nations (1984) *Convention against Torture and Other Cruel, Inhuman or Degrading Treatment or Punishment*. Accessed 28/11/2018 at: www.unhcr.org/uk/protection/migration/49e479d10/convention-against-torture-other-cruel-inhuman-degrading-treatment-punishment.html.

van Dijk, T.A. (2009) 'Free the victim: A critique of the western conception of victimhood.' *International Review of Victimology*, 16, 1, 1–33.

Van Parijis, P. (2004) 'Europe's linguistic challenge.' *European Journal of Sociology*, 45, 1, 113–154.

Wilson, K., Ruch, G., Lymbery, M. and Cooper, A. (2011) *Social Work: An Introduction to Contemporary Practice* (second edition). Harlow: Pearson Education Limited.

Narrative 5
Learning from Stella

I've been in Home Office accommodation since 2012. Five years, and it's very hard. I feel like I can't trust the housing officers, and I don't feel safe in the house as there's no respect for my dignity at all. The housing officers will open your room - looking for what? I think it's just another way of trying to break people down.

I always feel good when I'm out, but the moment I get to the front door I feeling like crying and so emotional. I don't sleep and I'm constantly thinking that maybe they put a camera in my room so I can't even relax in my room. At one point, one of the housing officers went into my room and took photos and when I found out, it broke me. I was thinking to end my life, because I don't know what they had seen in my room to use against me. I couldn't think straight for the whole week and even now I have nightmares about it. Each time you get a refusal they send you a letter straight away, to inform you that you need to leave the house. It's just too much. I think they should consider people's well-being, especially when they know someone is vulnerable. Often, they will put the letter on your bed so you're always having nightmares. The moment I open the door I'm looking for a letter and I feel like I want to throw up. What kind of life is that?

I know there are so many people in my situation but I think there are ways they could make it less difficult, even just little things, like if the housing officers stopped coming into people's rooms on a weekly basis. I just feel that they don't really care about people. In each house, there are people with mental health problems, and our safety is never considered. I strongly feel I can't trust them because they're from the Home Office; I'm scared of them. You know, there was one time when we had no heating in the house. I was having to carry boiling water to my room from downstairs, which wasn't safe. There is also no privacy within the house; other women I live with are very nosy and ask too many questions, and sometimes other people in the house will open my letters. But, when I complained to the housing officers, no one ever responded to me.

There are also problems in the house between the people sharing. They should allocate people's housing according to their health issues and other needs. I find it so difficult because you have your own health problems and we're sharing a bathroom. I have to clean the bathroom before and after using the shower, so you're doing too much for yourself as well, just to make sure you're safe. One bathroom for five women is not practical at all and, often, people don't get along if they're from different cultures and everyone has stress, depression and their own ways of coping. Some people put it on others. They can't direct it at the housing officers or the Home Office, so they get angry with the other women they live with.

I am so stressed out when I'm in the house. I'm better off outside; that's why I go out as early as 8 o'clock every day, even if I have no place or organisation to go to. It's better to be out of the accommodation because people are always fighting and usually just over little things, small and silly; they fight for the hoover, who is making noise, all those kind of things. Someone takes a shower and they don't clean the bathroom. Sometimes I think, am I dealing with young kids not women. Even if you ask someone quietly in a nice way to clean the bathroom, before you know it people are fighting. It's got so bad that I decided to just bathe in my room with a bucket, because I can't stand the dirty tub and sink, and I have my own health problems. For this same reason, I also decided to cook my food in my room with a microwave. That way I keep to myself and keep out of trouble. While I've been in Home Office accommodation, there have been two instances when a woman has been stabbed in the house by another woman. It always starts with an argument about cleaning in the bathroom and ends with violence.

I think that people with similar health issues should be housed together, like they do in other places. I know there's not enough houses to give each person their own flat but this will work if they've put people with similar health problems together. It will definitely help and improve people's mental health and physical health. Everyone is different and copes differently. Sometime, when I wake up I often feel so emotional. People who are close to me can see when I need support, and know straight away that they need to look after me today – they will follow up on me, to see how I am. This is why it's good to put people with the same health problems together, that way there will be another woman aware of your circumstances and difficulties. In the house, there used to be two other women with similar health problems to me, and they used to make sure they kept checking on me. There have been times in the past where they have been so worried about my safety and mental health that they have called the police or an ambulance.

I suffer from depression and anxiety, which is very bad, so any little thing can trigger me and I can feel so emotional and like I might even harm someone, and I don't want to; it will be better to harm myself than someone else. So, to keep myself safe, I took the advice of my social worker, to continue to get out of the house as often as I can. Sometimes she gives me a Costa card, worth maybe £15 so I go to Costa and get coffee, or sometimes she calls me to meet for a coffee and she says that what I'm doing is right for me. I find it useful because if you stay 24 hours in one place you can't think straight and you'll get yourself in trouble by fighting.

I do appreciate the Home Office giving us accommodation but feel they need to do more to support us. What's been useful for me is my social worker being very supportive. She's been working with me since 2012, and I receive a lot of support from my GP too. I think it's useful when a social worker is on your side and can advocate for you. Social workers can put complaints to the Home Office, call or write to them. Unfortunately, when you're an asylum seeker you are not considered important.

Chapter 10

Lessons from Community Work

Practices of Alliance with Asylum-Seeking Women

Hannah Berry

Social work in the UK is almost always centred on the individual, especially work with adults. It can also be over-focused on problems – on 'problem saturated' identities (White and Epston 1990, p.16). Yet we know that recovery and empowerment are social processes, processes ideally orientated towards hope. This chapter presents an example of facilitated group work that creates space for people to formulate their own identities beyond merely coping with the problems, needs and risks associated with being a refuge seeker. There are lessons to be learned from this kind of group work, where the workers accompany people in a process of collective reflection and facilitate action according to their own objectives. British social work may have become 'weighted…towards the notion of therapy' (Lynn 1999, p.945), but at different times and in different places the profession has understood the dual benefits of individual support and the restorative power of collective action against the structural oppressions which are, almost always, the ultimate cause of the problem.

In 2009, I had the good fortune to be awarded a practice-based doctoral studentship through the Third Sector Research Centre (TSRC).[1] I carried out the research within my own organisation, a community interest company called GAP Unit, taking Arise and Shine, our project with women who were refugees or seeking asylum, as my case study. The voices of women contained in this chapter derive from my PhD research.

GAP Unit is based in Manchester and specialises in participatory methods for empowering marginalised groups to 'have a voice' within local democratic processes. Central to our work with groups are the principles of popular education, which draw on the philosophy of the Brazilian theologian and educator Paulo Freire (1921–1997). My colleague and co-director, Carolina de Otezya, came of age in Venezuela's 'popular education' movement, which was inspired by Freire. Before coming to the UK, she trained as a social worker and spent over 20 years supporting the empowerment of people, especially women, who were facing poverty, injustice and marginalisation, helping them develop their organisations and networks, connect to power holders, assert their rights and demand change.

In many countries, above all in Latin America, there is a tradition of recognising the need to advance social justice within social work, while in the UK the 'Personal Caring approach' (Lynn 1999, p.939) has been largely dominant. Inevitably, as Freire pointed out, 'Social workers are conditioned by the structure of the society in which they live, in which they are formed' (Moch 2009, p.94). Nevertheless, there have always been other more radical currents in the mix, such as the programme taught at the University of Warwick from 1974 to 1986, which aimed to produce 'critical social workers who were committed…to enabling service users and others experiencing oppression to develop their consciousness of the structural forces which shaped their lives and their deprivations' and to help them 'resist them and help others to do the same, individually and collectively' (Leonard 1993, p.162). The philosophy of the Warwick school drew explicitly on the ideas of Freire (and of the Italian Marxist thinker Antonio Gramsci, who in turn influenced Freire's writing) (Mayo 1999). According to Lee (2001, p.36), 'the radical pedagogy of Freire is an underpinning of empowerment practice in

---

1   One of seven CASE (formerly knows as Collaborative Awards in Science and Engineering) studentships commissioned by the Taking Part? Capacity Building Cluster (CBC), a research cluster allied to the TSRC, itself a project of the Economic and Social Research Council (ESRC). An edited book, *Community Research for Community Development* (Mayo, Mendiwelso-Bendek and Packham 2013), has empirical chapters based on each of the CBC projects, including mine.

social work'. Indeed, most group work explicitly aimed at 'empowerment' could be said to owe its methods to Freire, whether in adult education, anti-oppressive community work practice, participatory action research perspectives or overseas development strategies. In a British context, the kind of work done by GAP Unit tends to be referred to as 'community development', as defined in this 2006 report on refugee integration:

> working within a community development framework, practitioners will work with and support community members, groups and local infrastructure to change power structures, to remove barriers that prevent people from participating in the issues that affect their lives, to challenge the attitudes of individuals and the discriminatory practice of institutions, and recognise the skills, knowledge and expertise that… members can contribute to their own communities. (Navarro 2006, p.vii)

One of Freire's main contributions was the idea that through interrogating the sources of their problems, exploring together their needs and developing strategies for meeting them, people acquire the power to free themselves, practically and mentally, from domination (Mazzer Barroso 2002). Becoming conscious, through dialogue, of the political causes of their oppression and entering a cycle of action and reflection in order to spiral towards greater freedom through demanding rights and resisting injustice, is a process Freire described as 'praxis', in which individual and group empowerment occur together. 'As people become aware of the conditions of their existence, they acquire the ability to intervene and change it' (Freire 1996, pp.80–1). Where oppressors or systems of power become tyrannical and resist all efforts at change, gaining knowledge of their situation is nevertheless vital for subjects of that power, who can develop tactics for resistance even if just 'in the private, personal space' (Hill Collins 2000, p.118) of their consciousness. 'Becoming empowered through self-knowledge, even within conditions that severely limit one's ability to act, is essential' (ibid.).

Freire placed great emphasis on the collective learning which comes from reflection on action, and the philosophy and techniques of Freirean practice guided both the Arise and Shine project and my study of it. Each phase of Arise and Shine, coming together with other women, collectively analysing their situation and formulating demands and taking action to get these heard was experienced by the participants as restorative and generative of new conceptual and social resources. At the heart of this evolving project was the Arise and Shine group: 14 women from ten countries who were at different stages in the asylum process. Over the course of four years, the group became both a space for giving and receiving mutual support and an action base for awareness raising about the injustices of the UK asylum system and the need for things to change. Through participant interviews, group discussions and my own reflections, I set out to create an account of our work together that would help other practitioners be effective, empowering allies to migrant women. As well as documenting what the women taught us about 'what works', my thesis (Berry 2013) explored some of the political and ethical dilemmas I encountered as an activist researcher. This chapter draws on the learning from the Arise and Shine project and considers the power of participatory group work as an important method for social work.

Group origins and initiation

Arise and Shine started out as a series of discussions with members of five women's organisations in Greater Manchester, during which participants were invited to share their experiences of the asylum system and how it could be improved. A 'learning exchange event' then gathered everyone together to consolidate the process of identifying concerns and targets for change, and to create new connections between groups, services and individuals. It was an opportunity for cultural exchange, with more than 80 women sharing music, dance, stories and food from their countries and celebrating their collective strength as women. It had been planned as a one-off event to inform participants of existing campaigns and other ways of taking action on the issues they had identified.

However, several women indicated that they were keen to continue collaborating with GAP Unit. This prompted the formation of the Arise and Shine Group, for which further funding was secured from North West Together We Can (NWTWC).[2] From then on, the project was driven by the participants' desire to do something together to fight back against the exclusions of the asylum system. The group became both a forum for mutual support and an action group, with GAP Unit drawing on our experience of facilitation and on our networks and resources to make it happen. Three of the women who joined were also core members of Women Asylum Seekers Together (WAST), a well-respected, self-organised, Manchester-based

---

2   The name used by the Regional Empowerment Agency in North West England (part of the National Empowerment Partnership set up by New Labour in 2007, disbanded in 2011).

group which was growing increasingly experienced in self-advocacy. One of them, Lydia Besong, was writing an educational play called *How I Became an Asylum Seeker*, and Arise and Shine participants realised it would be the perfect vehicle for the awareness raising they wanted to do. The play, which had had one 'work in progress' performance before the initial money ran out, dramatised scenes including a political murder in Africa, the queue at a UK reporting centre, the interior of an immigration removal centre and a WAST meeting, elaborating composite characters based on Lydia's friends and fellow asylum seekers. It was firmly in the Brechtian 'epic' theatre tradition, which challenges audiences to face and acknowledge injustice in society.

GAP Unit was able to rehire the original director to work with WAST to refine the production and add new scenes, while the Arise and Shine Group took on organising for it to be shown to audiences of public sector decision makers and staff engaged in frontline work with new migrants. The play was performed in theatres in two cities, on each occasion followed by an hour-long workshop bringing audience members into dialogue with the WAST actors and other Arise and Shine members.

A few months later, the women initiated the Educate! project, visiting schools to speak with children, young people and their teachers. Some of the WAST members had previously given talks in schools and felt it was important because 'if you go to a school with something that is so touching, if it touches this child she won't let the parents rest, she will always tell the parents "this is happening, this is happening"' (Lydia, participant).[3]

They believed that the work would generate 'support from the next generation, because they will know the real story, they will realise these things, because they've heard it direct from asylum seekers' (Naima, participant).

A final 'women's gathering' was held with the last of the money. Thereafter, the Arise and Shine Group reconvened every five or six months to catch up with each other, celebrate legal victories, share a meal and participate in some structured activities from Carolina's repertoire of popular education activities. Lydia said of these meetings:

Maybe you just say what was nice in the past weeks or, or what's also there. For me, it cheers you up… It makes you forget about even if

---

3   All quotes are from Arise and Shine participants, recorded during one-to-one interviews and focus group discussions. Their real first names are used in most cases but not all (according to their preference).

you have some other drawbacks…you focus on the nice things that happened to you, and also we are all friendly and together with each one.

'What's also there' refers to difficult experiences: periods of detention and threatened deportation, bereavements, health problems, the hardship of eviction and destitution. Women would respond with prayers, affirmation, expressions of solidarity and stories of their own to boost hope and resilience in anyone who was feeling down. Here, for example, Susan describes how hearing defiant tales from Lydia and Sofia, who had both just secured release from Yarl's Wood Immigration Removal Centre, helped with her paralysing fear that she could herself be detained any day:

> Staying at home, being alone, nobody can push me… But that mixing and sharing some words, those words are the ones who push me, which will push me, and having that confidence. No, if Sofia did go through it, Lydia managed it…I can as well!

The project unfolded according to its own logic, but my review of the literature revealed, retrospectively, that it was in many ways typical of projects being conceptualised by refugee and allied organisations right across the UK:

> A key part of community development is enabling people to articulate their own concerns and hopes. Projects in a northern mill town, a town in south east England and a city in Scotland have all provided support to asylum seekers and refugees to enable them to speak at conferences, seminars or workshops as well as visiting schools to talk about issues and raise awareness regarding asylum seekers and refugees and inviting refugees as guest speakers… In other neighbourhood settings workers were supporting women led groups with the current emphasis being on self-help and supporting the establishment of a women's group to enable them to advocate on behalf of other women who are asylum seekers and refugees. (Navarro 2006, p.13)

Learning from the Arise and Shine project

In terms of their legal status, the members of Arise and Shine were a mixture of recent and long-standing refugees, asylum seekers who had arrived recently or been waiting for years, and 'visa over-stayers' lost in a Home Office backlog but subject to the same conditions as asylum seekers (housed in the same sub-standard accommodation, in receipt of an income well below citizen benefit levels, not permitted to work or study – for more on the privations of the asylum system see Da Lomba 2010; Mulvey 2010; Querton 2012; Squire 2009). All had a strong faith, either Muslim or Christian. They were from Sudan, Bangladesh, Uganda, Cameroon, Ethiopia, Nigeria, Eritrea, Malawi, South Africa and Zimbabwe. Some were married, some widowed, some single. Those who were mothers had children ranging from toddlers to grown adults, either living with them or 'back home', or both. Levels of spoken English, formal education, and political and professional experience also varied considerably within the group. This diversity was a strength; all of the participants had chosen to be part of (or, at least, stayed with) the group because they knew they had something to contribute and to gain from one another.

Another differential was the extent of the women's involvement in other associational activities locally, in addition to Arise and Shine and their faith community. Some had a great number of voluntary commitments, partly to serve a distraction from their situation, as Sofia explained: 'When there is all kinds of stuff around the North West, I always go to participate… If I sit at home that is when I'm going to think, and I don't give myself chance to think.'

In contrast, for Rut and Fiona, Arise and Shine was more or less their first venture beyond two groups we had worked with in the first phase of the project. Rut had been attending a weekly women's session run by the Red Cross, a place to receive information, try different activities and learn or practise basic English in a caring, structured environment. Its services were aimed at newly arrived asylum seekers and included helping women get to know the city and to feel comfortable using public transport. The other, Refugee Mothers United (RMU), had started out supporting pregnant women but had broadened its remit to include all female asylum seekers. It operated a drop-in and offered various types of assistance, as Fiona explained:

> What RMU really helps is women who have got no relatives and maybe they are going to give birth, or women with children already… It can help them in the process, like to have a solicitor…which [GP] surgery you will have to register with…which school you have to take your children to.

Fiona felt that the professional counselling she was able to access through RMU had helped her cope with problems that had been threatening to overwhelm her, including the ongoing uncertainty of her legal case, the absence of her daughter, having no money and the demands of a small baby and a husband struggling with mental illness. She was also grateful for the birth partner RMU had provided and for the sense of community she got from its drop-in, saying of the coordinator:

> Jane is like our mother… Wherever we want to go, which numbers we need to call, which support we need, she knows already, because she's born here, and we are new to the system and sometimes we are new even in Preston. (Fiona)

However, she was clear that 'what is in RMU is not what is in GAP Unit' (Fiona). Both her and Rut's accounts indicated that Arise and Shine had complemented their other group, in particular through its focus on their predicament as asylum seekers, and its political framing. Freire believed that the conditions for political action are created when people who are oppressed begin to talk about their problems, freeing themselves from fatalism and isolation (Freire 1996, p.48). Rut commented that 'In my other group we never talk about asylum seekers; in that women's group there is no like these things, just we go English class…people they came tell us about project, and that's all.' Whereas, she said, 'from GAP group I can get a lot of information about asylum seeker and about people'.

By the end of the project, it was clear that the process had galvanised in Rut a sense of righteous anger at the petty discriminations she was facing, giving her courage, for example, to stand up to her landlords when she saw them bullying a neighbour who did not understand English. 'I have a confidence to speak for other people about our life…not like before shy and quiet,' she said. When I interviewed her she had just been granted leave to remain and was about to move to Birmingham, where she had lived before being 'dispersed' to Manchester, and was going with a determination to initiate discussions and a public advocacy process within the larger Ethiopian community there:

> because they don't have like this idea, a lot of my friends…all they have problems, but they can't say it. So, if we start – oh, there is a lot of sad, sad history you will hear – if you go there and you start like this organisation, we can talk for other people, contact organisations, it's good. (Rut)

Being involved with the play workshops, and then speaking with a class of ten-year-olds, Rut had not only come to see her experiences as the result of the asylum system being run according to a policy of deterrence rather than sanctuary, but crucially, had become aware that rather than feeling antipathy towards all asylum seekers, many British people have only a vague notion of what it means to seek asylum and are often sympathetic when they find out more. Other Arise and Shine participants had a similar revelation. The hostility and indifference they are exposed to as asylum seekers is cast in a different light by the realisation that they have superior knowledge to those who have merely absorbed negative populist assumptions. 'I'm telling you, they didn't know anything! They asked from a perspective whereby you see that someone completely doesn't know what is going on, who is a refugee and who is an asylum seeker!' said Fiona of the teachers she had talked with in one of the schools.

Before going into the school, Rut had been worried about her English, but the children's warm reception, intelligent questions and acceptance of what she had to say – so unlike the sceptical listening of Home Office officials to whom she had had to recount her story many times – had been very reassuring. One boy said he had heard that asylum seekers are given nice houses ahead of British people who are homeless, yet:

> When they explained to him not all asylum seeker have house, most of asylum seeker is living in charity house, like Boaz Trust, then he understand. He say 'Yeah'. Really understand. I like! (Rut)

Rut found it encouraging to see the impact of her intervention, which was reinforced when pupils sent her letters and pictures they had drawn. For Fiona, who had developed a level of apprehension and mistrust towards young British people, the school visits also broke an invisible barrier:

> At first I thought, these youth have grown in Europe, they won't be able to listen my ideas or my worries… I thought since they are not from suffering situations, how will they be able to listen? But they were very, very calm, and eager to listen more what I had to say. (Fiona)

Having begun thinking 15 minutes would feel interminable, she came to wish she had been allocated twice as long, because she had so much left to say. This was despite having found part of the talk quite upsetting, because she had found herself mentioning the child she had left in Uganda, something she usually kept concealed, even from herself. A barrage of questions followed from the curious students who identified with this nine-year-old and wanted to understand more. It was a difficult, emotional, but finally cathartic experience for Fiona, allowing her to process emotions she had been suppressing and to let go of some self-blame:

> The most important thing I got in the schools project was to talk about my daughter. I feel my daughter is part of me now, because I don't fear talking about her… The children asked, 'Why did you have to leave her back home?' And I was like, 'I didn't have enough money to bring her on board… It was through desperation that you needed to move out from your country to another one'… I will never forget about it, honestly, I will never forget about that. And it, it really filled in the gap between the youth and me. (Fiona)

After sharing this story at a conference, I was asked if we had not taken risks in exposing the women to such situations. Fiona's view was that 'it wasn't risky… We were not forced to talk about what we didn't want to talk' (although she pointed out that, unusually, we had not done a proper group evaluation that day; instead of going to a cafe 'to sit down, relax deeply, before you get your journey', the debrief had been done hastily on the bus on the way home). Of course, things might not have gone as well as they did, but what we were keen to avoid was the opposite tendency, apparent in many support organisations, of seeing asylum-seeking women through a prism of vulnerability, in need only of care and protection. This neglects the role of challenge and agency in people's recovery of personal strength in the face of experiences of racism and rejection, which is something that came across very powerfully in my interviews, putting me in mind of the 'cycle of liberation' referred to in liberation psychology, another Latin American contribution to combatting structural oppression (Johnson and Friedman 2014, p.126).

Fiona's definition of empowerment was 'letting me do things by myself'. For Lydia, it was 'making you feel like in your life never accept defeat, always know that you can break that wall'. For Elinah, empowerment happens when 'a situation comes, you just face it and you challenge it, sometimes without even thinking what you are doing…you see yourself rising to a level all the time'. Tendayi also attributed the recovery of her agency partly to what we undertook together. 'From the activities which we were doing, I realised "No, you are still Tendayi…the things which you were capable of doing, whether ten years ago, you are still capable of doing those things."' She appreciated the fact that GAP Unit staff would 'go in the background, behind the scenes, and you let us, you just say, "you do it", which is a very strong point about the organisation'.

RMU offered a different and valuable type of service, but the contrast is instructive. According to Fiona, 'We don't have whereby we are talking to each other about our problems. No. When everyone has problems in RMU, you just approach the manager.' RMU is centrally organised with a focus on meeting practical needs and providing individualised care. In Fiona's view, 'Simply, leave to remain has been bringing us there…and from there, everyone they get on with their business.' Running self-esteem sessions at RMU during the first phase of Arise and Shine, we saw that it was a new experience for the women to be encouraged to sit in a circle and talk to one another, whereas what Fiona had valued above all else with Arise and Shine was the chance to learn from the other women in the group:

> The women in GAP Unit…they were still strong, though they had a problem going on same as mine. Whereas in RMU the problem really takes its toll with the women. And I think the problem is because we expect from one person to do everything for us. So we don't look out there, to see how can we help ourselves. (Fiona)

As a result of the personal strength she had gained from spending time with older women she considered role models, Fiona said she had:

> come to realise that I'm the strongest person in RMU. And everyone thinks that I can be a support worker to other women. But they don't know where I've got the courage to do that, it's from going to GAP Unit. The women behave very different, strong… I'm always lifted by somebody else, that's how I am.

There were also some tangible outcomes from the public awareness raising. A new service for asylum-seeker mothers was initiated in Tameside, a school in Bury instituted an annual workshop with asylum seekers as part of its Year 9 Human Rights Day, and further speaking invitations were received by the women, including to give the keynote address at an NHS diversity and equality conference.

> People can take on board what they've seen in the play and what they've heard. And take it further…some people are public sector, others are private sector, you don't know who will carry what to where. (Fiona)

It was difficult to recruit anyone with significant political power to the events; those attending had no authority to end enforced destitution or amend national childcare policy. Nevertheless, there are many 'minor decisions where some play of power can be realized through discretion and individual agency' (Pannett 2011, p.189) by sympathetic officials. This kind of 'discretionary' practice is a tenet of radical social work and crucial for working alongside people who are marginalised on the basis of their immigration status. It requires social workers to identify and expand pockets of ethical practice in their workplace in order to deliver services in line with need and not with the encroaching demands of the increasingly bureaucratic contexts they are required to work in (Carey and Foster 2011).

Conclusion

The Arise and Shine meetings were never frequent. At the height of the project we met every few weeks, in addition to the workshops and events we were organising, but for most of the time it was every few months, moving to twice a year after Phase 3. I asked Fiona if it was a problem that we got together so infrequently and it turned out that she saw this as an advantage: 'Whenever it came, I was ready prepared, but I don't think if it was frequent I would manage... I found it very useful that there was a gap from one session to the other.'

This made sense to Carolina, remembering her work with communities in Venezuela. People have busy lives, and sometimes doing things too regularly can make them a chore, rather than something to wait for and look forward to. It is good to know that the pace can be slow and that meeting only sporadically will not automatically undermine a sense of continuity or intensity, because the costs can mount up. As the interviews also revealed, the provision of travel expenses, childcare (either a crèche or individual subsidy) and refreshments, ideally in the form of hot, home-cooked non-British food (much better received than cold sandwiches!), is very important in this kind of work. Room hire can be expensive too, especially if it needs to be in a city centre location for accessibility to those travelling in from elsewhere.

My research confirmed what makes for empowering community development work with women who are seeking asylum or refugees. The ingredients are simple: some ideas for action, some good volunteers and associates (including refugees themselves – two of the women became GAP Unit associates) and some money. The action can begin with swapping stories and experiences, which for those who are less politicised can be a process of 'conscientization' (Freire 1996, p.17). Formulation of demands and a strategy for targeting a particular audience, whether school children or national policy makers, comes next. According to Wroe (2012, p.48), who interviewed some of the same women for her research, a narrative approach to advocacy (as with the WAST play and the school workshops) 'is a way of ensuring that the agency lies with the subject of oppression or domination and that it is their desires that drive social change work, rather than the desires of a humanitarian organisation or campaigner'. This is important, since support organisations often inadvertently perpetuate the social exclusion of asylum seekers by acting as gatekeepers in their representation (Rainbird 2012).

The Arise and Shine process was 'owned' by the participants; they were not considered clients but were active members, making decisions, taking on tasks in disregard of perceived language barriers. Community development approaches did have quite such a good footing in the refugee sector nationally, though there were signs of weakening (with austerity and the disappearance of bodies like NWTWC) when I concluded my study in 2013. If, still, 'the dominant ideology about refugee people seeking asylum is that they are in need of support and services rather than empowerment' (Jones 2010, p.67) and 'support organizations continue to treat asylum seekers as lacking knowledge about the asylum system' (Rainbird 2012, p.415), the evidence of Arise and Shine is that this is inadequate. Tailored services offering therapeutic care and material support and advice are vital, but so are spaces for mutual collaborative work.

Ultimately, the success of Arise and Shine as a space for action in which participants could 'recognise themselves and be recognised for what they are or want to be' (Melucci 1996, pp.219–220) can be attributed in large part to intangible, relational factors. A member said of the Arise and Shine Group, 'This is my family where I can share issues freely, listen to others and support them where possible.' Recurrent words in discussions and interviews were 'genuine' and 'truthful', and they describe a collective achievement. 'The atmosphere which you created, it was very warm, a warm atmosphere. Welcoming. And instantly that's where the familiar relationship came from,' said Tendayi. However, it was she and the others who created the atmosphere, through their humour, thoughtfulness, hymn singing, optimism, sensitivity to one another and exuberance; we just set out the chairs. What GAP Unit provided was what Tendayi called 'the missing thing', that is:

> When you go to, to an organisation, they believe you. They value you as who you are. There's no suspicion, to say 'Hmmmmm you might be, this!' Showing empathy is one of the [most important things]. And believing…to say, 'What you are saying is true, although I don't agree with this, but what you are telling me is true.' (Tendayi)

Openness, shared respect for one another's faith and cultural identity, attentive listening to one another's ideas, trust in the process – these qualities developed automatically, without the setting of 'ground rules'. A final comment from Tendayi captures the essence of the project: 'GAP took us on a holistic nature, they didn't focus on one, on the campaigns that is strategic only, but all the whole, all what affects us – physical, social, emotional, spiritual, everything!'

Tips for empowering practice with people seeking asylum

Feedback from Arise and Shine participants gave rise to and confirmed the following practice knowledge:

- Practical considerations:
  - Having children cared for separately, away from the group, allows mothers to concentrate and contribute. Child-minding money should be given up front or a crèche provided.
  - Refreshments – ideally hot, home-cooked food – are essential. Women each brought a dish to Arise and Shine meetings, while at other events a participant cooked for everyone in return for expenses.
  - A warm meeting space gives important respite from the damp, cold, uncomfortable places many National Asylum Support Service-housed and destitute asylum seekers are living in.
  - Reimbursement of travel expenses should happen as a matter of course, rather than waiting for a request. It recognises the volunteers' contribution and prevents the relationship being one of patronage. It also demonstrates an understanding that their economic situation is outside their control, despite which, many people feel a sense of shame not to be earning their own living.
  - Even when people understand little English (and there is no one to translate for them), they benefit from being part of a group process and taking on appropriate tasks.
- Group work recommendations:
  - To facilitate well-structured, varied sessions, open with a warm-up exercise (such as an opportunity to share current challenges or recent achievements) and end with evaluation.

- Ensure everyone feels able to contribute to discussions and feels heard and valued.

- Show respect for religious sensibility, without necessarily making this explicit, to favour freedom of expression.

- Do not ask intrusive questions about people's history or asylum cases – participants should choose what they wish to share.

- Avoid seeing women asylum seekers through a prism of vulnerability – once trust is established, support them to leave their comfort zones and to challenge themselves. Understand that women are at different stages and need different kinds of support, but that all, over time, benefit from small, non-coercive opportunities to exercise agency and move beyond a passive service user role.

- Remember that open and honest communication, sensitivity to individual needs and a demonstratively caring approach are the necessary indicators of 'genuineness'. An important aspect of our project was the relative informality, for example some meetings were held in our own homes, reducing the risk of provider–client type relationships.

- Ensure that there is a thorough debrief after all actions and events, especially when these have been challenging. Sit down afterwards with refreshments to talk through how people felt and feel, what was achieved, what could have been better.

- Engage in regular ongoing evaluation as it is essential to the spirit of openness and learning within Freirian practice. Practitioners should encourage feedback and criticism from participants, in order to respond and adapt.

References

Berry, H. (2013) *Practices of Alliance and Solidarity with Asylum Seeking and Refugee Women – a Case Study* (Doctoral thesis). Accessed 23/11/2018 at: https://e-space. mmu.ac.uk/324985.

Carey, M. and Foster, V. (2011) 'Introducing "deviant" social work: Contextualising the limits of radical social work while understanding (fragmented) resistance within the social work labour process.' *British Journal of Social Work*, 41, 3, 576–593.

Da Lomba, S. (2010) 'Legal status and refugee integration: A UK perspective.' *Journal of Refugee Studies*, 23, 4, 411–414.

Freire, P. (1996) *Pedagogy of the Oppressed* (second revised edition). London: Penguin.

Hill Collins, P. (2000) *Black Feminist Thought: Knowledge, Consciousness, and the Politics of Empowerment.* New York, NY: Routledge.

Johnson, C.V. and Friedman, H.L. (2014) *The Praeger Handbook of Social Justice and Psychology*, Vol.1. Oxford: Praeger ABC-CLIO.

Jones, P.A. (2010) 'Refugee Community Organisations working in partnership: The quest for recognition.' Unpublished PhD thesis, University of Birmingham.

Lee, J.A.B. (2001) *The Empowerment Approach to Social Work Services: Building the Beloved Community* (second edition). New York, NY: Columbia University Press.

Leonard, P. (1993) 'Critical Pedagogy and State Welfare: Intellectual Encounters with Freire and Gramsci, 1974–1986.' In P. McLaren and P. Leonard (eds) *Paulo Freire: A Critical Encounter*, p.155–169. London: Routledge.

Lynn, E. (1999) 'Value bases in social work education.' *British Journal of Social Work*, 29, 6, 939–954.

Mayo, M., Mendiwelso-Bendek, Z. and Packham, C. (2013) *Community Research for Community Development.* London: Palgrave.

Mayo, P. (1999) *Gramsci, Freire and Adult Education: Possibilities for Transformative Action.* London: Zed Books.

Mazzer Barroso, M. (2002) *Reading Freire's Words: Are Freire's Ideas Applicable to Southern NGOs?* International Working Paper Series, 11. London: Centre for Civil Society, London School of Economics and Political Science.

Melucci, A. (1996) *Challenging Codes: Collective Action in the Information Age.* Cambridge: Cambridge University Press.

Moch, M. (2009) 'A critical understanding of social work by Paolo Freire.' *Journal of Progressive Human Services*, 20, 1, 92–7.

Mulvey, G. (2010) 'When policy creates politics: The problematizing of immigration and the consequences for refugee integration in the UK.' *Journal of Refugee Studies*, 23, 4, 437–462.

Navarro, A. (2006) *Refugee Integration and Cohesive Communities: Community Development in Practice.* London: Community Development Programme.

Pannett, L. (2011) 'Making a liveable life in Manchester: Doing justice to people seeking asylum.' Unpublished PhD thesis, University of Manchester.

Querton, C. (2012) *'I Feel Like as a Woman I'm not Welcome': A Gender Analysis of UK Asylum Law, Policy and Practice.* London: Asylum Aid.

Rainbird, S. (2012) 'Asylum seeker "vulnerability": The official explanation of service providers and the emotive responses of asylum seeker.' *Community Development Journal*, 47, 3, 405–422.

Squire, V. (2009) *The Exclusionary Politics of Asylum.* Basingstoke: Palgrave Macmillan.

White, M. and Epston, D. (1990) *Narrative Means to Therapeutic Ends.* London: Norton.

Wroe, L. (2012) 'A Study of refugee advocacy: Paradoxes of helping in a climate of hostility.' Unpublished PhD thesis, University of Manchester.

Chapter 11

Understanding Destitution and Finding Creative Solutions

How the Voluntary Sector and Social Care Can Support Each Other

Rachael Bee

I am a registered social worker in the UK who has been living and working alongside destitute asylum seekers since 2009. I work for Bristol Hospitality Network (BHN),[1] a charity set up in 2009 to extend solidarity to people seeking asylum and experiencing destitution through accommodation and creative community involvement. We have a small network of host households which have provided 84 destitute asylum seekers with accommodation and support since 2009, from a few months to a few years at a time. We also have a 12-bedroom house for men, which has offered sanctuary to 42 people. We run a weekly Welcome Centre for all asylum seekers and refugees, which offers a hot lunch for over one hundred people, specialist advocacy support service, ESOL (English for speakers of other languages) classes at two levels, therapeutic art space, bottomless tea and coffee and snacks, and games including pool and table tennis.

---

1   www.bhn.org.uk

Our members (we prefer this term to 'service users') are appeal rights exhausted,[2] have 'no recourse to public funds', no right to work,[3] no right to planned hospital treatment, have to travel five miles, often on foot, often as much as weekly, to sign on with the Home Office and are not able to rent a room or have a bank account. We therefore also provide £10 a week for some of our members because they have no other money. We can't afford to do this for all of our members (I'm sure you can imagine how difficult it is to decide who gets it and who doesn't). We have a small part-time staff team of four, over one hundred volunteers, no public funding and rely on small grants and individual donations to continue to operate. I have hosted 37 people (36 men and one woman) in my own home since 2009. The shortest time my guests stayed was for one week and the longest for two years. This has had its challenges!

In this chapter, I will share from my experience, through reflection and case study, how we can, when we all work together, work positively to challenge injustice and offer an alternative to the policies of successive governments leading to the forced destitution of refused asylum seekers (Refugee Council, no date). There is no simple answer. The challenges we face are so high, and so deeply part of the fabric of our society, that we have to learn how to fight them with campaigning, education and awareness-raising activities, and open our own homes and our own lives to those

2   The asylum system fails those seeking sanctuary in the UK and causes such unnecessary suffering to thousands of people in the UK via a policy of forced destitution. One element of this system that I want to draw out particularly is the continually peddled lie that the asylum system is linear. It is not, it is cyclical. Sanctuary seekers are rarely deported to many countries such as Somalia, Eritrea, Iraq and Iran from where many people claim asylum. Most of those accommodated by the No Accommodation Network (a national network supporting projects to accommodate destitute asylum seekers) are from these key countries. In BHN we have seen that 60 per cent of those who have been accommodated by us, when they moved on, were able to gain a form of refugee or humanitarian protection in the long term. Destitution is a policy that is part of the government's plan to make Britain a 'hostile environment' for sanctuary seekers. As most destitute asylum seekers have successfully been granted protection long term, it is abhorrent for this policy to continue and it is important for us as a profession to stand against it with all our power and influence, both politically via campaigning and also via creative resistance within social services departments.

3   The right to work is sometimes granted to those who apply for it but it is not really a right to work because it is only in shortage occupations, such as consultant brain surgeons or ballerinas. The No Accommodation Network and other refugee organisations are calling for the right to work to be extended to include work in *any profession*.

affected by them in the meantime. Read on, but be prepared to get pretty angry. In fact, I hope you do!

In 2009, when Dr Naomi Millner invited me to help her co-found Bristol Hospitality Network, I had been a qualified social worker for nearly two years. I was working in a new job as social worker for the Community Learning Difficulties Team. Alongside my training and first two years' in social work, I had also become involved with the campaign against unjust treatment of refused asylum seekers. I had also befriended a 19-year-old asylum seeker from Afghanistan. He changed my world, shifted my vision, unmasked to me the reality faced by so many destitute asylum seekers in the UK, hitherto hidden from my eyes. Let me tell you his story.

Mohammad

Mohammad[4] had arrived as a minor, but was age assessed as 18 (when in fact he was 16) and moved into shared National Asylum Support Service accommodation.[5] He was scared and alone and no one believed his story. He was devastated. In Afghanistan, his father had worked for the 'wrong' side and been killed, and a few years later they came for the whole family and bombed his house. His sister was badly injured but survived and his mother also escaped. He was out at the time. When he came home, the family immediately fled from Afghanistan and escaped to Pakistan. Later on, he was walking to the mosque and he saw a group of men from his area in Afghanistan talking to the imam. He tried to slip away but they saw him and shot at him. One bullet missed and the other got him in the upper arm. He has the scar. He ran and escaped to another part of Pakistan and then he was warned that these men knew where he was, so his family paid smugglers to get him out and he ended up coming to the UK under a lorry and claiming asylum.

Mohammad was age assessed (apparently, the facial hair and attempt to behave in a more grown-up way to impress the assessor backfired and he was assessed as 18) and so ended up in adult accommodation. Soon afterwards, his claim for asylum was refused. This was before BHN was founded. I asked around in my church and found a lovely couple who agreed to have him stay with them in their spare room. He stayed for six months. I was totally clueless at that time and tried to find out what organisations were helping

---

4   Not his real name.
5   The National Asylum Support Service is a Home Office accommodation provider for asylum seekers still in the process and not yet appeal rights exhausted; services are often outsourced and run by companies like G4S and Serco.

asylum seekers in the city. I took him to a drop-in and tried to get him advice. A local charity found him a solicitor, but the solicitor didn't bother to come to his court hearing and so my friends and I went and tried to help. We didn't understand the system and we were not solicitors, so we didn't help much in truth. He was refused again.

Later on that year, when he was signing at the police station with immigration, he was detained. Along with many other Afghan young men (Asylos 2017), he was deported to Afghanistan. Miraculously, on arrival he met an American journalist who interviewed him, knew the risk he faced in Afghanistan and counselled him to leave immediately, so he escaped from Afghanistan again and travelled to Pakistan, where he hoped the men who wanted to kill him would have left. Unfortunately, they had not and he was shot again. He escaped and his family again paid for him to be smuggled out of Pakistan and back to Europe. He finally got leave to remain in Italy in 2016. There is not much work in Italy for him, so he still struggles, but at least he is safe. The UK government has made much of the 'hostile environment' it is trying to create for sanctuary seekers in the UK. This young man faced that hostile environment in full, like so many other individuals caught in this system.

The process of walking alongside Mohammad as he struggled through all these barriers, and then the desolation I felt when all my efforts were worth nothing and he was removed and I knew how dangerous his next few hours and days would be, compelled me into action. I thought he would be killed. He nearly was. What we (Dr Millner and I) needed was to begin something that, by its existence, would both support those brothers and sisters seeking sanctuary here in the UK and who are facing destitution, and raise their voices above the clamour of xenophobia and fear of the 'other' that pervades our society. We didn't have lots of experience, or any money, or big houses. We had a burning fire under us, set by witnessing first-hand the suffering caused by this policy of forced destitution that made us move, made us ready to fight injustice and to open our homes to those in need. BHN came from that fire. It is still fed by it.

One thing I believe has been obscured in statutory work is the values-led nature of social work. Individual practitioners are often individually values-led, but few team or service managers retain values above budgetary constraint and senior management requirements. I've recently spoken to social work students about the work of BHN at Bristol University (where I trained). It brought back to me the focus on social work values in the training that I received, and the struggle I felt when entering statutory work as I realised that these values had been so deeply eroded in practice. In the voluntary sector, it is much more possible to live within and out of a values base that transcends 'work' and impacts all spheres of life. The reason I entered social work in the first place was because of a congruence between my values and the values of the social work profession. In BHN, we have been able to decide values as a whole 'family' and live from them – a 'luxury' I was not afforded in statutory work. We gathered as a family (of BHN members, volunteers and trustees) early on in the creation of BHN and we agreed what our values would be:

- solidarity (working alongside people, not merely giving aid)

- equality (people are people before labels)

- mutual empowerment (overcoming barriers together)

- hospitality (creating intercultural spaces of welcome)

- integrity (transparency in decision and action)

- creative resistance (living change imaginatively).[6]

These values are at the heart of what we do and are real, lived-out values with real meaning. Every day, as we live and volunteer/work together with BHN members in *integrity*, we create *intercultural spaces of welcome* from which we are able to *overcome barriers together* in *equality* and from a *solidarity* with one another built from a common aim to overcome the injustice of the asylum system (*creative resistance*). The international definition of social work (IFSW 2014) states that:

> Social work is a practice-based profession and an academic discipline that promotes social change and development, social cohesion, and the empowerment and liberation of people. Principles of social justice, human rights, collective responsibility and respect for diversities are central to social work. Underpinned by theories of social work, social sciences, humanities and indigenous knowledge, social work engages people and structures to address life challenges and enhance wellbeing.

---

6   I often get asked what this one means. For us, it means living out the change we want to see the rest of society transformed into (e.g. open spaces of hospitality and welcome for all) and then creating spaces where the voices of marginalised people can be heard louder because they are raised up by us and our power and opportunity to speak truth to power; gradually bringing their voices strongly and to the fore as we step out of the way.

This is the bread and butter of work outside the state, being free to live from values rather than state authority. We are able to do this because we are not constrained by any funding from statutory bodies, local government or political parties (we are funded by individual donors, small grant-making trusts and our in-house catering social enterprise). We are therefore free to live from our own values rather than expectations, targets and controls dictated from above. These values are real to us as a BHN family in how we support one another and journey together to a better world for all, but also to me as I share my home with two to five destitute asylum-seeking men.

Most people think that we are blurring boundaries and counsel us against it. Of course, we are blurring boundaries. When in statutory social work would you have the 'service users' live in your home, or know where you live, or have your home or mobile number? I have broken all the rules. But that is the right way for me to live for our members. Our members are from countries where family is everything. Community, not individual cultures. This means we have had to reassess what our cultural norms are in BHN. I have had my assumptions about the 'right' way to live shattered and reformed. What is needed for our members is belonging; rootedness in a new culture means finding a new family to belong to. BHN is that family for our members.

I must be honest, ungrudging hospitality is not always easy for me, particularly to those who never say thank you. Solidarity is not easy when it's easier to do something for someone than support them to do it for themselves. All of life becomes a place of learning about others and most deeply, myself, in my frailty and failure. I'm sometimes frustrated and cross when someone walks into my house for another demand, or I find the people I live with the most irritating individuals. But we are a family in BHN, and that's what family is like. It might be an odd one, but we press on together living our way out of the barriers that bind us into our boxes, creating a safer place for all where trust is built and kept over years, and, at least in our little enclave, Bristol can be a place of belonging for those cut adrift in the sea of fear in this unjust asylum system.

How does BHN interact with statutory services?

Case study: Kamil Ahmad

Kamil Ahmad (also mentioned in Chapter 5 by my colleague Rebecca Yeo) was a man who was referred to BHN some years ago. We placed him in our men's house and he seemed to settle in well. After about six months, his mental health began to deteriorate rapidly. Soon he had a mental health crisis and we could no longer support him in our volunteer-run hostel. We urgently contacted social services and they eventually assessed him and moved him to supported accommodation. He was assessed in 2013 under the old National Assistance Act legislation. His needs were considered 'destitute plus', which gave social services a duty to support him but no clear directives on how to support him (in 2014 these provisions were replaced by the Care Act). In this case, he was able to get supported accommodation, which seemed like a great solution for him and he seemed to recover from the episode over time. We saw him regularly at different drop-ins and in local shops where he seemed to be getting back on track. After some years of this support, he reported to the police that another person in the supported accommodation was threatening him. Some months later, this person killed him.

There is a lot to unpick here.

First, I am devastated that due to his high mental health needs we couldn't support him in our charity and years later he was murdered while in statutory provision. However, there are also questions to be answered about whether all options for alternative accommodation were followed up by statutory services once he had told them of the threats. It is also important to reflect on why his allegations were not taken seriously by those caring for him. Perhaps because his English was limited it was harder for people to really understand the seriousness of his allegations. Either way, it appears that the state did not adequately protect him and he was murdered.

Second, on a more positive note, he was believed when he was in crisis and given accommodation by the local authority on the basis of it and this is, from my experience working in this field, really rare. Usually, adults are accommodated only if they have children or there is a significant physical impairment that is undeniable. Small voluntary organisations are not set up to provide any specialist services, and local authorities should consider the mental health needs of destitute asylum seekers very carefully (as they did in this case), granting more destitute asylum seekers experiencing poor mental health statutory provision and support.

So, what can we learn?

Mental health practitioners have a particularly difficult role in assessing destitute asylum seekers in crisis. Suggestions for best practice in mental health are transferable to any field where Mental Health Act or Care Act assessments are carried out:

- It is not simple to work with the limited nuance you get when you use an interpreter to talk to someone. It is therefore vital that trusted face-to-face interpreters are used for assessments.

- Remember that asylum seekers have usually experienced trauma in their home country which is exacerbated by the trauma of leaving home and the dangerous journey to the UK and by the asylum system and the experience of destitution. You are usually assessing someone with multiple traumas that layer onto one another. It therefore takes longer to get to the underlying issues, so take extra time to assess properly. These are all complex cases because of trauma. Argue for the time to assess them properly.

- There are often a wide range of people involved in a person's support when they are without family in the UK, so use the care assessment widely to get a broader perspective on the needs of that person as seen through voluntary sector organisations or friends and supporters (even if you need to use an interpreter to include the views of a friend of the person).

These case studies are here to help explain the nature of this work with destitute asylum seekers, its struggles and its joy. However, it is unlikely that many social workers will live quite like this. I hope that the next suggestions for ways to get involved in support are accessible to all.

How can social workers support destitute asylum seekers during their day job?
Work less

It is likely that most social workers will not have the privilege of working directly with asylum seekers. However, in every city there are projects like Bristol Hospitality Network (BHN) crying out for the values-led work, social work skills, empathy and efficiency of good social workers. BHN is part of the No Accommodation Network (NACCOM),[7] and all NACCOM projects would benefit from the volunteer time and expertise of the social work community. We have a lot to give.

When I started in social work I thought I was starting a career. I would get a job and work for 20 years full time as a professional social worker. I was quite excited. Unfortunately for my social work career, the fire of BHN started under me and I was moved from that position. I gradually started to work fewer and fewer hours and have less and less money. It was okay. In the end, after volunteering about two or three days a week for five years, I got a part-time paid post managing the charity that I love, doing what I love to do every day. Maybe a few other social workers could work fewer hours too; make different choices; offer days not only evenings to voluntary sector organisations and help build the capacity of those organisations to help those that social workers are not usually allowed to support with statutory funding. Maybe your city has destitute asylum seekers but no NACCOM project. Start one! Why not? While reducing working hours is not feasible for everyone, perhaps you could take a day off now and then to offer training and support to voluntary sector organisations?

Take the destitution cases in your social work role

Get into a position to support destitute asylum-seeking families or asylum-seeking adults with physical impairments, or mental health difficulties, through showing an active interest in this area of work and requesting allocation of these cases from your team manager. This way you can develop an expertise that will lead to better service provision and an expansion of knowledge within statutory teams. You'll need to do some research first, to make sure you are up to date with the rules and how to use your powers to support destitute asylum seekers with temporary accommodation and support. There are a few individuals in every project who have needs that have been assessed as not meeting the (lower than usual) threshold for support under the Care Act, Slough Judgement and subsequent guidance (No Recourse to Public Funds (NRFP) Network 2018).[8] These individuals take a lot of additional time and energy from very overburdened charities. If social workers could work with us to support those who need additional

7   www.naccom.org.uk
8   The NRPF Network (2018) offers useful guidance on how to support families but do take independent legal advice in addition to your (possibly biased) social services in-house legal team to make sure.

help and cannot be hosted (using these powers), the voluntary sector could provide support to more destitute asylum seekers.

One woman whom we hosted needed social services supported accommodation. Gloria[9] from the Middle East was HIV positive and very unwell on medication that made her lethargic and sometimes unresponsive. She was also very depressed and was experiencing both post-traumatic stress disorder (PTSD) and the rejection of her family. She set fire to the chest of drawers in her room one day having fallen asleep under a burning candle. The flames were about to set fire to her wig (on her head at the time) when someone smelt smoke and burst into her room to put out the fire. She also developed hoarding tendencies and needed constant emotional support. I hosted her for a while, others also tried for some months, but in the end, it was clear she needed a supervised environment and better emotional support. She was granted social services support under the Care Act but this has been reassessed and removed many times and she is now homeless again.

Social workers are asking the wrong questions. For instance, if you ask her, 'Can you cook for yourself?' she will answer, 'Yes,' but she doesn't tell you that she cannot cook safely on her own! As a social worker you can take an interest in this area of work and be informed so that colleagues will choose to ask you for advice in that area and together you can build the skills of each team so that this doesn't happen. Maybe you've got a supportive senior practitioner and manager, maybe not. But you can still get the knowledge and skills yourself to ask the right questions in the right way using the right interpreter well, so that you can support a person in need to receive appropriate supported accommodation. Please do this.

Become a trustee or other volunteer for a local NACCOM project

Voluntary sector organisations need good governance and social work is actually a good training for the skills to be a helpful contributor on a board of trustees. Don't let anyone tell you that you are too young to be a trustee. Get involved. Charities often need social workers as advisors on issues like safeguarding and mental health. Why not offer your expertise over the phone in this way? Maybe you want to try something entirely unrelated to social work; you could volunteer for many NACCOM projects like BHN in

---

9   Not her real name.

many roles that are totally different from your day job. I would never have imagined that I would end up leading a project cooking food for hundreds of people! Until we created a new team for our catering social enterprise 'Moveable Feast' last year, I had organised this much of the time for three years. Sometimes just me and one member chef would cater for huge meals. I can now make much better curry! It's fun, and perhaps you will meet people who will become for you what Mohammad was for me – a person whom you meet and then you can never be the same again.

Campaign

Many refugee support organisations have a campaigning arm and are involved in challenging policy and guidance on the treatment of refugees, asylum seekers and other migrants. However, until now, few larger organisations have focused on campaigning against the very statutes that create destitution. I believe we are seeing a shift and we need to take hold of this moment. Perhaps you are struggling with work and home and can't fit in volunteering, maybe you can still help by adding your professional voice to the campaign to end destitution.

Still Human Still Here[10] campaigned for a fair asylum system without destitution playing a part in it for years. It has recently come under a new organisation, Asylum Matters,[11] which itself is now sitting under the City of Sanctuary movement. The Bristol City of Sanctuary group is building a campaign locally to say that destitution should not happen in the city. Get yourself signed up to the campaign updates for all these organisations and then respond when called to do so.

Befriend

The best campaigners are those who know those affected personally, so take time to befriend people seeking sanctuary. There are often schemes which enable you to do this in a more boundaried way (you don't have to do it the same way as me). You will then have a person in mind when you write to your MP; this will make your campaigning more effective and keep you both passionate for change and practical.

---

10 https://stillhumanstillhere.wordpress.com
11 https://cityofsanctuary.org/2017/04/20/city-of-sanctuary-hosts-new-advocacy-and-campaigns-project-asylum-matters

Our profession is under attack. We are being de-professionalised by the watering down of individual social worker authority, and the austerity agenda restricts our capacity to make real change. Social workers are not drawn to this work by the opportunity to have a career in exacerbating human misery! We want to make positive change in individuals and communities. We have social work values (British Association of Social Workers 2014) that should continue to inform all our practice and make us deeper practitioners who think for ourselves and are not pawns in the austerity game. It is time to be the change we want to see in the world.

I hope that those of you in statutory work will find a way to live into these values in social work teams across the UK. I also hope that those of you who are students will, as you move into the profession, find a way to hold on to the values you have been taught, in the face of the government's austerity policy and continuing indifference to human need. I also hope that as a profession we can move forward to challenge injustice wherever it is found and particularly that we will together challenge the injustice of the asylum system in the UK by activism, campaigning and practical action (in the voluntary sector and in statutory services).

Destitution should play no part in the asylum system. Help us end it.

References

Asylos (2017) 'Afghanistan: Situation of Young Male "Westernised" Returnees to Kabul.' Accessed 29/11/2018 at: https://asylos.eu/afghanistan-research-project.

British Association of Social Workers (2014) *The Code of Ethics for Social Work.* Accessed 28/11/2018 at: www.basw.co.uk/about-basw/code-ethics.

Care Act (2014) Accessed on 25/04/2019 at: https://www.legislation.gov.uk/ukpga/2014/23/contents/enacted.

IFSW (International Federation of Social Workers) (2014) 'Global Definition of Social Work.' Accessed 29/11/2018 at: www.ifsw.org/what-is-social-work/global-definition-of-social-work.

NRPF (No Recourse to Public Funds) Network (2018) Practice Guidance: Assessing and supporting children & families with NRPF. Accessed 28/11/2018 at: http://guidance.nrpfnetwork.org.uk/reader/practice-guidance-families.

Refugee Council (no date) 'The Facts about Asylum.' Accessed 28/11/2018 at: www.refugeecouncil.org.uk/policy_research/the_truth_about_asylum/facts_about_asylum_-_page_1.

Slough Judgement (2008) Accessed on 13/05/2019 at: https://publications.parliament.uk/pa/ld200708/ldjudgmt/jd080730/rmfc-1.htm.

Narrative 6
Learning from Andy

My name is Andy. I am 38 years old and I have been in the UK for 15 years. I am a failed asylum seeker and I am destitute.

My experience of getting legal help in the UK has been difficult. It has become harder since new government policies have cut the amount of lawyers you have access to. Lots of people don't have access to lawyers, which gives failed asylum seekers a massive disadvantage, and impacts on their mental health. Government policies on immigration mean that there is less funding, and fewer rights for immigrants. I think that if there is a change in UK government policy, it will make it easier for people to be treated fairly.

Being destitute has also been a massive challenge for me. I have been here for 15 years, sometimes finding myself on the streets, trying to find food and fighting the cold. Simple things become difficult: being hygienic, taking a shower, washing your clothes, brushing your teeth. You have to plan your day along those things. If you don't, it is easy to become depressed and get into a situation where you give up on yourself. I feel that destitution is a tactic from the government aimed at people who are failed asylum seekers, to try to make it tough for them so that they give up and volunteer to go home. I have been resilient so far, and I'm not going to give up.

My experience of community groups in my area has been fantastic. They have helped me, and I have met a lot of people who have been very kind and generous with their time and their energy. They have helped me a lot in my darkest hours, they have stood up to help me get accommodation and have access to food. Being part of groups has been fantastic for my well-being. Mingling with other people and doing different activities takes you away from what you are going through on a personal level, and it breaks up your day. I have learned a lot about plants and agriculture, and have had the opportunity to gain skills I might need in the future. It would be good to see even more groups that could provide people with more options for learning. Currently it is limited as to how you can study, college or university-wise. I find it helpful to spend time with other people through community groups – people who give you a positive vibe and energy. Being around the right people helps, and you can learn a lot.

I have been threatened with deportation on numerous occasions. This threat is something that has been created by the system to harass you and to intimidate you. But it's something that you always have to fight, and not give up. The Home Office is trying to break you down. If you continue to fight and be resilient, you can succeed.

I have been involved with a lot of activist and campaigning groups. I am the vice organising secretary for a political party that opposes the government in Zimbabwe. I am also the secretary for MiSol (Manchester Migrant Solidarity), and the co-chair for a charity called Destitute Immigrants. It keeps me busy. On Twitter, I speak out on the policies that the government makes, and the laws that affected me. I am also an ambassador for City of Sanctuary, where I speak at events about my fight, and how being an asylum seeker has impacted on my life. It keeps me busy and I like it. I feel like I'm contributing a little bit to the fight for humanity to be better, and for people to treat people better.

I have never had a social worker myself, although I have heard from other people that they can be quite helpful. If I was going to give a piece of advice to professionals working with people who are affected by these issues, it would be that you might not always get a thank you, or be shown appreciation by the people you are working with, but this is often because they are in a bad place. I would say that you shouldn't take it personally. People's energy and mindset are focused on other things, and it is important during these times to be patient with them and be sensitive. I believe that honesty is the best policy. Professionals should be honest with people about what they can help with and what they can't do too.

Chapter 12

Supporting Migrants and Asylum Seekers In and Beyond Immigration Detention in the UK

Joanne Vincett

At the peak of the migration crisis in Europe in 2015, the UK received 32,733 asylum-seeker applications, its highest number of applications since 2004; it has the ninth highest number of applications in the EU (Home Office 2016b). People seeking asylum in the UK may be detained (and re-detained) at any point in the process of their claims. But asylum seekers are not the only people in detention. Anyone subject to UK immigration control can be detained for administrative reasons, with no forewarning or permission to collect one's personal belongings, if already residing in the country, and no time limit in detention. Ensuing removal orders to one's country of origin can also be enforced with advance notice, anywhere between three months and a few hours prior to being escorted to the airport.

Migrants caught in this system of penal power live precarious lives of waiting and uncertainty, causing negative impact on their mental health and personal relationships (Turnbull 2016). Detainees may be separated from their family members and/or children, who may be placed into the care system, or they may have arrived in the UK as an unaccompanied minor and, after turning 18 years old, risk being sent back to a country with which they no longer identify. Although social workers and other frontline service workers may support people who have been detained or are at risk of being detained, or their family members, little is discussed in social work practice about how both supporters and those being supported may be affected by the detention regime.

From an inter-disciplinary perspective, this chapter aims to enhance our understanding of how migrants and asylum seekers may be impacted by immigration detention, and suggests possible activities to support them in and beyond detention. It provides an overview of the characteristics of immigration detention in the UK and inter-connected web of supporting and monitoring actors and relations inherent to the regime. This chapter also aims to be person-centred and offer constructive, practical guidance for human service workers, whether social work practitioners, managers or academics, while challenging them to maintain a critical stance towards the institutional structures and practices that may bound their thinking.

In the first section of this chapter, I provide an overview of who may be detained and why, how and where they may be detained. I emphasise the negative impact of detention on the emotional and mental well-being of detainees, particularly vulnerable people such as asylum seekers, women, people already suffering physical or mental health issues prior to detention (Bosworth and Kellezi 2015), and 'adults at risk' (Home Office 2016a, Section 11).

In the second section, I describe how the support services each facility offers detainees differ depending on the contractor for custodial care and operations tendered by the Home Office. I draw on my three-year doctoral research with Yarl's Wood Befrienders (YWB), a voluntary organisation that provides emotional support through a volunteer visiting scheme for detainees in Yarl's Wood Immigration Removal Centre (hereafter 'Yarl's Wood'). YWB is highlighted as an example of complementary voluntary sector support services that fills gaps in services offered by the centre to help detainees better cope with detention and decrease isolation (Vincett 2017).

In the final section, I discuss factors to consider for frontline service providers (practitioners and managers), social workers and academics/ students working with people who are at risk of being detained, currently in detention, about to be removed from the UK or recently released in the British community. I argue that this work requires compassion, empathy, resilience and safeguarding of those coping with the challenges of detention, but also self-care of the supporter. I conclude with key practical lessons to take away from this chapter.

Background of immigration detention in the UK - who may be detained, why and where

Anyone subject to UK immigration control and determined not to have a right to remain can be detained under the Immigration Act powers; however, detention is 'predominantly imposed as an administrative measure' (Kotsioni 2016, p.42). People can be detained upon arrival or after entry into the UK for various reasons, for example, not possessing the required travel documents to verify identification or to assess a child's age, or for 'overstaying' beyond a visa expiration date and failing to leave the UK.

People may be detained where they are living or working, on the street, while travelling, or at a required Home Office reporting appointment, at a designated police station or immigration reporting centre. If they are already living in the UK and detained outside their home, they are not permitted to return home and collect their belongings. Therefore, many arrive at detention facilities traumatised, confused and feeling like criminals, and with only the clothes they were wearing and possessions they were carrying when Home Office contracted escorts arrested them.

In 2016, a total of 28,908 people were detained in the UK (Home Office 2017a). The UK's immigration detention facilities are the second largest in Europe, with the capacity to hold approximately 5000 people at any given time (McGinley 2015). At the end of September 2017, 3125 people were in detention, 90 per cent men and 10 per cent women (Home Office 2017c).[1] The vast majority of them are held in eight immigration removal centres (IRCs) and three short-term holding facilities located near ports and airports across the UK. Some IRCs were previously prisons and are still managed by Her Majesty's Prison Service, but the Home Office has contracted most of them out to multinational companies to manage (e.g. G4S, GEO Group, Mitie Plc, Serco Plc) (Global Detention Project 2016; Silverman and Hajela 2015).

Prisons are also used as detention facilities, with an additional 330 people detained there at the end of the third quarter of 2017 (Home Office 2017c). Approximately 600 total places are available for immigration detainees (Silverman and Hajela 2015), whether or not they have criminal convictions or completed their criminal sentences (Bosworth 2009). Although detention should be used as 'a last resort' in cases of imminent removal from the UK, it is often used to prevent people from absconding or to continue

---

1   Data is from 30 November 2017, the most recent immigration statistics released by the UK Home Office at the time of writing.

their incarceration if the Home Office considers them a risk to the public (Hasselberg 2014; Refugee Council 2015).

Foreign national offenders who have served a criminal sentence in the UK may remain detained in prisons or transferred to immigration removal centres as they await their deportation. In some cases, they may not be notified in advance that they will not be released, but instead transferred to an IRC and remain in confinement, which raises issues of human rights. The 'automatic deportation of foreign criminals' was made possible by the UK Borders Act 2007 (McGuinness 2017, p.5) and later accelerated by Operation Nexus, beginning in 2012 as a plan between police forces and the Home Office to target deportation of 'high harm' offenders (e.g. involving weapons/firearms or serious violence, including sexual). Justified by protecting the public's safety, Operation Nexus has been criticised, and unsuccessfully legally challenged, that it 'had widened beyond its original remit' (McGuinness 2017, p.11) to lower-level criminal acts committed.

Nonetheless, foreign national offenders are a small group of people in detention compared to about 60 per cent[2] of detainees who are asylum seekers, as of the end of the third quarter in 2017 (Home Office 2017c). In 2015, at the height of the migration crisis in Europe, the UK reached its highest number of asylum-seeker applications since 2004, with 32,733 applications (Home Office 2016b). Adults seeking asylum (over age 18) can be detained at any point during the application process, for example at Home Office screening interviews to establish identity or age disputes, while awaiting an immigration caseworker's decision to allow or deny their entry into the UK or after the Home Office refuses their asylum claim and they have exhausted their appeals. Asylum seekers may also remain in detention while awaiting transfer to another European country where their asylum claim will be processed (in cases under the Dublin regulations where the Home Office establishes they have travelled through another European country prior to arriving the UK; see Right to Remain 2016). The common thread in all these cases, irrespective of the reasons for being detained, is the unknown and indeterminate time people remain detained.

---

2   This figure accounts for the people who have claimed asylum at some stage, according to the most recent statistics released quarterly by the Home Office at the time of writing this chapter. The Home Office acknowledges that 'the percentage increased from Q4 2016 due to previous under recording of some categories of asylum case types' (Home Office 2017a, Immigration Statistics Detention tables - dt_01 to pr_01, Notes).

In 2002, the Home Office changed the name of its facilities from 'immigration detention centre' to 'immigration removal centre' in the Nationality, Immigration and Asylum Act 2002, to emphasise removal intentions, but many people remain detained for months or years, and some detainees may not even be 'removable' (i.e. without identification or travel documents or considered 'stateless' from losing citizenship or nationality). In 2016, in Yarl's Wood, the main centre for women, including a small unit for families with children over age 18, only 21 per cent of people were removed from the UK, compared to the national average of 47 per cent across IRCs. In other words, 79 per cent of people detained in Yarl's Wood were eventually released into the community, leaving many 'questioning the initial decisions to detain' (Independent Monitoring Board 2017, p.15). It is not surprising that these centres have been referred to as 'symbolic spaces of suspension and liminality, where detainees are asked to "wait out" their status regularisations' (Silverman and Massa 2012, p.679).

Vulnerable people

Although in December 2010, the UK coalition government declared that it would end the immigration detention of children under the age of 18 years, children are still detained in disputed age cases, particularly if they are unaccompanied. Those accompanied by family are held together in Tinsley House near Gatwick Airport. The UN Committee on the Rights of the Child (UNCRC) has expressed eight key areas of concern about the UK's governmental practices. One contentious matter is how immigration officers subjectively assess the ages of children, resulting in some 'assessed as adults based on their physical appearance' (UNCRC 2016, p.20). The UNCRC has recommended that the UK government completely 'cease the detention of asylum-seeking and migrant children' (2016, p.21).

Another controversial practice by the Home Office is the postponed detention of young migrants who arrive as unaccompanied minors, termed 'young arrivers', and who, on turning 18 years of age, can be detained and face removal/deportation back to countries with which they no longer identify themselves (Godshaw 2017). Often, they have been through traumatic incidents before arriving in the UK and then placed into the care system, which can also vary in quality across the country. When they reach 18 and are deemed adults, the protective measures for minors are lifted (Godshaw 2017). They are threatened to be uprooted from the place where they sought safety and belonging, and sent back to where they may no longer feel any personal connection or know the language.

Some advocacy groups argue that certain types of vulnerable people, such as young arrivers (Godshaw 2017) and women (Girma *et al.* 2015), should be recognised as 'adults at risk' and, therefore, not suitable for detention. But the Home Office's list of specific categories of 'adults at risk' is limited to the following people, under the 2016 Immigration Act (Home Office 2016a, Section 11):

- those who suffer mental health ilnesses including post-traumatic stress disorder

- victims of torture, human trafficking or modern slavery, or sexual or gender-based violence (e.g. female genital mutilation)

- severely physically disabled people or those with grave health conditions

- pregnant women (not to be detained more than 72 hours; however, this limit can be 'extended up to one week with Ministerial approval' [Home Office 2016a, footnote 4])

- people aged 70 or over

- transgender or intersex individuals.

However, the Home Office acknowledges that this 'will not mean that no one at risk will ever be detained' (Home Office 2016a, Section 3). For example, individuals at risk can still be detained prior to their removal from the UK, except in certain cases of modern slavery. Controversy as to the subjective nature of assessing some of these at-risk categories is ongoing.

The impact of indefinite detention on emotional well-being and mental health

Regardless of people's migration stories and histories, the act of confinement in itself makes detainees vulnerable, especially when they may feel powerless to affect the outcome and receive no notice of the duration. The UK is the only country in Europe to have a policy of indefinite detention (Global Detention Project 2016) and there are ongoing campaigns for reform.[3]

---

3   See www.detentionforum.org.uk and https://detentionaction.org.uk

Although the majority, about 82 per cent of detainees, were held for less than two months as of the end of 2016, about 17 per cent were detained for two months to one year, and 1 per cent from one year to four years (Home Office 2017a).

Detention facilities vary in design, in mobility within the compound and in quality of custodial care, mostly provided by Home Office contracted multinational firms and the National Health Service (NHS). The controversial temporal and spatial nature of confinement makes IRCs similar to prisons, and a few facilities that were former prisons have had no interior transformations after being converted to IRCs. Segregation units used to isolate detainees for various reasons, such as punitive or physical health, are deemed justifiable by detention centre staff. Termed 'removal from association', detainees may be taken to individual isolation 'cells', and some facilities have separate solitary confinement rooms for mental health reasons (Independent Monitoring Board 2017). But whereas inmates in prison have a finite number of days to count down until being released, immigration detainees count the days up, with no idea when and how they will leave the detention centre. The accumulated stress and anxiety from an unknown future, fear of removal, isolation and denial of liberty have detrimental effects on migrants' physical and mental health (British Medical Association Medical Ethics Committee 2017; Steel *et al.* 2011).

The negative impact of long-term and indefinite detention on detainees' emotional well-being and mental health has been repeatedly demonstrated in academic studies and practitioner reports, with subsequent recommendations to the Home Office on policy reform but with no significant success (Bosworth and Kellezi 2012, 2015; British Medical Association Medical Ethics Committee 2017; Centre for Mental Health 2017; Connelly *et al.* 2015; Her Majesty's Inspectorate of Prisons 2015; Shaw 2016). Pregnant women (Girma *et al.* 2015; Shaw 2016) and people suffering physical or mental health issues are particularly at risk of compounded distress from confinement in detention (Bosworth and Kellezi 2015). Research has identified that extremely vulnerable people, such as women and asylum seekers, tend to have higher levels of depression (Bosworth and Kellezi 2015).

Similarly, the Centre for Mental Health's (2017) assessment of IRCs in England found the level of mental distress to be significantly higher in Yarl's Wood, the main IRC for women. Kellezi and Bosworth's (2016) study on mental health, suicidal thoughts and self-harm in Yarl's Wood emphasises the gender-specific issues and the multiple sources of support women seek to cope with life in detention, including contact with people outside the centre via mobile phone and in person, such as with family, friends and visitors from charities. The following section describes the services offered inside detention centres and how they are monitored. It highlights Yarl's Wood as an example and draws on an ethnographic study from 2016 to 2018 of the charity Yarl's Wood Befrienders, which offers befriending support for women detained there.

Services inside detention centres – monitoring custodial services in IRCs

Services for detainees offered inside detention facilities and offered by the voluntary sector greatly vary across the facilities. To learn more about a specific IRC, the Independent Monitoring Board (IMB) produces public annual reports that review each removal centre and some short-term holding facilities.[4] IMB members are independent volunteers who have unrestricted access inside the facilities and make monthly visits to monitor the day-to-day living conditions and ensure that duty of care and human dignity are upheld. The IMB also plays a vital role in handling formal complaints from detainees and feeding them back to IRC management.

Her Majesty's Inspectorate of Prisons (HMIP) is another independent monitoring body for IRCs, but a statutory one in order to fulfil the UK's obligation under the Optional Protocol to the UN Convention against Torture and other Cruel, Inhuman or Degrading Treatment or Punishment (HMIP 2017b). HMIP visits are unannounced and less frequent than IMB visits, once every two years for approximately eight days (HMIP 2017a) or up to 19 days (HMIP 2015). HMIP visits are more like inspections or audits to assess facilities based on four 'healthy establishment' tests (safety, respect, activities and preparation for removal and release) by gathering qualitative and quantitative data from detainees, staff members and other stakeholders (HMIP 2017a, p.11). Although both IMB and HMIP make recommendations to the Home Office and contractors for improvements, with updates in subsequent reports as to the level of progress made, following the recommendations is by discretion and not obligatory.

---

4   See www.imb.org.uk

An example: Yarl's Wood Immigration Removal Centre[5]

Yarl's Wood is the main IRC for women, with a small unit for families with children over age 18 and a short-term holding facility for men. It has been the centre of public scrutiny in recent years due to allegations of derogatory and abusive staff treatment of female detainees, as reported by *Channel 4 News* in March 2015 (Lampard and Marsden 2016), and ongoing complaints about healthcare services (Independent Monitoring Board 2016). Since then, it has undergone positive changes in custodial staff, mental health services and social activities offered for emotional support (Independent Monitoring Board 2017), with continued pressure from advocacy groups, monitoring bodies and independent evaluations (see Lampard and Marsden 2016; Shaw 2016).

In Yarl's Wood, with a monthly average of 302 detainees in 2016 (Independent Monitoring Board 2017), all detainees undergo a 'reception process' on arrival, and are offered medical appointments with contracted healthcare staff and an induction programme to explain the rules, regulations and services of the facility. They are allocated a bed in an ensuite single or twin room with furnishings such as a wardrobe and television/DVD with Freeview stations. They are given a tour and issued basic mobile phones without cameras and internet access capability, but with £10 credit. Yarl's Wood is a 'cashless' environment and detainees receive £0.71 per day in their accounts which are managed by a local credit union. In addition, there are select paid work opportunities throughout the centre to earn £1 per hour (e.g. hairdresser, cleaner, post room assistant). The Home Office has been publically criticised for paying 'slave wages', labour exploitation and excluding detainees from minimum wage legislation, and is being legally challenged (*The Guardian* 2017).

Yarl's Wood was designed as a 'relaxed regime' compared to prisons during the expansion of the British detention estate in the early 2000s (Shaw 2004, p.8), and detainees are called 'residents', rather than 'inmates' as in prisons. Activities are unstructured and detainees can manage their own schedules and move freely within the centre during the day, but are locked within their residential units at night. Professional counsellors on site, through the Kaleidoscope charity, offer group talking therapies and sessions to improve emotional well-being. 'Welfare officers' are also available to assist

---

5   The services and activities available to detainees can change depending on the contracted management of the centre. What is described in this section is what was current at the time of writing.

detainees with matters relating to their bank accounts, personal property, bail applications, filing complaints, or voluntary return and resettlement. Access to legal advice may be one of the most crucial services, and weekly surgeries are offered by the Legal Service Commission, but on a limited basis, and are usually oversubscribed.

Other activities for detainees include: arts and crafts, cooking together with up to six other detainees in the 'cultural kitchen', badminton, aerobics and yoga in the sports hall, film viewings in a small cinema, basic English-speaking classes, and hair, nail and beauty treatments in the salon. There are also rooms for legal appointments, religious activities (a multi-faith prayer room, Sheikh and Buddhist temples), a library, post room with fax and copy machines to manage their legal cases, and an IT room with limited access to websites (social media sites and Skype are blocked). There is an internal shop with consumable and non-consumable goods, including the possibility to order culturally specific items. Despite the amenities available, few detainees see their temporary 'residence' as a holiday resort.

Family and friends may visit at designated social visiting hours in the visits hall under surveillance. Aside from sparse legal visitors, detainees have limited physical contact with the outside world, unless their family and friends live nearby, and they can often feel isolated. Therefore, social visits from local charities, community or faith-based groups and volunteer visitor groups are welcomed.

The volunteer visitor group: Yarl's Wood Befrienders

There is a volunteer visitor group attached to every IRC across the UK which can be contacted through the umbrella organisation called AVID (Association of Visitors to Immigration Detainees).[6] Volunteer visitors are independent of the immigration regime. They offer a listening ear, and emotional and practical support and advice (e.g. clothing, shoes, blankets, mobile phone credit, suitcases, assistance with forms and writing letters). Visitor groups offer a range of support services, such as visiting schemes, campaigning, legal casework and post-release support.

Since Yarl's Wood was first built in 2001, the charity Yarl's Wood Befrienders (YWB) has been running a one-to-one visiting scheme that matches trained volunteers in the community with detainees who request a befriender. Befrienders visit their allocated detainees once a week for the

---

6   http://aviddetention.org.uk

entire duration they are detained. With the UK's policy of no time limit in detention, the uncertainty of how long a person is detained can create emotional and mental turmoil. People are continuously entering and leaving detention with no advance notice of when they will be detained, released or removed. Families are separated and personal relationships are disrupted. In my immersive research with the charity on befriending, I often visited detainees who were mothers in agony at being separated from their children:

> She had two boys [in China], 13 and 9 years old. One lived with her older sister, the other lived with her mother. She had been in touch with them at the beginning when she first arrived in the UK, but then couldn't get through to them and she couldn't even remember their phone numbers now. She broke down sobbing. (Fieldnotes, April 2016)

In 2016–17, YWB visited 222 women individually (YWB 2017). Around half were seeking asylum as victims of trafficking, physical or sexual violence/abuse, female genital mutilation, torture, forced marriage, or because they were in danger of persecution for their sexual, religious or political affiliation. Volunteer visitors may signpost detainees to supporting charities relevant to their cases, such as Medical Justice, UK Lesbian & Gay Immigration Group, Hibiscus, Bail for Immigration Detainees (BID), the Salvation Army and the Modern Slavery Helpline, the Helen Bamber Foundation, Women for Refugee Women, and local refugee support organisations. Befrienders have also acted as 'first responders' for the National Referral Mechanism (NRM) to identify potential victims of trafficking or modern slavery (Home Office 2017b).

With the stress and trauma of first arriving in a detention centre, detainees may not be aware of their rights to free legal advice at the surgeries offered inside detention centres or to apply for release on bail after seven days (BID 2016). Volunteer visitors offer their support in the spirit of compassion to help detainees build awareness of the services offered in the IRC. Some befrienders have written letters to their MPs and the Home Office in support of a detainee's release, helped detainees write letters and formal complaints and fill out forms, or contacted detainees' solicitors or family members on their behalf (Vincett 2017). Detainees with no English skills or literacy or who have learning disabilities are more vulnerable and necessitate additional support since IRCs may not be inclusive of diverse needs.

Factors to consider for frontline support service workers – self-care for the vulnerable supporter

'Going the extra mile' requires compassion, empathy, resilience and safeguarding of those coping with the challenges of detention, but also entails self-care of those in supporting roles. Following the British Medical Association Medical Ethics Committee's (2017) recommendation, healthcare professionals and organisations with frontline support service workers should 'provide training and continued support in health and well-being issues for all those working with detained individuals' (p.8). People released into the community may continue to feel as if they are in an extension of detention and require ongoing support as well (Klein and Williams 2012).

Supporters and advocates in prolonged contact with vulnerable or suffering individuals are at risk of vicarious (or secondary) trauma (Jirek 2015) or compassion fatigue (Vincett 2018). This involves those in supporting roles who are affected by the trauma of those individuals experiencing distress through the continual shared pain and suffering and empathic interaction (Bride 2012; Jirek 2015). Pearlman and McKay (2008) point out the harm in the 'cumulative effect of contact' with suffering individuals, plus the helper's sense of 'responsibility to help and at times inability to fulfill that commitment' (p.1). In my research fieldnotes, I often described feeling helpless in alleviating detainees' suffering. In the following excerpt, I illustrate mixed empathic emotions during a telephone call with a woman I befriended. After I referred her to the Salvation Army as a victim of sex trafficking, she was interviewed, released and given government accommodation in Glasgow.

> I feel so helpless. I tell her I don't know how I can help her. I'm going through things in my head about what I can do. … She starts to cry. I feel so horrible not being able to do anything for her and not knowing more technical Mandarin words. I can feel this whole issue weighing on the back of my mind. … I tell her that I'm going to find another charity there in Glasgow that may be able to help her. I'm so afraid of overpromising. … I hang up the phone and feel so dejected. (Fieldnotes, April 2016)

Practitioners, researchers and students are equally likely to be impacted at any stage of their research or client/participant relationship. Stress can affect paid staff or unpaid volunteers, regardless of their level of expertise. Even experienced individuals can be affected by the ups and downs of the emotional rollercoaster often associated with supporting migrants and asylum seekers in or at risk of detention.

Conclusion

As Kotsioni (2016, p.49) rightly points out, 'the act of migration is stressful in its own right as it involves uprooting, multiple losses, separation from family members, disruption of daily life, and uncertainty about the future'. Migrants and asylum seekers may have ended their journeys from the countries they departed, but they embark on a new one of settling and building new lives while continuing to live in fear of detention and removal, or live in limbo in detention. Whether or not they have been through the detention system, it is important for support workers to be familiar with the process of how people are detained and the environment where they are held in order to better understand what they have endured or are at risk of enduring. Particularly for those who have been detained before, even being released in the community is often not the end of emotional turmoil. Compassion, courage and emotional resilience are required to effectively support people who are in/out/at risk of detention or being re-detained. Special attention and sensitivity need to be taken towards minors and more vulnerable adults at risk, including those with learning, literacy and language disadvantages.

Safeguarding of those in support roles is equally important as safeguarding clients. Frontline service workers, volunteers and researchers must be prepared for the emotional labour that is inherent in this area of work. In the emotionally charged setting of immigration detention and the surrounding context, managing our emotions can present challenges while attending to others' emotions. Training in resilience and creating a self-care plan incorporating mental health resources to refer to is essential should predicaments arise. Ongoing self-care is required in order to sustain supporting roles and serve those who most need our assistance.

Key lessons for frontline support service workers

- Support service workers should undertake training on cultural sensitivity and diversity awareness, and on issues that may specifically affect people who identify themselves as LGBTIQ (lesbian, gay, bisexual, transgender/transsexual, intersex, queer).

- For clients who may not speak English or another language in common, use professional interpreters or seek volunteers to communicate with them and check with clients on the quality and understanding of interpreters.

- Obtain contact information for the Independent Monitoring Board representatives for each applicable immigration removal centre where clients may be detained. Encourage clients to report any complaints about the facilities or staff treatment to the IMB. Assist with writing any letters together with clients who have learning disabilities, or literacy issues, or lack English language skills.

- Maintain regular contact with detained clients to demonstrate support. Visit in person, if at all possible, or refer them to a community volunteer visitor group and correspond with the volunteer visitor(s) (see AVID).

- Even if you may not fully understand the evolving legal frameworks governing immigration detention, work closely with other volunteers and practitioners assisting in the client's legal case and charities specialising in the immigration and asylum system (for a succinct, regularly updated guide with recommended action plans for people going through the British system, see the Right to Remain toolkit[7]).

- Safeguard people who are in/out of detention and at risk of being detained by not sharing their personal information with other parties unless they grant permission. Uphold and regularly review data protection policies to ensure compliance since they can change over time.

- Undertake formal training on emotional resilience, well-being and mental health issues that may be encountered, such as vicarious (or secondary) trauma or compassion fatigue, and have access to regular professional supervision.

- Practise compassion for clients, and yourself; prepare a self-care plan to lead a healthy lifestyle with a list of resources to call on should emotional predicaments arise.

---

7   https://righttoremain.org.uk/toolkit

References

Bail for Immigration Detainees (BID) (2016) *How to Get Out of Detention: The Self-Help Guide for Detainees*. London: BID.

Bosworth, M. (2009) *Visiting Foreign National Prisoners: Findings from a Scoping Study*. Oxford: Association of Visitors to Immigration Detainees.

Bosworth, M. and Kellezi, B. (2012) *Quality of Life in Detention: Results from MQLD Questionnaire Data Collected in IRC Yarl's Wood, IRC Tinsley House, and IRC Brook House, August 2010–June 2011*. Oxford: Centre for Criminology, University of Oxford.

Bosworth, M. and Kellezi, B. (2015) *Quality of Life in Detention: Results from MQLD Questionnaire Data Collected in IRC Campsfield House, IRC Yarl's Wood, IRC Colnbrook, and IRC Dover, September 2013–August 2014*. Oxford: Centre for Criminology, University of Oxford.

Bride, B.E. (2012) 'Secondary Traumatic Stress.' In C.R. Figley (ed.) *Encyclopaedia of Trauma: An Interdisciplinary Guide*, pp.601–602. Thousand Oaks, CA: Sage.

British Medical Association Medical Ethics Committee (BMA) (2017) *Locked Up, Locked Out: Health and Human Rights in Immigration Detention*. London: BMA.

Centre for Mental Health (2017) *Immigration Removal Centres in England: A Mental Health Needs Analysis*. Accessed 29/11/2018 at: www.centreformentalhealth.org.uk/immigration-removal-centres-england.

Connelly, E., Eadie, N., Mabruk, J. and McGinley, A. (2015) *Rethinking 'Vulnerability' in Detention: A Crisis of Harm*. London: The Detention Forum.

Girma, M., Kershaw, I., Lousley, G., Radice, S. and Walter, N. (2015) *I Am Human: Refugee Women's Experiences of Detention in the UK*. London: Women for Refugee Women.

Global Detention Project (2016) *United Kingdom Immigration Detention Profile*. Geneva: Global Detention Project.

Godshaw, D. (2017) *Don't Dump Me in a Foreign Land: Immigration Detention and Young Arrivers*. Crawley: Gatwick Detainees Welfare Group.

Guardian, The (2017) 'Immigration detainees bring legal challenge against £1 an hour "slave" wages.' 28 June. Accessed 28/11/2018 at: www.theguardian.com/uk-news/2017/jun/28/immigration-detainees-legal-challenge-slave-wages.

Hasselberg, I. (2014) 'Coerced to leave: Punishment and the surveillance of foreign-national offenders in the UK.' *Surveillance & Society*, 12, 4, 471–484.

HMIP (Her Majesty's Inspectorate of Prisons) (2015) *Report on the Unannounced Inspection of Yarl's Wood Immigration Removal Centre, 13 April–1 May 2015*. London: HMSO.

HMIP (Her Majesty's Inspectorate of Prisons) (2017a) *Report on an Unannounced Inspection of Yarl's Wood Immigration Removal Centre, 5–7, 12–16 June 2017*. London: HMSO.

HMIP (Her Majesty's Inspectorate of Prisons) (2017b) *Inspection Framework*. London: HMIP. Accessed on 13/05/2019 at: www.justiceinspectorates.gov.uk/hmiprisons/wp-content/uploads/sites/4/2014/02/1.-INSPECTION-FRAMEWORK-May-2017-1.pdf.

Home Office (2016a) *Immigration Act 2016: Guidance on Adults at Risk in Immigration Detention*. London: HMSO.

Home Office (2016b) *National Statistics: Summary*. London: HMSO.

Home Office (2017a) *Immigration Statistics, October to December 2016: Detention Data Tables - dt_01 to pr_01*. London: HMSO.

Home Office (2017b) *National Referral Mechanism Guidance: Adult (England and Wales)*. London: HMSO.

Home Office (2017c) *National Statistics: How Many People are Detained or Returned?* London: HMSO.

Independent Monitoring Board (IMB) (2016) *Annual Report 2015: Yarl's Wood Independent Monitoring Board*. Accessed 28/11/2018 at: www.imb.org.uk/report/yarls-wood-2015-annual-report.

Independent Monitoring Board (IMB) (2017) *Annual Report of the Independent Monitoring Board at Yarl's Wood Immigration Removal Centre*. Accessed 28/11/2018 at: www.imb.org.uk/app/uploads/2017/06/Yarls-Wood-2016-1-1.pdf.

Jirek, S.L. (2015) 'Soul pain: The hidden toll of working with survivors of physical and sexual violence.' *SAGE Open*, 5, 3, 1–13.

Kellezi, B. and Bosworth, M. (2016) *Mental Health, Suicidal Thoughts and Self-Harm Inside Immigration Detention*. Accessed 28/11/2018 at: https://papers.ssrn.com/sol3/papers.cfm?abstract_id=2867358.

Klein, A. and Williams, L. (2012) 'Immigration detention in the community: Research on the experiences of migrants released from detention centres in the UK.' *Population, Space and Place*, 18, 6, 741–753.

Kotsioni, I. (2016) 'Detention of migrants and asylum-seekers: The challenge for humanitarian actors.' *Refugee Survey Quarterly*, 35, 2, 41–55.

Lampard, K. and Marsden, E. (2016) *Independent Investigation into Concerns about Yarl's Wood Immigration Removal Centre*. Accessed 28/11/2018 at: www.verita.net/wp-content/uploads/2016/04/Independent-investigation-into-concerns-about-Yarls-Wood-immigration-removal-centre-Serco-plc-Kate-Lampard-Ed-Marsden-January-2016-1.pdf.

McGinley, A. (2015) *Hidden Stories*. London: Association of Visitors to Immigration Detainees.

McGuinness, T. (2017) *Deportation of Foreign National Offenders*. Briefing Paper 8062. London: House of Commons.

Nationality, Immigration and Asylum Act (2002) Accessed on 13/05/2019 at: http://www.legislation.gov.uk/ukpga/2002/41/schedule/3.

Pearlman, L.A. and McKay, L. (2008) *Vicarious Trauma*. Pasadena, CA: Headington Institute.

Refugee Council (2015) *Detention in the Asylum System*. London: British Refugee Council.

Right to Remain (2016) *Right to Remain Toolkit*. London: Right to Remain.

Shaw, S. (2004) *Report of the Inquiry into the Disturbance and Fire at Yarl's Wood Removal Centre*. London: HMSO.

Shaw, S. (2016) *Review into the Welfare in Detention of Vulnerable Persons: A Report to the Home Office by Stephen Shaw*. London: HMSO.

Silverman, S.J. and Hajela, R. (2015) *Immigration Detention in the UK*. Oxford: The Migration Observatory, University of Oxford.

Silverman, S.J. and Massa, E. (2012) 'Why immigration detention is unique.' *Population Space and Place*, 18, 6, 677–686.

Steel, Z., Liddell, B.J., Bateman-Steel, C.R. and Zwi, A.B. (2011) 'Global protection and the health impact of migration interception.' *Plos Medicine*, 8, 6, 1–5.

Turnbull, S. (2016) '"Stuck in the middle": Waiting and uncertainty in immigration detention.' *Time & Society*, 25, 1, 61–79.

UN Committee on the Rights of the Child (UNCRC) (2016) *Concluding Observations on the Fifth Periodic Report of the United Kingdom of Great Britain and Northern Ireland.* Geneva, Switzerland: UNCRC. Accessed on 12/3/2017 at: www.unicef. org.uk/babyfriendly/wp-content/uploads/sites/2/2016/08/UK-CRC-Concluding-observations-2016-2.pdf.

Vincett, J. (2017) 'Befriending kinships in immigration detention in the UK.' *Discover Society* 44. Accessed 28/11/2018 at: https://discoversociety.org/2017/05/02/befriending-kinships-in-immigration-detention-in-the-uk.

Vincett, J. (2018) 'Researcher self-care in organizational ethnography: Lessons from overcoming compassion fatigue.' *Journal of Organizational Ethnography*, 7, 1, 44–58.

Yarl's Wood Befrienders (YWB) (2017) *Yarl's Wood Befrienders: Trustees' Annual Report for the Year Ended March 2017.* Accessed 28/11/2018 at: http://apps. charitycommission.gov.uk/Accounts/Ends60/0001143160_AC_20170331_E_C. PDF.

Narrative 7
Learning from Aida

My name is Aida. I am an asylum seeker. I came to the UK in 2006. Until now, I haven't received a decision from the Home Office, but I am a strong woman.

After I claimed asylum, I had to sign at Dallas Court. The last time I went, they sent me to Yarl's Wood. I strongly feel that they must close all detention. Yarl's Wood is very hard, I was threated by officers when I refused to eat. They open your door at 9am, and, one time, they were very scary when they couldn't see me because I was in the bathroom. They thought I has escaped, but that place is not somewhere you can escape from. The walls are so high. Even if you did, it is in the forest not a town, so which road can you go?

Even after you leave detention, it is very hard. I came here to save my life, my family were killed in my country. I was tortured, but I feel like I am suffering double torture in this country. My mental health is not good, nothing is good for me, it is very hard. The process of waiting is so hard; we've all been waiting so long. I am so tired of waiting. All the problems are because of the Home Office. If the Home Office did a good job, there would be no sickness or mental health problems. They need to provide amnesty; give all asylum seekers papers and allow us to work so we can give taxes to this country.

It can be difficult with solicitors; I've changed solicitors several times. The solicitor I had in detention could not represent me for free after I left, so I had to find another one. When I left detention, the organisation Women Asylum Seekers Together (WAST) helped me find my current solicitor. There are many different organisations that support you in Yarl's Wood: Growing Together, Refugee and Asylum Seeker Participatory Action Research (RAPAR), Sanctuary, WAST. RAPAR sent someone to see me in Yarl's Wood to bring me clothes. Outside detention, too, there are many good community groups in Manchester who are helping me with everything. They do many things for me, like paying for my transport when I wanted to go to Liverpool to make a fresh claim. When I was in a tent, they gave me money. Accessing community groups and seeing people helps when you're stressed but when you go home and see your four walls, the stress comes back again. You're thinking about what will happen tomorrow, what letter will I receive?

I experienced destitution for a long time. In 2010, I started receiving vouchers that you could use in the supermarket: £35. It was hard, but I survived. It's a little better now, because they give you a card that you can use in all the shops, but you can't withdraw money. Sometimes you need cash, especially for public transport. I live in Old Trafford and it is too far to walk to Piccadilly, but sometimes I don't have money for a ticket. I feel this is an injustice.

I would like it if social workers intervened and spoke to the Home Office, to help us. When I first came here, my foot was broken and they gave me a social worker. She helped me a lot and did everything for me, for one year, and left me once my foot was healed. But, I was worried every time I saw her because I was thinking she was working for the Home Office and they had sent her. Confidence is important, and I wasn't sure if my social worker would tell the Home Office things I told her.

Chapter 13

Age Assessments of Unaccompanied Minors

Observations from an Appropriate Adult

Elaine Ortiz

I work as an appropriate adult for young people undergoing age assessments in relation to their status in the UK. I have attended good age assessments that were conducted respectfully. I have also attended others that were conducted like an interrogation. The former group of social workers had received training on conducting age assessments. As a result, they understood the process and its potential impact on the young person. Based on my role and experiences to date, I advocate for a child-centred and rights-based model of age assessment, so that when it must be carried out under current legislation and policies (Section 55 of the Borders, Citizenship and Immigration Act 2009; Home Office 2018; Modern Slavery Act 2015 (Section 51)), it can be done in a way that acknowledges the specific health, cultural and communication needs of unaccompanied minors.

That said, I do not feel that age assessments should be conducted. It is my view, and the view of many others in the field – including social workers themselves (British Association of Social Workers (BASW) 2015b) – that we should always work on the premise that the child is the age that they claim to be. The House of Lords Joint Committee on Human Rights (2013, p.26) asserts that 'if assessed incorrectly, children could be accommodated inappropriately, supported insufficiently and be placed at risk of harm, detention and deportation'. There is no reliable medically evidenced method for assessing age (BASW 2015a; Doctors of the World 2015), and all age assessment methods – medical or otherwise – are 'complex, often intrusive and unreliable' (Asylum Information Database 2015, p.6; also Immigration Law Practitioners' Association 2007). The process is 'no more than a best guess' (BASW 2015a, p.2).

All procedures need to implement the benefit of the doubt principle which is recognised in the legal principles governing age assessments (Home Office 2018). Only if there is a significant concern that the individual is not a child should such a process be considered. However, current guidance stipulates that the procedure can be invoked if a child is suspected to be an adult, their age is doubted by the Home Office and they have little or no reliable evidence of their age (ibid.). An imbalance in current practice is that there are guidelines and procedures to dispute the age of an unaccompanied minor, but not to establish it (Refugee Studies Centre 2010). In line with the existing social work guidance, I would propose that the focus of any assessment should be making sure that appropriate services are offered (Association of Directors of Children's Services (ADCS) 2015), and that all procedures are carried out in the best interest of the child and uphold a child-centred and child-friendly perspective (UNICEF 2013).

If and when an age assessment is deemed to be required, there must be consideration of several factors. First concerns an understanding of the trauma experienced by many unaccompanied young people. This has implications for communication during the actual age assessment. Second, the age assessment meeting should be a formality that takes place within broader multidisciplinary practice. Such practice should focus on the young person's overall needs and processes to ensure that identified needs are met regardless of the outcome of the assessment. Finally, social workers should be required to undergo specialist training to carry them out. While each one of these points is linked to the other, I shall talk about them in turn.

Communicating about trauma and understanding traumatic experiences

Children who undergo age-assessment interviews may have experienced trafficking and abuse in their country of origin and during the migration journey (Boyden et al. 2002; Every Child Protected Against Trafficking (ECPAT) UK and Missing People 2016; Mougne 2010; UNICEF 2017). Such traumatic experiences can have an impact on their well-being and their communication skills (Kaplan et al. 2016). While the ADCS (2015) guidance for age assessments highlights these issues and stipulates that assessments should account for these various factors, it is my observation that they are frequently ignored. ADCS (2015, p.6) stresses that:

> Age disputing a child or young person can affect the way they engage with their social worker, and the repeated questioning of their credibility and identity can leave children and young people feeling angry and bewildered. In this context, it is important that age assessments are not undertaken unless absolutely necessary.

Questioning children about traumatic events needs to be handled with care and specialist training should be offered to all practitioners who are required to complete age assessments (ibid.). Instead, I've witnessed social workers just stating, 'Next question!', after exploring traumatic events which children have experienced or even the making of inappropriate comments, questioning and disbelieving the child.

When an unaccompanied asylum-seeking child first arrives in the UK they are bombarded with information. There will be placement meetings, social workers and carers to meet, they have to enrol at school, take English classes – numerous new people, systems and processes that can be overwhelming for a young person. Having your age disputed amid this rapid change can lead to further feelings of stress, anxiety, loss and isolation. A young man I work with constantly points out how his documentation states that his age is disputed. He found it deeply upsetting to be told that he was lying about his age. Unaccompanied minors also talk to each other and hear 'horror stories' about what happens in the age-assessment interviews. During the interview, children I work with noted that they are so nervous of 'tripping up' that they retreat. Things that are really important for them to say they don't bring up. The same happens with their asylum applications. Things that I know about them haven't come up because they usually only have one session with a lawyer and they get so worked up about it because they are desperate to get it right. As they are worked up and stressed, they don't say important issues like 'I'm at risk of death if I return home.' If they have a good lawyer, the lawyer will ask children to provide that information specifically, but this may not always be the case.

Research also tells us that consistent testimonies are difficult to obtain from children – further compounded during the age assessments through the use of interpreters in a process fraught with anxiety (Bianchini 2011; UNICEF 2013). Even the Home Office (2016, p.34) guidelines for processing children's asylum claims stresses that 'children do not often provide as much detail as adults in recalling experiences and may often express their fears differently from adults'.

Social workers need to be trained to conduct interviews that don't sound like an interrogation and to ask questions that don't sound like accusations. Examples I've witnessed include – 'So, all the men left the women. What are women doing now? They are just left to fight the Taliban on their own!', or going into details about the torture young people experienced, without an explanation as to why they need to know such details or any consideration as to what the impact of this will be on the young person concerned. In another age assessment, a social worker just kept repeating the same question – 'So how old are you? Why don't you know your date of birth?' She could not get her head around differences between the Jalali and Gregorian calendars – or that a child may struggle to explain these differences. This happened after six sessions of age assessment. Good practice requires a social worker to look this information up between sessions, rather than expect a child to explain why they may not know their date of birth as calculated in a Gregorian calendar (ADCS 2015). Equally, social workers conducting such assessments should have knowledge about different communication styles, attitudes towards authority and all other relevant cultural information that applies to the context in which the child grew up (ibid.).

A good age assessment I attended was like a conversation. There was less disbelief. Social workers asked for information and said thank you. It was respectful, appropriate, child-friendly and done in one session, with ample involvement of other professionals. Furthermore, we need to think carefully how information is provided to a child before, during and after the age-assessment interview(s) (ADCS 2015; UNICEF 2013). Even when written information is presented – which rarely happens – it needs to be in a language and format a child can understand (The Children's Society 2012). Focus should be on building rapport with the child and making them feel safe (ADCS 2015).

A need for preparation and follow-up

During the age assessment, social workers focus on the timeline, to see if it matches their understanding as to when the child should have been at school or other life course markers. However, that cannot be worked out in a couple of interviews. Mental preparation is important – just feeling supported to know that they may go into a hostile environment. Environments in which age assessments are conducted are hostile because there is a culture of disbelief (The Children's Society 2012; Immigration Law Practitioners' Association 2007) and I don't think young people are prepared for that mentally. They close off instead. Such a culture places them at risk of harm and exploitation and enables the best interests of the child to be ignored. Children themselves report that they find the process very difficult and upsetting, leaving them with feelings of distrust (ADCS 2015). ECPAT (in Joint Committee on Human Rights 2013) stresses that the act of disbelief itself has further consequences for the mental health of unaccompanied children.

Instead of the interview being the point at which all the information is gathered, it should be preceded by life story work – with a family map worked out with the children prior to the assessment. Such work may be difficult for a child and young person to do with social workers (Kohli 2005), but easier if conducted by someone the child or young person knows and trusts. This, and other forms of preparation, would be highly relevant. Children need to have an opportunity to address any relevant gaps or inconsistencies in information (ADCS 2015).

This doesn't just apply to the age-assessment process. When we worked with young people in the Calais camp through the Hummingbird Project (initially running the health clinic and then a safe space for young people), it took a long time to build relationships with them. Young people have travelled across the continent, sometimes further, and you are just another adult who potentially can be part of the government, trying to find out information about them. During the Calais camp evictions, some young people closed up again because they started to fear that we had started to work – or had worked throughout – with the French government. We constantly had to prove that we were not linked to the government through the police, immigration or other services. They had no trust in authorities, particularly the police. The same mistrust can apply to social workers who act as agents of the local government (Kohli 2005). We had to work very hard to develop trust within the Hummingbird Safe Space, as we wanted the young people to have a degree of trust in the police, so that they would be able to call them if they were in danger. However, they were adamantly of a view that the police were the ones who would harm them, either in their own countries or in Europe. In their eyes, police were the abusers. Getting the young people we work with to understand authority – and also the rule of law – has been a huge challenge.

This is particularly important as unaccompanied young people don't understand how child protection services link to the rule of law. In their countries, rule of law may only be linked to military activity and actual harm inflicted on them and their families. You can see why they would close off, considering their experiences. It takes them a long time to work out differences between social workers, teachers and police and to understand how the rule of law connects all public service professionals in this country.

Good intensive preparation work would help prepare the young people for the age-assessment process, but there is limited guidance on such preparatory work. Recent age-assessment guidance for Scotland (Scottish Government 2018) highlights issues which I have found relevant in my experience to date. These guidelines stress that the age assessment should be carried out by someone who is trained and who knows which information is relevant, and who ensures that prior support for the young person is available through the appointment of appropriate adults or other advocates. That would also help to make the age-assessment process itself more of a formality. It doesn't have to be so intense. The way age assessments can be currently set up feels as if it is the biggest test of the young person's life. More collaborative work with the professionals who are already involved with the young person is crucial. Processes should include observation of their behaviour and relationships over several encounters and allow input from all who play a role in the child's life (Bianchini 2011). Time is needed to build trust with the individual who may be a separated child and to allow for proper recollection and sharing of information about the child's own story (Separated Children in Europe Programme 2012). This would enable the process to serve a purpose of a holistic assessment of vulnerability and needs, focusing on the young person's entire life (Separated Children in Europe Programme 2012; UNICEF 2013).

Support should also continue after the age assessment, to ensure young people are not further traumatised by the experience. A follow-up after the session should be provided by a counsellor or another social worker, to check if the person is okay, have a cup of tea, and provide information on whom to contact and what their support network is like. If a child is in foster care, they have the benefit of going back to their carers, who will – it is hoped – know to look after them and be available to talk if need be. But we don't know enough about family networks when we have family reunifications, because they have been set up quickly and without sufficient follow-up and prior checks. We don't know if family bonds actually exist to ensure that the child is supported afterwards. What we are seeing, more recently, is that when a child is placed with family members these placements are breaking down. We are making an assumption that the family placement is a best option, but we don't know, as not all local authorities conduct comprehensive assessments. Hence, there should be more consideration as to where children are accommodated and if they are sufficiently supported within that placement (ADCS 2015).

The worst age assessment I have attended included four to five meetings, each spanning several hours. Each was conducted as an interrogation. The questions that are asked in any age assessments bring up traumas. In each one I have attended, children were asked about incidents of sexual, physical abuse or torture they had experienced and witnessed. Without relevant support prior, during and after an interview which explores such issues, such assessments do not constitute child-friendly practice. Professional practice of any kind cannot explore a child's traumatic experiences and then expect the child to just get on with their day. None of the assessments I attended included a follow-up with the young people. The only information provided in the end was 'Thank you, we'll be in touch in a couple of weeks, a month...'

Need for multidisciplinary and inter-agency work

Multidisciplinary and inter-agency collaboration with the child's support networks is relevant throughout this process, as highlighted in a range of relevant literature (ADCS 2015; BASW 2015a; Separated Children in Europe Programme 2012). An age assessment should be done in collaboration with other services and professionals who are already involved with the young person and who can vouch for him or her. During the Hummingbird Project work in the Calais camp, we slowly got to know the stories of young people we worked with there, and who we have continued to support in the UK. This took place over a prolonged period – sometimes lasting over a year. As someone who has worked with young people since the start of the Hummingbird Project in 2015, I know what has happened to them – we drew pictures about it, we explored it in the safe space we ran. None of this may come out in the age-assessment interview, either because there is no time to do so, or it is conducted as an interrogation and from a position of mistrust.

However, despite writing letters of support for the young people undergoing this process or attending the meeting as an appropriate adult supporting them, I feel we have not been heard, or our perspective considered, in the majority of cases. In a particular case, a young 16-year-old man we were supporting was assessed as being 19 years of age. At the age-assessment meeting, I wasn't allowed to talk or contribute. After the meeting, I was asked to put any information I wanted to share in writing but I do not believe this was considered. As an appropriate adult, I should be able to challenge interviewers if I feel the interview is not being conducted appropriately (Coram 2017), but to date, none of my challenges have been heard or responded to.

Beyond taking part in the assessments, I also liaise with the child's family or foster carers, as well as their schools and other people involved in their life. I spoke to the teachers at the school attended by one of the children I support, and they were asking about the age-assessment process. It is important for them to know, because the child we work with may be 'worked up' before and upset afterwards. Teachers need that information to understand a child's behaviour. Good practice is to communicate with people around the child and to check how they are behaving. If a child experienced an incident or a bereavement, professionals involved in their lives should make sure they are looked after. The biggest concern is that such support may not be available throughout the country. It depends on the services that are available locally and which contacts followed the child along their journey. This, more than anything, should urge all professionals and volunteers to liaise more closely with each other throughout the assessment process.

Conclusion

Where an unaccompanied minor disagrees with the assessment made, they can seek a judicial review of the decision, and the court's determination of age binds both parties. Data from the Home Office Immigration Statistics for 2008–12 suggests that age was disputed in approximately 30 per cent of cases of unaccompanied asylum-seeking children presenting a claim, but the data available is insufficient to provide insight into the outcomes of such challenges (Joint Committee on Human Rights 2013). The BASW (2015a) statement on age assessments stipulates that social workers who take part in age assessments should ensure that unaccompanied minors are helped to challenge the outcome of this process, to raise awareness of oppressive and unfair practice.

The potential conflict of interest embedded in the age-assessment process has been recognised in relevant literature (Bianchini 2011; Joint Committee on Human Rights 2013). Local authorities are responsible for both assessments and the costs of care for those determined to be children through subjective and fallible procedures (Bianchini 2011). Similar recognition was noted in relation to age-assessment practices across Europe (Separated Children in Europe Programme 2012, p.8), as 'prevailing cultural constructs and perceptions of childhood based on European parameters cannot be considered as objective criteria in questioning the declared age of separated children'.

It is a shame that the data on the number and outcome of the age-assessment appeals is not readily available, as it would enable a more nuanced exploration on the benefits and shortcomings of the current processes. As an appropriate adult, I wish I had observed more examples of good practice, particularly as it concerns young people who have experienced trauma and persecution, not only in their country of origin but during their journey to the UK. The concern I have is that the social workers who I felt didn't conduct this process well are likely to do many more age assessments in the future.

I appreciate that some social workers will find this difficult to read. Experiences shared in the chapter are the ones I have had to date, many of which weren't positive. Nonetheless, the practice I advocate for is rooted in relevant legislation, guidance and research – but it isn't the practice I predominately encountered when supporting the young people I work with. The focus of any assessment should be to make sure that appropriate services are offered and that all procedures are carried out in the best interests of the child, and to uphold a child-centred and child-friendly perspective. This is in line with the benefit of the doubt principle embedded in the relevant legislation and policies. All social workers conducting age assessments need to undertake relevant training. Such training needs to focus on developing empathy with young people and an understanding of migrant journeys, including the impact of trauma on unaccompanied minors, communication skills and analytical skills relevant for engagement with culture-specific customs and communication. Finally, the process, if conducted, needs to be rooted in multidisciplinary practice prior to, during and after the assessment meetings. However, most of all, I would urge social workers to consider the advice from BASW (2015b) about whether they want to take part in such ethically questionable practices in the first place.

References

ADCS (Association of Directors of Children's Services) (2015) *Age Assessment Guidance.* Accessed 08/09/2017 at: http://adcs.org.uk/assets/documentation/Age_Assessment_Guidance_2015_Final.pdf.

Asylum Information Database (2015) *Detriment of the Doubt: Age Assessment of Unaccompanied Asylum-Seeking Children.* Accessed 08/09/2017 at: www.asylumlawdatabase.eu/sites/www.asylumlawdatabase.eu/files/aldfiles/AIDA%20Brief%205_AgeAssessment.pdf.

BASW (British Association of Social Workers) (2015a) *BASW Position Statement: Age Assessment/Age Determination.* Accessed 30/10/2018 at: www.basw.co.uk/resources/basw-position-statement-age-assessmentage-determination.

BASW (2015b) *ADCS Age Assessment Guidance.* Accessed 30/10/2018 at: www.basw.co.uk/resources/adcs-age-assessment-guidance.

Bianchini, K. (2011) 'Unaccompanied asylum-seeker children: Flawed processes and protection gaps in the UK.' *Forced Migration Review,* 37, 52–53.

Borders, Citizenship and Immigration Act (2009) London: HMSO.

Boyden, J., de Berry, J., Feeny, T. and Hart, J. (2002) *Children Affected by Conflict in South Asia: A Review of Trends and Issues Identified through Secondary Research.* Oxford: University of Oxford Refugee Studies Centre.

The Children's Society (2012) *Into the Unknown: Children's Journeys Through the Asylum Process.* Accessed 08/09/2017 at: www.childrenssociety.org.uk/sites/default/files/tcs/into-the-unknown--childrens-journeys-through-the-asylum-process--the-childrens-society.pdf.

Coram (2017) *Acting as an Appropriate Adult at an Age Assessment.* Accessed 30/10/2018 at: www.childrenslegalcentre.com/resources/appropriate-adult-age-assessment.

Doctors of the World (2015) *Age Assessment for Unaccompanied Minors: When European Countries Deny Children Their Childhood.* Accessed 08/09/2017 at: https://mdmeuroblog.files.wordpress.com/2014/01/age-determination-def.pdf.

ECPAT (Every Child Protected Against Trafficking) UK and Missing People (2016) *Heading Back to Harm: A Study on Trafficked and Unaccompanied Children Going Missing from Care in the UK.* London: ECPAT.

Home Office (2016) *Processing Children's Asylum Claims.* Accessed 08/09/2017 at: www.gov.uk/government/publications/processing-an-asylum-application-from-a-child-instruction.

Home Office (2018) *Assessing Age for Asylum Applicants.* Accessed 30/10/2018 at: www.gov.uk/government/publications/assessing-age-instruction.

Immigration Law Practitioners' Association (2007) *When Is a Child not a Child? Asylum, Age Disputes and the Process of Age Assessment.* Prepared by Heaven Crawley. Accessed 08/09/2017 at: www.ilpa.org.uk/data/resources/13266/ILPA-Age-Dispute-Report.pdf.

Joint Committee on Human Rights (2013) *Human Rights of Unaccompanied Migrant Children and Young People in the UK: First Report of Session 2013–14.* HL paper 9 HC 196. London: The Stationery Office.

Kaplan, I., Stolk, Y., Valibhoy, M., Tucker, A. and Baker, J. (2016) 'Cognitive assessment of refugee children: Effects of trauma and new language acquisition.' *Transcultural Psychiatry,* 53,1, 81–109.

Kohli, R.K. (2005) 'The sound of silence: Listening to what unaccompanied asylum-seeking children say and do not say.' *British Journal of Social Work,* 36, 5, 707–721.

Modern Slavery Act (2015) London: HMSO.

Mougne, C. (2010) *Trees Only Move in the Wind: A Study of Unaccompanied Afghan Children in Europe.* Geneva: UNHCR.

Refugee Studies Centre (2010) *Negotiating Childhood: Age Assessment in the UK Asylum System.* Accessed 08/09/2017 at: www.rsc.ox.ac.uk/publications/negotiating-childhood-age-assessment-in-the-uk-asylum-system.

Scottish Government (2018) *Age Assessment: Practice Guidance*. Accessed 30/10/2018 at: www.gov.scot/publications/age-assessment-practice-guidance-scotland-good-practice-guidance-support-social/pages/7.

Separated Children in Europe Programme (2012) *Position Paper on Age Assessment in the Context of Separated Children in Europe*. Accessed 08/09/2017 at: www.scepnetwork.org/images/16/163.pdf.

UNICEF (2013) *Age Assessment: A Technical Note*. Accessed 08/09/2017 at: www.unicef.org/protection/files/Age_Assessment_Note_final_version_(English).pdf.

UNICEF (2017) *Harrowing Journeys: Children and Youth on the Move Across the Mediterranean Sea, at Risk of Trafficking and Exploitation*. New York, NY: UNICEF.

From 'Translation Machine' to Trusted Colleague

Interpreters in Social Work

Annemarie Morsch

Introduction

We cannot begin to practise social work until we can communicate with service users. Every individual has specific communication needs, and we must strive to meet these, whether service users are adults with dementia, children or young people, older adults, those with mental ill-health, or those who speak a first language other than ours. We must find the tools to reach them if we are to do our job. This chapter looks briefly at some issues involved when this communication effort involves interpreter-mediated work.

Almost one in five primary school pupils is known to have a first language other than English (Department for Education 2015), and in work with these families we would almost certainly need to use an interpreter. Given the enormous number of languages spoken by refugee, asylum seeker or other non-English-speaking members of society, even practitioners who are bi- or multi-lingual should be prepared for this type of practice. Among others, both Lord Laming's Victoria Climbié Inquiry and the Serious Case Review into Daniel Pelka's death recommended that interpreters be used in communicating with children and families whose first language is not English (Coventry Safeguarding Children Board 2013; Department for Health and Home Office 2003). The potential impact of not communicating effectively with these children or the adults caring for them can be catastrophic.

Interpreter-mediated work also reflects our professional duty not to discriminate against service users on the grounds of language: in accordance with the 1998 Human Rights Act, in striving for anti-oppressive practice, in working to the Recognising Diversity and Human Rights values in the British Association of Social Workers (2014) *Code of Ethics*, or as reflected in the concept of linguistic justice. Refugees and asylum seekers in particular have often experienced almost unimaginable oppression and power inequities before our work with them begins. As social workers, we seek to establish a more balanced power dynamic, and enabling these individuals to speak their own language is fundamental to this.

So why is this work often seen by practitioners as problematic? What does good practice look like, and can interpreter-mediated work be a positive element of social work?

Is the work inherently problematic?

Having worked extensively as an interpreter and in social work with refugee families where most casework involves interpreters, I would find it difficult to argue that work in this complex triad dynamic is easy for any participant. It is significantly different from and more challenging than social work without an interpreter and is often described by practitioners in actively negative terms: as 'immensely difficult' (Abdulla and Payne 1997, p.86) or 'a hindrance' or 'disability' (Hadziabdic *et al.* 2009, p.461, p.465). Pinpointing the 'necessary evil' argument, Križ and Skivenes (2010, p.1361) find social workers believing that 'working through interpreters, while the only way to overcome the hurdle of the lack of a common language, reduces the quality and extent of information they receive from children and carers'.

Perhaps among the reasons this sentiment is so widespread is the expectation, particularly from inexperienced practitioners, that interpreters function as 'translation machines'. The (scant) literature appears to demonstrate a preference from practitioners for a 'non-person' model (Westermeyer 1990), with the interpreter expected to act as 'a disengaged presence', 'a communication aid' (Hadziabdic and Hjelm 2013, p.72, p.73) or a 'translation machine' (Miller *et al.* 2005, p.30). There is a clear sense that service providers expect an interpreter to be effectively a 'non-person' and consequently any interpreter behaviour falling outside this definition of the role is seen as transgressive, informing a negative assessment of interpreter-mediated work. Nevertheless, using face-to-face professional interpreters means introducing a third human being, and thus creating two additional relationships: service user–interpreter and interpreter–social worker.

The power imbalances and additional relationships can be difficult to negotiate. Tribe and Thompson (2009, p.4) believe negative feelings around this work arise partly from the fact that 'engaging in three-way relationships can be unfamiliar for clinicians'; Brämberg and Sandman (2012, p.164) describe service providers 'feeling a loss of control of sessions'; and service providers' feelings of 'exclusion' are widely described (Freed 1988; Križ and Skivenes 2010; Tribe 1999). Furthermore, the service user–interpreter relationship, while often transitory, must be substantial, and deep enough to allow the interpreter to act as the 'voice' of the service user. This requires a profound degree of trust and rapport between those two individuals.

In triadic communication, interlocutors can feel 'outnumbered' when communication does not directly include them, and these feelings can be heightened when the language spoken by other participants is not understood. Feelings of exclusion can affect all parties: 'The triangular relationship may lead to any one member being or feeling excluded from the consultation at any one time' (Tribe 1999, p.573). Service providers may feel this most deeply; however, interpreters' practice takes place exclusively within this dynamic, and service users experience it constantly, while practitioners 'may feel threatened by the presence of a third person in "their" consulting room' (ibid.) or anxious about 'the exposure of having a witness to their work' (Boyles and Talbot 2017, p.11). This can be particularly unsettling for social workers, who are unlikely to have received any training in working with this complex dynamic. Awareness and ownership of these feelings, together with reflexive practice, may help to mitigate some of this discomfort.

More practical concerns are also likely to inform the work. These can include a 'lack of interpreters with proficiency in a particular language, difficulties in the availability of interpreters and access to the interpreter agency' (Hadziabdic and Hjelm 2013, p.74). Inadequate interpreter provision is widely identified as a problem. Okitikpi and Aymer (2003, p.219) discuss limited access to interpreters faced by social workers, adding that 'waiting times were long for specialist services'. Such barriers to good practice cannot help but influence practitioners.

Discussing interpretation in the health service (which frequently has access to the same, limited pool of interpreters as local authority workers), Bischoff and colleagues (2003, p.511) state that 'there are generally institutional constraints by which organisations decide not to dismiss the use of unqualified personnel and not to implement qualified interpreter services'. Financial implications of interpreter use should also be acknowledged: despite better outcomes achieved by using trained interpreters, 'training is a quality label and the cost of using a trained interpreter is thus higher than for an untrained one' (Hadziabdic and Hjelm 2013, p.70). It seems understandable that workers in the current context see the need for interpreters as a drain on limited resources. Consequently, family members may be used, despite awareness that this is bad practice. Discussing social workers' reluctant use of child interpreters, Lucas (2015, p.156) observes that 'the phenomenon…raises questions about the adequacy of provision and support for families and social workers to engage with interpreting services effectively'. Finding qualified, available, appropriate interpreters though language service agencies can be a struggle at best and impossible at worst.

Given our unrealistic expectations of being able to work with a non-person interpreting machine, the addition of a third person and additional relationships to an already complex dynamic, frequently poor provision of services, and financial implications for over-stretched organisations, it is unsurprising that while we acknowledge the necessity of working with interpreters, their use is often seen as problematic. As this work is unlikely to disappear, practitioners must ask the logical questions: how can these obstacles be reduced, and what might good practice look like within this context?

What does good practice look like?

Some barriers to good practice are beyond the control of the practitioners who must deal with their implications; we are unable to influence the choice of contracted language agencies, train linguists in minority languages, improve or introduce social-work-specific training for available interpreters. Fortunately, there are key aspects of interpreter-mediated practice that are under our control, namely those reflecting our own practice in preparation for, during and following this work.

This third person is not a 'translation machine'

The interpreter's identity influences the work and consideration must be given to aspects of their identity which may affect a service user's trust in this person to act as their voice. Hadziabdic and Hjelm (2013, p.72) list 'ethnic origin, religious background, gender, language or dialect, social group, appearance and attitude', but other elements such as experience in relevant settings, or tribal or political identity may also contribute. Language and dialect specifications are particularly crucial of course, and it is essential to check both that the correct 'version' of a language is recorded when booking an interpreter, and that understanding is checked carefully when the service user and interpreter are first introduced. It is entirely possible to state preferences on the basis of all of these aspects of identity when making an interpreter booking. While such requests are not always respected or honoured it is certainly worth asking the questions.

Practice example: a Sudanese refugee, persecuted for his sexuality in an Islamic country en route to the UK, said that he did not want a male interpreter, as it was difficult to speak about his torture in front of men, and that women wearing the hijab reminded him of the discrimination he experienced there. We found a female Arabic interpreter who does not wear the hijab and he felt safe to express himself fully.

Where the service user and interpreter come from a small community this can lead to significant reluctance to share difficult or sensitive information. Service users may indicate a preference for interpreters unconnected to 'their country of origin or their local network' (Raval 2005, p.204) and, where this is not possible, concerns should be addressed, and may be allayed somewhat through an explicit commitment by the interpreter to their professional duty of confidentiality.

An expectation of being able to use interpreters as impersonal machines rests on a 'cognitivist model of language', assuming an interpreter simply matches 'a word from one lexicon to a word of equivalent meaning from the other' (Thomas, Shah and Thornton 2009, p.14). In reality, language transfer is more complex; there is often no direct equivalence of meaning between different languages. For example, there is no word for anxiety/depression in Urdu (Searight and Searight 2009), words around sexual abuse are not easily translated into some Asian languages (Chand 2005), and Turkish patients are often more uncomfortable than English ones when confronted with the word 'depression' (Tribe 1999). If the practitioner does not acknowledge this cultural difference and provide an appropriate explanation of new or difficult concepts then the interpreter must do so in order to facilitate understanding, and may not use the practitioner's preferred terms. An experienced, well-trained interpreter may feel empowered to interject, requesting an explanation. Not providing a service user-appropriate framing initially, however, increases the risk that crucial misunderstandings will arise.

Practice example: when interpreting in hospital, a consultant advised of a child's 'elevated stroke risk'. As the interpreter, I was thus given the choice of using the 'equivalent' medical term which the mother, with little formal schooling, was unlikely to know, or hoping that she would feel able to ask for an explanation, reframing the sentence to include a basic explanation of a stroke, drawn from my personal understanding, or interjecting and asking the consultant to provide an explanation the mother would understand.

Language itself can become a productive focus in these cases. Tribe and Thompson (2009, p.8) find 'co-reflecting about language, meaning and the use of an interpreter with clients…very instructive and illuminating, often accessing areas of clients that might otherwise not have come to light'. I often experienced this as an interpreter, with a lack of directly equivalent concepts being a useful way into discussing differences in individual or cultural understandings of particular issues.

Interpreters work more effectively if service providers adapt their speech to the changed dynamic. This can include speaking in shorter sentences, using less jargon, or reformulating questions (Boyles and Talbot 2017; Brämberg and Sandman 2012; Farooq and Fear 2003; Raval 1996). Using 'clear language makes it more possible to interpret accurately' (Raval 1996, p.35). The interpreter also needs to be able to see the faces of both other interlocutors, and a triangular arrangement is the most practical for this. The social worker should address the service user directly, and in the first person (Boyles and Talbot 2017). It is in the interests of practitioners to facilitate the interpreter's job by communicating in a way which is simpler to interpret; the more empowered the interpreter is to do the job well, the better the session for everyone.

A final advantage of the interpreter's personhood lies in their ability outside the session (ideally in a post-session briefing) to provide information about cultural values and norms. Interpreters are 'inevitably value-impregnated individuals' (Patel 2003, p.224) and so, while such information can be useful, we must be wary of unquestioningly accepting an interpreter's cultural insights as valid for specific service users. Tribe and Thompson (2009, p.6) recommend that 'ideas taken from such interchanges…should be shared with clients in a spirit of open enquiry rather than reified into a fixed and rigid idea of another's "culture"'. This suggests a model where cultural differences are identified (likely by the interpreter, who often has access to both cultures) and then discussed openly.

Working within a triad

To facilitate shared understanding and strategy, interpreters can be given background information and instruction to support their practice in a short pre-session briefing. This can include practical details, such as copies of relevant forms, acronyms or vocabulary, an idea of the objective of the session and issues which may arise (some of which may be meaningful or triggering, particularly if the interpreter is from the same cultural background as the service user). All of this should help the interpreter work more effectively.

Interpreters are often not 'given sufficient information, preparatory time, or support in order to familiarize themselves with the specialized ways in which practitioners work' (Raval 2005, p.200) and a briefing can be a useful opportunity to establish ground rules or discuss working preferences, which may differ from those of other practitioners or other settings.

Within sessions, social workers should be assertive and direct the interpreter: ask them to interpret if they are not consistently doing so, seek clarification, control the conversational flow. Assertiveness on the part of social workers is reported by Westlake and Jones (2017, p.19) as 'enabl[ing] workers to structure sessions in ways that involved the client more fully', and a social worker quoted by Sawrikar (2015, p.402) explains the need sometimes to say 'stop. Tell me what just happened. And ask me the questions.' If a social worker notices the conversation becoming dominated by the interpreter, or by the interpreter–service user relationship, it is within their power to change this dynamic. The social worker is the lead professional, and can and should manage the interaction.

Practice example: a kind and relatively inexperienced Kinyarwanda interpreter was clearly answering questions posed by service users during our session. I consistently reminded her in session to interpret everything that was said back to me, and we discussed this afterwards, when I also explained that I might select relevant information deliberately when responding to these questions, for reasons she may not be privy to. Her practice has greatly improved.

Tribe and Thompson (2009, p.6) find interpreter involvement to have a significant symbolic value to the relationship with the service user, showing 'how far the [practitioner] is prepared to go to meet them', while Raval (1996) found that having the interpreter present allowed difficult issues (such as racism and cultural difference) to be discussed. As a first step towards creating rapport, arranging an interpreter is invaluable in showing determination to hear the service user voice, but is not enough in and of itself. The social worker will need to make greater than usual effort to build a trusting relationship, involving active listening and significant reflective communication.

Where a trusting interpreter–service user rapport is established, and having checked that the service user and interpreter are happy to work together, it is often productive to maintain consistency, booking the same interpreter for future sessions. It can feel safer for service users to trust their story to a consistent interpreter rather than having to build this rapport with a new individual each time they see you. Language agencies should be able to facilitate this.

Having a third party in the room not only provides a useful opportunity for reflexive practice and observation of the service user's verbal and extra-linguistic communication during periods where the other two interlocutors are communicating, but can also create a sense of shared understanding. In traumatic work, the presence of a third person can create a communal sense of witnessing, and 'joint enterprise'. Miller *et al.* (2005, p.33) describe therapists valuing the interpreter's presence to 'share the intensity of the client's emotional experiences' with subjects, stating that 'it was traumatizing…and having the interpreter there with you was so immensely comforting because you know that you could process it together'. Service users also 'liked the fact that two people heard their stories – the more people that know about these terrible things the better' (Bot and Wadensjö 2004, p.375). Reflection with interpreters following this type of difficult work often leads to insights or questions which may not have arisen without access to this additional informed viewpoint.

Practical considerations

Planning sufficient time for interpreter-mediated work is essential. An interpreted session will take at least twice as long as an equivalent non-interpreted session. All utterances are expressed twice, and while this in itself adds time, it is also time consuming to explain systems and concepts which differ across cultures. 'You might get allocated one case, but it is equivalent to two' (social worker, quoted in Sawrikar 2015, p.402), and clearly the extra time required for these cases should be reflected in caseloads.

Where additional time is not considered in scheduling this work, practitioners can feel rushed, omitting or forgetting things, or working in 'target-oriented' ways, as noted by a social worker quoted in Westlake and Jones (2017, p.12) who felt 'focused on communicating the essentials:

"right, this is what I need to do today, this is what I need to get across'"
(p.12). This risks neglecting important rapport-building elements of social
work, key to creating trusting relationships. Rapport building can take
the form of profiting from the interpreter's presence, for example to check
understanding of other issues, question appropriate interpreter provision by
other services, or create resources (such as notes in English to give to other
agencies or appointment reminders in the service user's language).

Following a session, debriefings are useful for interpreters and
practitioners alike. They 'allow clarifications, deeper understanding,
descriptions of cultural dictates and explanations of specific behaviour'
(Freed 1988, p.317), as well as considerations of 'difficulties that arose and
how they might be dealt with' (Tribe 1999, p.573). Spending a few minutes
discussing noteworthy aspects of the session can have a real impact. This is
also an opportunity to provide feedback and support to the interpreter, who
has no other access to evaluation or critique of their practice; an interpreter's
work is seen only by the practitioner and the service user. Few interpreting
agencies provide supervision and, as a result of confidentiality requirements,
without a practitioner's immediate post-session support it can be impossible
for these colleagues, who have experienced the same potentially difficult or
traumatic session as the practitioner (expressing all emotions in the first
person), to process their emotional response to the work.

Lastly, if there are problems with an interpreter's practice (if they were
unprofessional, were not working within the boundaries of their role or were
incompetent) then this must be reported to the relevant agency. Again, the
practitioner and the service user are the only witnesses to their practice and
if this is not challenged, it will go unreported and continue to contribute to
negative perceptions of interpreter-mediated work.

Conclusion

While those speaking a second language 'may be able to communicate their
thoughts adequately in a language used in a school, work or market setting…
they may be unable to communicate their *feelings* freely' (Westermeyer
1990, p.745, my emphasis). Good practice with interpreters is essential if
we are to empower service users to express themselves fully, enabling the
free expression of feelings necessary for good social work practice. Believing
that simply booking an interpreter resolves all communication issues where
there is a language barrier is unrealistic and contributes to the perception
of this work as problematic. It is unarguable that work with an interpreter

demands additional effort, before, during and after the session. If workers recognise and are prepared to do this work, to plan, reflect on barriers, and make the extra communication effort required, this practice has the potential to be both productive and rewarding.

References

Abdulla, M. and Payne, D. (1997) 'Good practice in working with interpreters.' *Probation Journal*, 44, 86–88.

BASW (British Association of Social Workers) (2014) *The Code of Ethics for Social Work: Statement of Principles*. Accessed 03/03/2018 at: http://cdn.basw.co.uk/upload/basw_23237-8.pdf.

Bischoff, A., Bovier, P.A., Rrustemi, I., Gariazzo, F., Eytan, A. and Loutan, L. (2003) 'Language barriers between nurses and asylum seekers: Their impact on symptom reporting and referral.' *Social Science & Medicine*, 57, 503–512.

Bot, H. and Wadensjö, C. (2004) 'The Presence of a Third Party: A Dialogical View on Interpreter-Assisted Treatment.' In J.P. Wilson and B. Drožđek (eds) *Broken Spirits. The Treatment of Traumatized Asylum Seekers, Refugees, War and Torture Victims*, pp.355–378. Hove: Brunner-Routledge.

Boyles, J. and Talbot, N. (2017) *Working with Interpreters in Psychological Therapy*. Abingdon: Routledge.

Brämberg, E.B. and Sandman, L. (2012) 'Communication through in-person interpreters: A qualitative study of home care providers' and social workers' views.' *Journal of Clinical Nursing*, 22, 159–167.

Chand, A. (2005) 'Do you speak English? Language barriers in child protection social work with minority ethnic families.' *British Journal of Social Work*, 35, 6, 807–821.

Coventry Safeguarding Children Board (2013) *Serious Case Review Re Daniel Pelka, Born 15th July 2007, Died 3rd March 2012*. Accessed 23/11/2018 at: www.scie-socialcareonline.org.uk/serious-case-review-re-daniel-pelka-born-15th-july-2007-died-3rd-march-2012-overview-report/r/a11G0000002W3m7IAC.

Department for Health and Home Office (2003) *The Victoria Climbié Inquiry: Report of an Inquiry by Lord Laming*. Accessed 23/11/2018 at: http://webarchive.nationalarchives.gov.uk/20130401151715/https://www.education.gov.uk/publications/eOrderingDownload/CM-5730PDF.pdf.

Department for Education (2015) *Statistical First Release: Schools, Pupils and Their Characteristics*. January. Accessed 23/11/2018 at: www.gov.uk/government/uploads/system/uploads/attachment_data/file/433680/SFR16_2015_Main_Text.pdf.

Farooq, S. and Fear, C. (2003) 'Working through interpreters.' *Advances in Psychiatric Treatment*, 9, 104–109.

Freed, A.O. (1988) 'Interviewing through an interpreter.' *Social Work*, 33, 4, 315–319.

Hadziabdic, E., Heikkilä, K., Albin, B. and Hjelm, K. (2009) 'Migrants' perceptions of using interpreters in health care.' *International Nursing Review*, 56, 461–469.

Hadziabdic, E. and Hjelm, K. (2013) 'Working with interpreters: Practical advice for use of an interpreter in healthcare.' *International Journal of Evidence-Based Healthcare*, 11, 69–76.

Human Rights Act (1998) London: The Stationery Office.

Križ, K. and Skivenes, M. (2010) 'Lost in translation: How child welfare workers in Norway and England experience language difficulties when working with minority ethnic families.' *British Journal of Social Work*, 40, 1353–1367.

Lucas, S.E. (2015) 'Child interpreting in social work: Competence versus legitimacy.' *Transnational Social Review*, 5, 2, 145–160.

Miller, K., Martell, Z., Pazdinek, L., Carruth, M. and Lopez, F. (2005) 'The role of interpreters in psychotherapy with refugees: An exploratory study.' *American Journal of Orthopsychiatry*, 75, 1, 27–39.

Okitikpi, T. and Aymer, C. (2003) 'Social work with African refugee children and their families.' *Child and Family Social Work*, 8, 213–222.

Patel, N. (2003) 'Speaking with the Silent: Addressing Issues of Disempowerment when Working with Refugee People.' In R. Tribe. and H. Raval (eds) *Working with Interpreters in Mental Health*, pp.219–237. Hove: Brunner-Routledge.

Raval, H. (1996) 'A systemic perspective on working with interpreters.' *Clinical Child Psychology and Psychiatry*, 1, 1, 29–43.

Raval, H. (2005) 'Being heard and understood in the context of seeking asylum and refuge: Communicating with the help of bilingual co-workers.' *Clinical Child Psychology and Psychiatry*, 10, 197–217.

Sawrikar, P. (2015) 'Using interpreters in child protection matters.' *Child and Family Social Work*, 20, 396–406.

Searight, H.R. and Searight, B.K. (2009) 'Working with foreign language interpreters: Recommendations for psychological practice.' *Professional Psychology: Research and Practice*, 40, 5, 444–451.

Thomas, P., Shah, A. and Thornton, T. (2009) 'Language, games and the role of interpreters in psychiatric diagnosis: A Wittgensteinian thought experiment.' *Medical Humanities*, 35, 13–18.

Tribe, R. (1999) 'Bridging the gap or damming the flow? Some observations on using interpreters/bicultural workers when working with refugee clients, many of whom have been tortured.' *British Journal of Medical Psychology*, 72, 567–576.

Tribe, R. and Thompson, K. (2009) 'Opportunity for development or necessary nuisance? The case for viewing working with interpreters as a bonus in therapeutic work.' *International Journal of Migration, Health and Social Care*, 5, 2, 4–12.

Westermeyer, J. (1990) 'Working with an interpreter in psychiatric assessment and treatment.' *Journal of Nervous and Mental Disease*, 178, 12, 745–749.

Westlake, D. and Jones, R.K. (2017) 'Breaking down language barriers: A practice-near study of social work using interpreters.' *British Journal of Social Work*, doi: 10.1093/bjsw/bcx073.

Narrative 8
Learning from Ken

After making my asylum application I was full of hope. I'd read through the guidance on how to make an application and what the decision makers analyse when making a decision. I was full of hope, full of joy and thinking, 'Yes, my life will be fine.' But when I got the negative decision, I realised this wasn't the case. I had submitted a lot of evidence, some of which was ignored by the decision maker. It is not logical. Once you read their position, you see it is not something that would make sense to anyone. They were picking out certain things to support their opinion, but when they did this, pieces of evidence would start to contradict each other. In my application, I explained that in [my country of origin] I had a secret Facebook account to try to get into a relationship. One of the comments used against me was that the Facebook account contained a picture of a man kissing a woman, which was ridiculous. To start with, it was a painting, not a photo. And it was of two men holding each other. I had specifically chosen to use a painting rather than a photo to make it clear, as people were thinking I was someone else when I used the photos I had found on the Internet. How someone can claim that, I don't know.

They also said I had not submitted evidence that I owned the Facebook profile, and therefore evidence from it cannot be taken into account. But in another paragraph, they say, 'That account has a photo of a man and a woman therefore...' So they are saying that evidence to support your claim cannot be taken from this account, but we will take evidence from this account to use against you. It was really disappointing. The whole process has been a lot of stress.

In my own documents, it is clear. My lawyer said that they 'failed to acknowledge some evidence'. That is not the words I would use, I would say they are lying and covering up. There are paragraphs where I refer to the same thing over and over; how can you fail to acknowledge something like that? When I was studying in the UK and my ex-boyfriend was in [his country of origin], he made an application to join me. It was initially denied but then he went to court and was allowed over. I used this case as evidence of my sexuality, but because this is convincing evidence, they decided to ignore this completely. I talked about our lifestyle and even provided council tax bills showing that he lived with me, but the decision maker just ignored it.

All asylum seekers are suffering from the same problem, which is that the UK is not offering asylum. The decision on my asylum application shows a blatant attempt to disregard evidence and deny asylum. In my case, I feel that I can clearly indicate that the system is unfair. It is not even incompetence, it goes beyond someone just not doing their work properly. They have put in effort to lie.

I became depressed for the first time. The whole system is really stressful; you don't know what is happening. You are given 14 days from the date of the decision to find a lawyer, go to court and gather evidence. It's all way too much. They have a whole year to do whatever they are doing and then give you just 14 days. I made the application by myself because I thought it would be easy. They rushed me to submit information but then ended up taking their time once they had it. It was really, really stressful. You are about to lose everything, but you have to spend loads of money on lawyers. By the time they made their decision I was in a relationship, so my relationship was going to be split up as my boyfriend was in the UK. I was going to lose my house and lose my job.

My initial solution to dealing with depression was to not think about it. But then I started getting really strong anxiety attacks. There was a time when my rugby team were away for a tournament and we were in a pub celebrating. I was trying really hard not to show what was happening. But I was having such strong anxiety attacks that I had to go to the toilet to sit for a while. I went to the GP and was given anti-depressants, and they referred me to the [local] Mind group. With time, I have learned how to cope with these stressful situations and I have read books on mindfulness. Now I have finally managed to come off the medication and not fall back into depression.

I find it very weird that in the UK legal system they say that if you come into the country and do not make an asylum claim immediately then that is a strike against you. That is very illogical thinking. Would such a rule be applied to victims of domestic abuse? Would they say, 'You didn't complain within ten seconds of being abused, therefore it didn't happen?' It doesn't make sense psychologically. When I came to the UK I was worried about going to a gay club. It took me six months to a year to finally go. It took two months to just find out where the clubs were. On the third month, I would pass outside them, but I was worried someone would see me looking in. Today I can walk in without feeling anything, I can tell people at work that I am gay. But it takes time for someone to go from hiding and feeling fearful to being open. It doesn't happen when you land at the airport, you don't feel on that day, 'All my fears are over, I can be free!' I think any psychologist would tell you that you don't move from being fearful and hiding to being open in the eight hours it takes for a plane to arrive in the UK.

I've not really felt any discrimination in the UK, I've felt very welcome. I'm in [my local] rugby team and they have really made me feel comfortable to say I am gay. I was lucky in that I was already in the UK when I made my claim for asylum. I had already had support from gay groups like Pride Without Borders. It may be different for someone in the LGBT community compared to other asylum seekers, as they may not have a community they can go to, to talk about what is happening to them. For example, people from Syria may find other Syrian people who have similar problems. LGBT people may not have a place they can go to for support, especially if they are isolated. The only service I have accessed for LGBT asylum seekers is Pride Without Borders. But within the wider gay community there are many clubs and teams that you can join to socialise. They are for everyone, whether you are an immigrant or UK born.

Pride Without Borders is easy to access, but you need to know it exists to access it. Before Pride last year, I didn't know it existed. I would not have been able to access it at all. You would have to be out and involved in the gay community to access it. It would be easier to access if there were more of these groups, and if they were more spread out across the country and if there was a bit more advertising. When you claim asylum, they send you a bundle of documents about where you can get help. It would be good if information about groups like Pride Without Borders was included in that bundle.

I have not had any issues accessing NHS services because I was already registered with a GP from my time as a student. I have not had a problem there. I did a course of cognitive behavioural therapy (CBT) through both the NHS and MIND. While I was waiting for the NHS course to start, I began CBT with MIND. They were teaching the same things, but in the NHS they would give you lots of information in a short amount of time, whereas the MIND CBT took it a lot slower and was more relaxed and welcoming. The course content in the NHS was good, but the delivery could be improved on.

To improve my mental health, I have been listening to audiobooks and a Tai Chi group which I found through my GP's well-being service. I found the meditation and Tai Chi very useful, but it was £3 a session so I had to stop and begin meditating by myself using my headphones instead.

My advice to Home Office decision makers would be to be careful about your practice and question whether what you are being asked to do is legal. I worry that staff could be made into scapegoats if something changes or there is a scandal.

The higher-ups will protect themselves and I have a sense, and a feeling, that case owners and frontline staff are being pressured into making outrageous decisions. There was a time I was signing in and they wanted to detain me. I explained that I still had a court proceeding going on. They accepted it, but to cover their backs they wanted to call their office. Whoever they spoke to did not want them to let me go, and insisted they call my lawyer. They did and my lawyer confirmed it. The office then insisted that they call the court as well. They did, and it was confirmed. This time they didn't call the office back, and they let me go. The person in the office pushing people to make negative decisions will not get prosecuted if anything goes wrong.

Chapter 15

Concluding Thoughts
Ways Forward for a Social Work Without Borders

Lauren Wroe, Rachel Larkin and Reima Ana Maglajlic

Around the time the ideas for this book were coming to fruition, Colin Turbett, author of *Doing Radical Social Work* (2014) and a retired children's services manager, spoke at a gathering of the Plan C organisation (an anti-capitalist organisation concerned with social justice[1]). He was advising a crowd of health and social care workers on how to practise ethically, and how to change systems and defend the rights of the individuals and families we work with, particularly in the context of austerity, the increasing surveillance of families, and the blaming of people for their marginalisation by society (Featherstone *et al.* 2018). Colin insisted that the first thing we have to do, if we are to carve out a place for ourselves as social workers committed to social justice, is to be brilliant at our work. This, he argued, gives us credibility. It gives us capital to be heard and to inform decisions, and it ensures that wherever we practise, and whomever we practise with, we remain vigilant about working in accordance with the values of our profession.

Knowledge, critical debate and critical reflection are all key to effecting change in social work policy and practice. As Hannah Berry, drawing on Hill Collins (2000), reminds us in her chapter:

> Where oppressors or systems of power become tyrannical and resist all efforts at change, gaining knowledge of their situation is nevertheless vital for subjects of that power, who can develop tactics for resistance

---

1   www.weareplanc.org

even if just 'in the private, personal space' (Hill Collins 2000, p.118) of their consciousness. 'Becoming empowered through self-knowledge, even within conditions that severely limit one's ability to act, is essential' (ibid.).

This book, then, is a celebration of brilliant work that challenges, resists and carves out a space for itself in increasingly pressured contexts. By listening to the individuals and families we work alongside, and drawing on theory and knowledge from academia and our colleagues in other disciplines, we hope to contribute to a knowledge base that lays the foundations for future brilliant practice. This book contributes to the learning, reflection and skill development that equips social workers to do this essential work. Importantly, we also hope to have contributed to a social work without borders that centres, and partners with, the individuals and families we work with, one where we resist austerity and hostility together, alongside one another.

In this conclusion, we synthesise the major themes emerging from the chapters, and explore ways forward for a social work without borders. We propose that social work can, and should, play a key role in supporting asylum seekers, refugees and migrants and we must think critically about the intersection of race, class and borders if we are to challenge discourse about who is safeguarded and who is policed. Finally, drawing on the calls from our contributors, we promote collectivity as a vital tool in resisting hostility and in emboldening individual practitioners to take action.

There is a role for social workers with asylum seekers, refugees and migrants

There has been too much reliance on analyses that highlight the role of the media in the demonisation of social work; this appears an inadequate analysis when considered carefully. Surely, the logic of such an analysis is that social work practitioners are too incompetent to be feared. Our research with young people and their families suggests, however, that fear of an authoritarian state is often to be found among those who experience racism and oppression and feel alienated and disconnected. (Featherstone *et al.* 2018, pp.160–161)

Like Henrietta, whose voice we heard at the start of this book, we believe that social workers 'really play an important role for asylum seekers' (see Learning from Henrietta). Of course, we want to see social workers using their skills to promote social justice for those impacted by borders, but we must remember that social work is also important because social work interventions (or the lack of them) have critical and long-lasting effects on the individuals and families we work with. Social work is important because it is powerful and so it is crucial that we use this power carefully, with *care*, and with constant reflection on the conflicting agendas that dictate and govern our work (Robinson and Masocha 2017).

There remains a relative lack of literature, based on research, theory or practice, for social work with asylum seekers, refugees and migrants. Without a critical knowledge base, or the reflexive spaces to consider these in the workplace, the danger is that practitioners may fall back on their own unexamined constructions of the refugee or migrant, constructions which may exclude (Larkin 2015; Wroe 2018). Social work provision for people with irregular immigration status is a complex area of work. It is too easy for the best intentions of practitioners to get lost in a web of (lacking) legal entitlements, local policy, office hearsay and received cultures of practice.

For example, there is no statutory guidance for social workers supporting families with NRPF and the Social Care Institute for Excellence's *Good Practice Guidance in Social Care with Refugees and Asylum Seekers* has not been updated since 2015. This results in confusion among practitioners and potentially devastating consequences for families who are refused support. This has, no doubt, contributed to poor practice in some local authorities where 'failed' asylum-seeking and migrant families are being threatened with family separation in lieu of the provision of child-in-need support (*The Guardian* 2017). How do we resist poor practice if we are not versed in the values of our profession and the legal and human rights of those we support, or if we do not have space to critically reflect on practices and discourses that work to exclude the individuals and families we work with? There is an urgent need therefore for proper consideration to be paid to the knowledge and skills required to do this work, and for the social work curriculum to reflect this.

What all of the contributors to this book make very clear is that there is a role for social workers in supporting asylum seekers, refugees and migrants. Social workers have a role to play, not just because of the duties laid out (or obscured) in law and policy, but because of the social justice dimension of our profession. While the nature of our role is often framed by organisational processes, and by the legal and policy context, it is also shaped by us as practitioners. We are not simply enactors of law and policy; therefore, we cannot avoid our professional responsibilities, collectively or individually, towards people adversely affected by the immigration system in the UK.

Case study: a role for social workers

In 2017, one of the editors in her voluntary role with the charitable organisation Social Workers Without Borders (SWWB) advocated for a local authority children's services referral to be opened for a young person who had been 'assessed' by the Home Office as being 18 and had been placed in adult accommodation for asylum seekers in the north of the UK. This young person had not been age assessed. He said he was 16. He did not know the area, or how to cook, or how to use public transport, and he could not speak English. He was sharing a room with another adult male. The referral came from the solicitor that had represented this young man in the unofficial Calais refugee camp.

SWWB made a referral to the local authority to raise concerns that a young person was living in their area without access to support. The referral was initially declined, stating that as the young person had been 'assessed' as over 18, there was no role for children's services. SWWB responded, highlighting the risks posed to this young person, and advocated for a Merton compliant age assessment[2] by the local authority to challenge the age given by the Home Office.

A referral was opened and the young person was allocated a social worker. The social worker called SWWB and asked for further details about the young person's situation. It was then that SWWB was able to share information, with the young person's consent, about his journey to Calais, his time in the camp, his thoughts and feelings about being in the UK and importantly his disorientation and fear of being left in an unknown town, in an unknown country, without support. The social worker admitted that she knew very little about asylum-seeking young people and the kind of journeys they have taken. The social worker was alarmed and incredulous at hearing this young person's story and agreed to to stay in touch with SWWB, who would act as an advocate for the young person.

The social worker went on to arrange an assessment, to familiarise herself with the relevant guidance and to arrange an interpreter. She also linked the young person in with a local refugee organisation, and held a collection in her office for winter clothes and toiletries while they waited for the assessment date.

The young person was assessed as being 16. He was accommodated by the local authority who helped him to access legal advice. He was eventually granted leave to remain.

---

2   Under UK case law, age assessments must comply with the findings of *R (B) v Merton* LBC [2003] 4 All ER 280, where the court provided guidance on how age assessments should be conducted. This is known as being 'Merton compliant'.

'If they take you in the morning, they will be coming for us that night'[3]: migration as a route to the securitisation of social work

The social work profession has been critiqued for acting as part of the 'surveillance society', as 'agents of immigration control' (Cohen 2004, p.8) and, undoubtedly, this book has multiple examples of excluding practices. We need to pay attention to these examples, uncomfortable as they are to hear, if we are going to identify and challenge this practice when it occurs. As we argued at the start of this book, a commitment to social work practice premised on human rights and social justice is just as much about the defence of the rights of the individuals and families we work with as it is about the defence of our values as a profession and our right to care.

A clear warning from the chapters of this book, one that echoes that laid down by Hayes and Humphries (2004), is of the increasing encroachment of border regulation and monitoring into social work practice. In her chapter on asylum-seeking children in and leaving care, Anna Gupta (Chapter 8) highlights the challenges of practising social work from a human rights perspective:

> The contradictions social workers face in relation to adhering to their professional values, alongside the social work task increasingly having become embedded in restrictive immigration control, makes work with unaccompanied asylum-seeking children particularly challenging for workers striving to promote social justice and human rights.

Experienced practitioners Jude Boyles, Anna Turner and Katy Tolman make a similar call, documenting how these conflicting demands undermine social workers' commitment to those they are ostensibly positioned to support (Chapter 9):

> In our experience, it is not uncommon for social workers to become entwined in a bureaucratic system of resource management and, in the process, discount the needs and rights of a survivor at risk of homelessness/immigration detention and/or removal.

The securitisation of social work, through the instrumentalising of welfare as a mechanism of social control, is garnering increasing concern from professionals (Featherstone *et al.* 2018; McKendrick and Finch 2017;

---

3   From 'An Open Letter to My Sister, Angela Y. Davis' by James Baldwin. Reprinted in 2016.

Stanley 2018). However, as Rebecca Yeo reminds us in her timely exploration of disability and asylum seeking (Chapter 5), this has always been the reality for some families and individuals. Citing Tony Benn's famous warning, 'the way a government treats refugees…shows how they would treat the rest of us if they thought they could get away with it', Rebecca points out that the treatment of those deemed less worthy, in this case asylum seekers and disabled people, has laid the foundation for the exclusionary treatment of increasing categories of people. We are seeing service cuts and neo-liberal notions of choice and responsibility seep into areas of social work and welfare practice that previously have only been aimed at those already considered beyond the border.

The learning from this book, then, goes beyond the imposed definitions of 'asylum seeker', 'migrant', 'refugee' or 'citizen'. As Lucy Mort demonstrates in her chapter Migration and Austerity (Chapter 4), the policing of borders in expanding areas of public and private life, often built on the premise of 'otherness' (Ahmed 2000), is impacting on migrant and non-migrant alike. Importantly, in the context of the results of the 2016 UK EU membership referendum, the shifting and yet unknown definitions of belonging and rights will work to reposition borders and escalate the 'othering' of a broader category of people. While all categories of migrants do not experience the brutality of borders equally, due to the well-documented racialisation of border control (de Noronha 2018), we must prepare ourselves as a profession to resist an intensification of immigration surveillance in the arena of welfare provision and care. It is crucial, as we move into this new era of immigration management, that we are mindful of how we construct notions of who is deserving of support, and who is not. As Rebecca Yeo reminds us in her chapter Disability and Forced Migration (Chapter 5):

> The problems with presenting anyone as undeserving may be obvious, but campaigns presenting particular people as exceptionally deserving are similarly problematic. If someone's worth depends on being exceptional, then the implication is that others are less deserving.

Despite the complex web of political and media discourse, government policy, immigration law and service cuts, marching across the pages of this book is a defiant commitment to ethical practice and the ideas and skills to realise it. We have heard numerous examples of practitioners working to resist, mitigate and disrupt the impact of a hostile political environment, working creatively within their everyday roles, and creating spaces where experiences can be held and contained, while drawing on collective voices to instigate change. These are roots we need to develop and grow, if social work is going to more rigorously and effectively challenge discourses which dehumanise, and resist processes which exclude.

Resisting borders in social work: a case study from practice

Luke de Noronha recounts below the story of a man he met in Jamaica as part of his doctoral work on the deportation of ex-offenders from the UK and to Jamaica (de Noronha 2018).

I met Darel in Jamaica in September 2016. He had been deported a few days earlier on a charter flight with 41 other Jamaican nationals. Darel, aged 31, had lived in London since he was 7. He has six children in London, and was the primary carer for four of them.

When I met him in Jamaica, he was disoriented and frightened. He had no money, no support network, and spent his days inside on his phone speaking with his children.

Darel had never been to prison, but he had received three convictions for possession of marijuana. He was deported under Operation Nexus after the police claimed he was a 'suspected gang member'. Darel was not a member of any gang, he just grew up on an estate, smoked weed and was black. On this basis, he was exiled from his children, his partner, his family, his friends, and his home in the world.

Darel...did not understand the law and was not entitled to legal aid. He was subject to the most extraordinary form of state power, and yet his story was not news. It is this vulnerability to state power, and the illegibility and invisibility of Darel's suffering, that alerts us to the mechanics of race and class in the operation of the border.

What could a social work response to family separation at the intersection of race, class and border control look like?

Social Workers Without Borders (SWWB) works with the organisation Bail for Immigration Detainees (BID)[4] conducting best interest assessments for families who are separated by detention and/or the threat of deportation. SWWB conducts these assessments in light of children and families' the European Convention on Human Rights, Article 8 rights to 'private and family life'.

BID reports that in 2018 it worked with over 150 families separated by detention, deportation and removal from the UK under immigration rules (Cobain 2018). Restrictions on legal aid provision mean there is no legal aid available for families who are appealing immigration decisions in relation to their Article 8 rights. SWWB, supporting the work of BID, coordinates a network of volunteer social workers to conduct assessments at family homes and in detention centres, so that the families facing the most brutal arm of the immigration system have the chance to have their rights considered in front of a court. For many of these families, like Darel, a parent is detained after committing minor offences which are then used to justify their deporation from the UK. SWWB works across the deserving–undeserving nexus that plagues some areas of social work and refugee advocacy work (Wroe 2018), by making a collective decision to use resources to support migrant families who face separation by the criminal justice and immigration system. In line with domestic legislation and international rights treaties, and its commitment to the rights of families and children, SWWB believes that every child has a right to be brought up in their family, unless there are safety reasons that render this inappropriate. This is the case regardless of a parent's race, immigration status or involvement with the criminal justice system.

Not all families have the means to access social work or other expert reports in the absence of legal aid funding. Social work volunteers are filling this gap, while at the same time speaking out to hold the Home Office accountable for its family separation practices.

---

4   www.biduk.org

Collective action

> British social work may have become 'weighted…towards the notion of therapy' (Lynn 1999, p.945), but at different times and in different places the profession has understood the dual benefits of individual support and the restorative power of collective action against the structural oppressions which are, almost always, the ultimate cause of the problem. (Hannah Berry, Chapter 10)

Resistance has long played a role in professional social work, yet it is under-theorised and often individualised (Strier and Bershtling 2016). A key theme that emerged from the contributors to this book was a call for collectivity, based on a recognition of the strength and solidarity which can come from collective action. Social work has always been a contested profession, internally and externally, and it has struggled to find spaces where collective voices can develop. We recognise that austerity policies have further undermined social work organisations, in both voluntary and statutory sectors, and that this has added to the daily demands of practice, leaving little emotional or practical space for social workers to give to collective action. Yet this book is testament to the passion and commitment that exists within the profession, across services and sectors, a commitment we can take strength from and which we can take forward into our own work.

So what does this 'resistance' look like? Strier and Bershtling (2016, p.115) offer us this:

> resistance may differ in its level of visibility and recognition. It may be carried in subtle, indirect ways or in overt, articulated actions. These acts of opposition may be individual or collective, material or symbolic, conscious or unconscious, spontaneous or well-orchestrated, local or global, grounded in everyday professional life or other relevant spheres of professional participation. These professional actions can be targeted against both the practical and discursive aspects of the oppressive reality to be resisted.

Resistance can be an individual act of defiance, an act of care in the face of hostility or of generosity in the face of scarcity. Rachael Bee's account of her transition from statutory social work to establishing the destitution project the Bristol Hospitality Network (Chapter 11) is a powerful and inspiring example of what one person can do when they push at the boundaries of what it means to be a social worker: an example, perhaps, of the re-imagining of professional boundaries where the 'professional body of social work codes of conduct has no clocking on and off times and applies equally on the dance floor as in the office!' (Suryia Nayak, Chapter 3).

Yet Rachael could not have done this work alone, without the support of colleagues, family and friends and the relationships formed with those whom her project supports. Collective action is a rallying call from the pages of this book and this is achieved by creating networks of social workers dedicated to a theoretically informed, rights-based practice.

Collectivity can be a powerful tool at the micro-level, as well as the regional or national level, and they support each other. The sharing of knowledge, within teams and organisations, can be a constructive first step to build a shared sense of purpose. Creating spaces in workplaces to discuss and share the dilemmas, as well as the successes, can lead to debates about what type of social work practitioners want to foreground in their work. Involving the people we work with in meaningful dialogue, and asking them about their experiences of social care services in diverse and creative ways, can also create a sense of collectivity across the boundaries that too often separate us. In the same way, opening ourselves up to dialogue with colleagues from other agencies, and allowing ourselves to hear their perspectives, also fosters collectivity. This is a global issue and there is a wealth of knowledge, ideas and skills beyond our own locality, which can both improve our own work and sustain us through the difficult times.

Summarising her experience of establishing the charity Social Workers Without Borders, Lynn King (Chapter 2) reflects on how her experience of experimenting with collective work activism, at the intersection of social work and border control, has resulted in her feeling proud, for the first time, to be a social worker. It is this pride in our professional community that is too often absent, and that arguably differentiates social work from, say, the health or teaching professions. However, it is this pride that affords professionals the confidence to collectively stand up and speak out against attacks on our values and on the lives of the people we work with. Is this why we have seen resistance to the recording and sharing of nationality data with the Home Office by Docs Not Cops and Schools ABC, yet nothing from social work on the embedding of immigration officials in NRPF teams?

While this book is a celebration and provides multiple examples of excellent social work practice, we are mindful of the potted and often contested history of social work. Where social work is practised without an ethical value base, not grounded in social justice and human rights, it can have devastating consequences. Silence is complicity. That is why it is crucial that we frequently revisit the question of social work autonomy from the state. How do we practise ethical social work with asylum seekers, refugees and migrants, in and against (London Edinburgh Weekend Return Group 1979) the very systems that seek to violently exclude them? While this book makes a contribution to this question, it is a matter for ongoing, collective reflection and political action. Social work is political. Whether we revisit its roots in the Charitable Organisations Society individual casework model for the 'deserving and undeserving' (Lymbery 2005) or the social work of the Black Power movement (Bell 2014), we are engaged in political work.

In her chapter, Black Feminist Diaspora Spaces of Social Work Critical Reflexivity, Suria Nayak (Chapter 3) confronts us with this thought: 'the challenge amounts to social work choosing, for it is a choice, whether to stand by waiting for liberation to happen or to be instrumental in the struggle'. The voices brought together in this book speak to numerous struggles: the struggle of social work to maintain its position as a caring profession based on principles of human rights and social justice, and the struggle against borders by those who seek to cross them. Social work without borders, then, is about the intersectionality of these struggles (Nayak and Robbins 2018). It is about pushing at the borders of what it means to do social work and pushing borders out of social work practice.

References

Ahmed, S. (2000) *Strange Encounters: Embodied Others in Post-Coloniality.* London: Routledge.

Bell, J.M. (2014) *The Black Power Movement and American Social Work.* New York, NY: Columbia University Press.

Cobain, I. (2018) 'UK immigration authorities separating children from parents.' Accessed 29/11/2018 at: www.theguardian.com/uk-news/2018/jul/03/uk-immigration-authorities-separating-children-from-parents.

Cohen, S. (2004) 'Foreword: Breaking the Links and Pulling the Plug'. In D. Hayes and B. Humphries (eds) *Social Work, Immigration and Asylum: Debates, Dilemmas and Ethical Issues for Social Work and Social Care Practice,* pp.7–10. London: Jessica Kingsley Publishers.

Davis, A. (2016) *If They Come in the Morning... Voices of Resistance.* London: Verso.

de Noronha, L. (2018) Race, class and Brexit: Thinking from detention. Accessed 28/11/2018 at: www.versobooks.com/blogs/3675-race-class-and-brexit-thinking-from-detention.

European Convention on Human Rights (1950) Accessed on 16/11/2018 at: www.echr. coe. int/Documents/Convention_ENG.pdf.

Featherstone, B., Gupta, A., Morris, K. and White, S. (2018) *Protecting Children: A Social Model.* Bristol: Policy Press.

Guardian, The (2017) 'Destitute immigrants in the UK are threatened with having children removed.' 13 June. Accessed 29/11/2018 at: www.theguardian.com/uk-news/2017/jun/13/destitute-immigrants-uk-threatened-with-having-children-removed.

Hayes, D. and Humphries, B. (2004) *Social Work, Immigration and Asylum: Debates, Dilemmas and Ethical Social Work and Social Care Practice.* London: Jessica Kingsley Publishers.

Hill Collins, P. (2000) *Black Feminist Thought: Knowledge, Consciousness, and the Politics of Empowerment.* New York, NY: Routledge.

Larkin, R. (2015) 'Understanding the "lived experience" of unaccompanied young women: Challenges and opportunities for social work.' *Practice,* 27, 5, 297–313.

London Edinburgh Weekend Return Group (1979). 'In and against the state.' Accessed 30/11/2018 at: http://libcom.org/library/against-state-1979.

Lymbery, M. (2005) *Social Work with Older People: Context, Policy and Practice.* London: Sage.

McKendrick, D. and Finch, J. (2017) '"Under heavy manners?": Social work, radicalisation, troubled families and non-linear war.' *British Journal of Social Work,* 47, 2, 308–324.

Nayak, S. and Robbins, R. (2018) *Intersectionality in Social Work: Activism and Practice in Context.* London: Routledge.

R (B) v Merton LBC [2003] 4 All ER 280.

Robinson, K. and Masocha, S. (2017) 'Divergent practices in statutory and voluntary-sector settings? Social work with asylum seekers.' *British Journal of Social Work,* 47, 5, 1517–1533.

Social Care Institute for Excellence (2015) *Good Practice in Social Care for Refugees and Asylum Seekers.* Accessed 27/11/2018 at: www.scie.org.uk/publications/guides/guide37-good-practice-in-social-care-with-refugees-and-asylum-seekers.

Stanley, T. (2018) 'The relevance of risk work theory to practice: The case of statutory social work and the risk of radicalisation in the UK.' *Health, Risk & Society,* 20, 1–2, 104–112.

Strier, R. and Bershtling, O. (2016) 'Professional resistance in social work: Counterpractice assemblages.' *Social Work,* 61, 2, 111–118.

Turbett, C. (2014) *Doing Radical Social Work.* London: Palgrave Macmillan.

Wroe, L. (2018) '"It really is about telling people who asylum seekers really are, because we are human like anybody else": Negotiating victimhood in refugee advocacy work.' *Discourse and Society,* 29, 3, 324–323.

Contributors

Editors

Lauren Wroe is a registered social worker, a social work academic and an activist. Lauren is a co-founder of the charity Social Workers Without Borders and a research fellow at the Contextual Safeguarding Team at the International Centre Researching Child Sexual Exploitation Violence and Trafficking at the University of Bedfordshire. Lauren has worked and campaigned alongside people navigating the asylum and immigration system for 14 years and since qualifying as a social worker has worked in children's and adults' services in the statutory and voluntary sector. Lauren is interested in exploring everyday problems from a social justice perspective and has researched, evaluated and published work relating to child protection, social work systems and borders internationally and in the UK.

Rachel Larkin is a registered social worker with over 25 years of experience in practice, in frontline and leadership roles, and in both statutory children and families services and in the voluntary sector. Since 2008 Rachel has worked as an independent reviewing officer for looked-after children, working directly with young people who have migrated to the UK. In 2018 she completed a professional doctorate at the University of Sussex, researching social work with unaccompanied young women and examining the ways in which young women and practitioners understand each other. She is interested in the ways that social workers and young people think and feel about each other, and how this may affect what happens to young people within social work services.

Reima Ana Maglajlic is a senior lecturer in social work at the University of Sussex. Rea's practice and research focuses on health and social care reform in conflict and post-conflict countries, particularly in relation to mental health. Since starting her post at the University of Sussex in 2013, she volunteers in local charities and initiatives that support unaccompanied minors and destitute asylum seekers, primarily offering casework supervision and support for the development of new practice initiatives.

Chapter authors

Jen Ang is founding co-director of JustRight Scotland and an experienced human rights lawyer who has specialised in working with trafficked children and young people, and those seeking international protection. She leads JustRight for All, which is a legal research, policy and training hub. Jen is also a lecturer in law at the Open University, and an advocate of open access to education for all.

Rachael Bee is the manager of Bristol Hospitality Network, a charity working in solidarity with destitute refused asylum seekers in Bristol. Rachael co-founded the charity in 2008 with Dr Naomi Millner and has been working for it since 2014. Previously, Rachael was a social worker in hospital discharge and then in the community team for adults with learning difficulties. She has hosted over 35 refused asylum seekers since 2008 in her own home.

Hannah Berry is a community development worker and activist. In 2013, she completed a doctorate on 'Practices of alliance and solidarity with asylum-seeking women', drawing on her work with GAP Unit, a small Manchester-based organisation inspired by the popular education movement and the philosophy of Paulo Freire. She now coordinates an older people's Equalities Board as part of Ambition for Ageing, a five-year third-sector programme aimed at reducing social isolation among older people in some of the more deprived neighbourhoods of Greater Manchester.

Jude Boyles is a BACP senior accredited psychological therapist, having qualified in June 1994. She currently manages therapeutic services for resettled Syrian refugees for the Refugee Council. In 2003, Jude established the first Freedom from Torture (FFT) rehabilitation centre outside FFT's headquarters in London. Jude managed the service for 14 years until April 2017. As part of this role, she provided supervision to therapists and practitioners working in the refugee field in the region. Before specialising in refugee therapy, Jude worked as a crisis counsellor for 11 years within a non-medical mental health crisis service, having worked within Rape Crisis and Women's Aid services for many years prior to qualifying.

Natalia Farmer is a research associate in the School for Business and Society at Glasgow Caledonian University, Scotland. Her doctoral research at the Asylum Seeker Housing Project has focused on the tensions between immigration legislation and social work practice, exploring the issue of 'no recourse to public funds' (NRPF). Her recent publication *No Recourse to Public Funds: Insecure Immigration Status and Destitution: The Role of Social Work?* (2017) is drawn from her research and examines the barriers destitute NRPF families encounter when attempting to access local authority support. She has provided written and oral evidence to the Scottish government's Equality and Human Rights Committee, which informed the report *Hidden Lives – New Beginnings: Destitution, Asylum and Insecure Immigration Status in Scotland* (2017). Other research interests include the science and technology studies methodological approach of controversy analysis. She is currently an editorial board member of *Critical and Radical Social Work*.

Anna Gupta is a professor of social work at Royal Holloway University of London. She teaches on the qualifying and post-qualifying social work programmes in the Centre for Social Work in the School of Law. Her research interests include child protection and poverty, unaccompanied migrant youth, children in care and adoption. She has recently completed an ESRC-funded research seminar series on unaccompanied children seeking asylum, as well as a BASW-funded study exploring the role of the social worker in adoption with a focus on ethics and human rights.

Lynn King has been a local authority social worker since 2006 and is currently the practice development lead for adult social work in Kent. She is a qualified best interest assessor and practice educator. In 2016, Lynn co-founded the charity Social Workers Without Borders (SWWB) in response to the refugee crisis at the French and UK border in Calais. Since 2016, she has helped to coordinate over a hundred assessments of best interests/ human rights undertaken by volunteer social workers for SWWB, across the UK and in France.

Annemarie Morsch was a translator and interpreter for over ten years, having emigrated to the UK as a child and studied modern languages (obtaining a master's in translation studies and a diploma in public service interpreting). She interpreted primarily with refugees and asylum seekers in the health service, in a wide variety of settings. She retrained as a social worker, qualifying in 2014, and is now a project worker at the Refugee Council in Sheffield, where she supports resettlement refugees in their integration and works closely with interpreters.

Lucy Mort completed a doctorate in social care and social work at Manchester Metropolitan University in 2017. Her thesis explored how austerity and the 'hostile environment' are experienced by both migrants and refugees and by those providing support to migrants and refugees in the voluntary sector. A qualified social worker, Lucy has eight years' experience of working with migrants, asylum seekers and refugees. Since her doctorate, Lucy has been working in a practice context with migrant women with 'no recourse to public funds' who have experienced gender-based violence, and with the Syrian Vulnerable Persons Resettlement Programme. She is working on several publications from her thesis, and has recently joined the Institute for Public Policy Research as a research fellow.

Suryia Nayak is a senior lecturer in social work at the University of Salford. Suryia has been working with Black feminism for over 35 years, campaigning for social justice in ending violence against women and girls, primarily within the Rape Crisis Movement. She has set up services and spaces dedicated to Black and Asian women. Suryia applies models of education as liberation and the activism of Black feminism to raise consciousness about the psychological and political impact of oppressive social constructions. She also works as a psychoanalytic therapist and supervisor and is training to be a group analyst.

Elaine Ortiz has worked for many years in child protection for organisations such as the National Society for the Prevention of Cruelty to Children (NSPCC) Child Protection Helpline, in residential care and as a rape crisis worker at the St Mary's Centre in Manchester. In June 2015, she set up the Hummingbird Project, which initially worked directly with refugees in camps in northern France and also in the UK. Following the closure of the refugee camp in Calais, Elaine became the director of the Hummingbird Project as a registered charity which runs a number of services and projects across the UK and Europe in order to ensure refugees and unaccompanied minors receive the vital support they need and deserve, as they work their way towards a better life.

Katy Tolman qualified as a social worker in 2016 and completed her assessed and supported year in employment (ASYE) in a local authority children and families team. Katy has worked with refugees and people seeking asylum both pre- and post-qualifying, including working specifically with survivors of torture. She has volunteered with Social Workers Without Borders since its inception, first as a student and then as a professional. Katy currently works as an intercountry social worker in the fields of international child protection and family reunification.

Anna Turner is a Manchester-based social worker, currently working for the NHS in an early intervention in psychosis team. Prior to this, Anna spent ten years developing and coordinating services for a charity sector organisation, working with refugees and people seeking asylum. Anna has developed and led on a number of projects and created a working model of therapeutic social work with torture survivors in exile. She continues to be active across services working with refugees and people seeking asylum as an external supervisor, trainer and trustee member. She is in her final year of studying for a diploma in transactional analysis in psychotherapy.

Joanne Vincett is a doctoral researcher in the Faculty of Business and Law at the Open University in Milton Keynes. She is also a trustee overseeing fundraising on the board of Yarl's Wood Befrienders, a voluntary organisation that offers emotional and practical support to people detained in Yarl's Wood Immigration Removal Centre in the UK. Her current ethnographic research explores how volunteers practise compassion and emotional resilience while befriending detained migrants and asylum seekers.

Rebecca Yeo worked in the international development sector for many years, focusing on issues of disability and poverty in different parts of the world. When she began volunteering in the UK asylum sector she realised that the existence and needs of disabled asylum seekers were being largely ignored. From 2009 to 2012, Rebecca worked with the UK Disabled People's Council, coordinating research with disabled people living in a wide range of different circumstances. It was then that she began working with disabled asylum seekers. Since then, Rebecca has continued working on similar issues, mostly in the UK, but also in Berlin for six months in 2017.

Subject Index

Aboriginals 21
accommodation 95–6
  assessing support 100–2
  close proximity to the issues 102–4
  key points for practice 104–6
  lessons from controversial inquiries 97–8
  raising awareness through
    the media 98–100
Afghanistan 144, 156, 166, 175–9, 207–8
Against Borders for Children 72
age assessments 23, 147–8, 223
  ages dispute and age assessment 128–30
  R (B) v London Borough of Merton
    [2003] EWHC 1689 147, 270
age assessments of unaccompanied asylum-
  seeking children (UASC) 239–40, 246–7
  communicating about trauma
    and understanding traumatic
    experiences 240–2
  need for multidisciplinary and
    inter-agency work 245–6
  need for preparation and follow-up 242–5
Age of Legal Capacity (Scotland) Act 1991 119
Ahmad, Kamil 22, 77–8, 85, 88, 92, 211
  Kamil's experiences 78–80
Albania 144, 156
Ang, Jen 22–3, 280
appeal rights exhausted (ARE) 101,
  125, 148, 155, 172, 206, 222
Arab Spring 27
Arise and Shine project 190–2, 200–2
  group origins and initiation 192–4
  learning from the Arise and
    Shine project 194–200
  tips for empowering practice with
    people seeking asylum 202–3

Asylum Matters 215
Asylum Seeker Housing (ASH) Project,
  Glasgow 95, 97–100, 102, 104, 107–8
asylum seekers 7, 17–19, 21, 27, 57–8
  Aida's experience 237–8
  Andy's experience 217–18
  determination of child asylum
    claims 134–7
  European migrant crisis 18, 27,
    63–4, 96, 117, 219, 222
  Henrietta's experience 13–15, 268
  impact of austerity policies 58–60
  Jan's experience 115–16
  Kamil's experiences 78–80
  learning from the Arise and
    Shine project 194–200
  Ken's experience 263–6
  Mary's experience 39–41
  mental health 70–1, 212
  processing of child asylum claims 131–4
  role for social workers with asylum seekers,
    refugees and migrants 268–70
  Sam's experience 75–6
  Stella's experience 185–7
  tips for empowering practice with
    people seeking asylum 202–3
  torture survivors 164–5
asylum seekers with disabilities 77–8, 92
  Ahmad, Kamil 78–80
  data 89
  hostile environment policies 80–7
  inclusion 89–90
  proposed ways forward 90–2
  safeguarding vulnerable people 87–9
Asylum Support Appeals Project
  (ASAP) 101–2

austerity 7–9, 19, 71–3, 201
    global focus 63–4
    impact of austerity policies 58–60, 149
AVID (Association of Visitors to
    Immigration Detainees) 228

Bail for Immigration Detainees
    (BID) 34–5, 229, 274
Baldwin, James 'An Open Letter to
    My Sister, Angela Y. Davis' 271
Bangladesh 195
Becoming Adult 151, 155–6, 157
Bee, Rachael 23, 275–6, 280
Benn, Tony 92, 272
Berry, Hannah 23, 267, 280
Besong, Lydia How I Became
    an Asylum Seeker 193
best interest assessments 30–3, 34–5
black feminist diaspora 41–3, 53–4
    border consciousness 43–5
    critical reflexivity 45
    logic of context 50–1
    logic of the collective 47–8
    logic of the erotic 51–3
    logic of time and heritage 48–50
Black Power 277
Borders, Citizenship and Immigration Act
    2009 Section 55 121, 125–6, 131, 145
Boyles, Jude 23, 271, 280–1
Brexit 95, 123
Bristol Hospitality Network
    (BHN) 205–7, 275
    Ahmad, Kamil 211
    how can social workers support
        destitute asylum seekers? 212–16
    mental health work 212
    Mohammad 207–10
Bristol Refugee Rights 17
British Association of Social
    Workers (BASW) 32, 59, 73
Brook House Immigration Removal Centre 99

Calais migrant camp, France 18,
    27–36, 89, 181, 243, 245, 270
    Jungle Books Kids Space 29
    legal shelter 30
Cameron, David 67
Cameroon 179–80, 195
Cardiff University 83
Care Act 2014 36, 211, 212, 213, 214
    Section 18(1) 79
Care Leavers (England) Regulations 2010 148
CASE (Collaborative Awards in
    Science and Engineering) 190

Channel 4 News 227
Charitable Organisations Society 277
Charity Commission 33
child and adolescent mental health
    services (CAMHS) 172, 173
children 117–18, 138–9
    age dispute and age assessment 128–30
    asylum decision 137–8
    asylum process 131
        case studies 126–8, 135–7
        child-specific assessment
            of the claim 135
        child-specific persecution 135
        responsible adult 131–2
        service of decision 134
        shift in burden of proof 134–5
        Statement of Evidence
            Form (SEF) 132–3
        substantive asylum interview 133–4
        welfare interview 132
    Calais migrant camp, France 27–32
    challenges and barriers facing children
        and young people 126–8, 130–1
    child first, migrant second 118–19
    child welfare legislation 124–5
    children's rights in international
        and domestic law 119–24
    children's rights in UK domestic law 124–6
    torture survivors 169, 172–3, 175–9
    trafficking 128, 240
    see age assessments of unaccompanied
        asylum-seeking children
        (UASC) children
    see unaccompanied asylum-
        seeking children (UASC)
Children (Leaving Care) Act 2000 146
Children (Northern Ireland) Order 1995 124
Children (Scotland) Act 1995 124
Children Act 1989 124, 143, 146, 147
    Section 17 20, 69, 148, 179
    Section 20 148, 149
Children's Society 132
Chile 91
City of Sanctuary 215
Clearsprings Group 98
Climbié, Victoria 251
Cohen, Steve 8
Common Assessment Framework 173
community groups 23, 189–92, 200–2
    group origin and initiation 192–4
    learning from the Arise and
        Shine project 194–200
    tips for empowering practice with
        people seeking asylum 202–3

COMPASS (Commercial and Operational
    Managers Procuring Asylum
    Support Services) 98, 107
Conservative government 20, 60, 88
controversies 95–6, 110
    assessing support 100–2
    close proximity to the issues 102–4
    contemporary immigration context 96–7
    key points for practice 104–6
    lessons from controversial inquiries 97–8
    raising awareness through
        the media 98–100
    social work and NRPF (no resource
        to public funds) 106–9
Convention on the Rights of
    the Child (CRC) 30–1
criminals 222
Croydon LBC 147

Democratic Republic of the
    Congo (DRC) 171–5
Department for Work and Pensions 69, 84
deportation 8, 61, 67, 69, 274
Destitute Domestic Violence
    (DDV) Concession 69
destitution 19, 20, 22, 205–7
    Ahmad, Kamil 211
    how can social workers support
        destitute asylum seekers? 212–16
    how does BHN interact with
        statutory services? 211–12
    Mohammad 207–10
detention 8, 23, 61, 71, 85–6,
    194, 219–20, 231–2
    background of immigration
        detention in the UK 221–3
    factors to consider for frontline
        support service workers 230–1
    impact of indefinite detention on emotional
        well-being and mental health 224–6
    key lessons for frontline support
        service workers 231–2
    services inside detention centres 226–9
    vulnerable people 223–4
disabilities 77–8, 92
    Ahmad, Kamil 78–80, 92
    current initiatives for disabled
        asylum seekers 87–90
    disablism 81–5
    hostile environment policies 80–7
    proposed ways forward 90–2
Disability Living Allowance 83–4
Docs Not Cops 21, 72, 276

domestic abuse 69–70
Driver and Vehicle Licensing
    Agency (DVLA) 61
Dublin III 30, 123–4, 222
Duncan Lewis 30, 34
Dungavel Immigration Removal Centre 100

Early Help 173
Ebrahimi, Bijan 88
Economic and Social Research
    Council (ESRC) 190
Eritrea 144, 156, 195, 206
ESOL (English for speakers of
    other languages) 67, 205
Ethiopia 195, 196
European Convention on Human Rights
    (ECHR) 1950 122, 125, 148, 154, 274
European Union (EU) 18, 27, 272
European Union Common European
    Asylum System (CEAS) 123–4
Eurozone crisis 63–4
Every Child Matters 172
Every Child Protected Against
    Trafficking (ECPAT) 243
Exchange Model 169–70

family reunification 30, 244–5
family separation 274
Farmer, Natalia 22, 281
Freire, Paulo 190–1
Freud, David 83

G4S 61, 98, 99, 103, 221
GAP Unit, Manchester 190–1,
    192–3, 196, 198–9, 200–2
gatekeeping 8, 62, 108, 201
Gender Participation Unit 23
gender-specific abuses 165, 229
General Data Protection
    Regulation (GDPR) 32
Geneva Convention 122
GEO Group 221
Glanville, Philip 108
global crises 63–4
Global North 65
Global South 65, 69
Go Home vans 61, 97
Gramsci, Antonio 190
Greece 63
    Leros migrant camp 18
    migrant camps 181
Grenfell Tower disaster 59, 62
    public inquiry 97

Growing Together Levenshulme 17
Guardian, The 81
Gupta, Anna 23, 271, 281

Hayes, Debra 19
Health Care Professions Council
    (HCPC) 32–3
Helen Bamber Foundation 229
hepatitis C 102
Her Majesty's Inspectorate of
    Prisons (HMIP) 226
Her Majesty's Prison Service 221
Hibiscus 229
Hillingdon LBC 147
    Hillingdon judgement 146–7
Hillsborough Stadium Disaster
    Inquiry Report 97
HIV 102–3, 214
Home Office 8, 33, 35, 62, 69, 78, 81, 84–7,
    92, 102, 104, 106, 194, 197, 206, 276
    child asylum seekers 121, 125–6, 128,
        131–4, 145–7, 154, 159, 246
    detention 221, 222–4, 225, 229
    Home Affairs Committee 97–8, 99, 100
    Home Office Immigration
        Statistics 2008–12 246
    torture survivors 168
    'hostile environment' policies 18,
        19–22, 60–2, 72, 100, 157, 206
    asylum seekers with disabilities 80–7
human rights 81, 82, 83, 85, 104,
    144, 157, 158, 163
Human Rights Act 1998 34, 125, 252
Hummingbird Project 243, 245
Humphries, Beth 7, 19
Hussein, Saddam 85

Imkaan 47
immigration 7–9, 18–21, 57,
    95–6, 110, 219–20
    contemporary immigration context 96–7
immigration acts 82
    Borders, Citizenship and Immigration
        Act 2009 121, 125–6, 131, 145, 239
    Immigration Act 2014 61, 62, 96
    Immigration Act 2016 61, 62, 96,
        137, 148, 157, 221, 224
    Immigration and Asylum Act 1999
        7, 19, 82, 83–4, 87, 104, 107
    Nationality, Immigration and
        Asylum Act 2002 107, 125
Immigration Law Practitioners'
    Association 176–7

Immigration Removal Centres
    (IRCs) 23, 99, 100, 219–20
    background of immigration
        detention in the UK 221–4
    Her Majesty's Inspectorate of
        Prisons (HMIP) 226
    impact of indefinite detention on emotional
        well-being and mental health 224–6
    Independent Monitoring
        Board (IMB) 226, 232
    services inside detention centres 226–9
Independent Monitoring Board
    (IMB) 226, 232
International Convention on the Elimination
    of All Forms of Racial Discrimination 81
International Federation of Social
    Workers (IFSW) 28
interpreters 23–4, 80, 128, 152–3, 170,
    212, 214, 232, 251–2, 259–60
    is the work inherently problematic? 252–4
    practical considerations 258–9
    third person is not a 'translation
        machine' 254–6
    what does good practice look like? 254
    working within a triad 257–8
intersectionality 65–6
Iran 144, 206
Iraq 77, 78–9, 80, 85, 144, 206

Jamaica 273

Kaleidoscope 227
Kent CC 147
Kent County Council 18
Kids In Need of Defence (KIND) 34
King, Lynn 18, 22, 276, 281
    Social Work Without Borders
        (SWWB) 27–36
Kramer, Lyndsey 27
Kwanzaa 46

labour exploitation 66–7, 227
Labour government 145, 192
Larkin, Rachel 279
Latin America 190, 198
Lawyers Without Borders 33
legal issues 22–3
Legal Service Commission 228
local authorities 8, 20, 69
    unaccompanied asylum-seeking
        children (UASC) 145, 146–7,
        149–51, 153–4, 156–7, 246

Maglajlic, Reima 279–80
Malawi 195
marginalisation 22
Maternity Action 68
May, Theresa 60, 88, 100, 157
media 98–100
Medical Justice 229
mental health 70–1, 212
    child asylum seekers 152–3, 154, 156
    impact of indefinite detention on emotional
        well-being and mental health 224–6
    torture survivors 169, 176, 178–80
Mental Health Act 2017 212
Merton judgement 147, 270
#MeToo 95
Mid-Staffordshire NHS Foundation
    Trust Public Inquiry 97
migrants 18–24, 57–8
    European migrant crisis 18, 27,
        63–4, 96, 117, 219, 222
    global focus 63–4
    hostility towards migrants 60–2
    impact of austerity policies 58–60
    intersectionality 65–6
    mental health 70–1, 212
    NRPF (no resource to public funds) 68–70
    precarity 66–8
    role for social workers with asylum seekers,
        refugees and migrants 268–70
Millner, Naomi 207, 208
Mitie Plc 221
Modern Slavery Helpline 229
Morgan, Louise 28
Morsch, Annemarie 23–4, 281–2
Mort, Lucy 19–20, 22, 272, 282

National Asylum Support Service (NASS) 60
National Health Service (NHS)
    61, 62, 81, 199, 225
National Referral Mechanism (NRM) 128, 229
Nationality, Immigration and Asylum
    Act 2002 107, 125, 223
Nayak, Suryia 21–2, 276, 277, 282
NGOs (non-governmental
    organisations) 163, 164
Nigeria 195
No Accommodation Network
    (NACCOM) 206, 213, 214–15
North West Together We Can
    (NWTWC) 192, 201

NRPF (no resource to public funds)
    20, 22, 68–70, 206, 269, 276
    categories of people affected 68–9
    social work and NRPF (no resource
        to public funds) 106–9

Office of the Immigration Services
    Commissioner (OISC) 101
Operation Nexus 222
Orchard & Shipman (O&S) 99, 102
Ortiz, Elaine 23, 282
Otezya, Carolina de 190, 193, 200

Pakistan 166
Pelka, Daniel 251
Pinochet, Augusto 91
Plan C 267
political changes 9
Portugal 63
post-traumatic stress disorder
    (PTSD) 168, 176, 214
precarity 66–8
    child asylum seekers leaving care 154–7
pregnancy 103–4, 195, 225
Project 17 20
public inquiries 97–8

R (B) v London Borough of Merton
    [2003] EWHC 1689 147, 270
R (Behre) v London Borough of
    Hillingdon [2003] EWHC 2075 146
racism 19, 22, 61, 81
rape 165, 166
Red Cross 195
Refugee Convention 1951 81,
    82, 122, 134, 135
Refugee Council 68
Refugee Mothers United
    (RMU) 195–6, 198–9
refugees 18–19, 21, 57–8
    European migrant crisis 18, 27,
        63–4, 96, 117, 219, 222
    impact of austerity policies 58–60
    mental health 70–1, 212
    role for social workers with asylum seekers,
        refugees and migrants 268–70
    torture survivors 163–4, 166–7, 180–1
Regional Empowerment Agency 192
Right to Remain 232
Rights of Children and Young Persons
    (Wales) Measure 2011 124
rule of law 243–4
Rwanda 86

Safety4Sisters 73
Salvation Army 229, 230
Samaritans 85
Schools ABC 21, 276
science and technology studies (STS) 95
Scottish Guardianship Service 132, 152, 158
Scottish Refugee Council (SRC) 99, 100
Second World War 81, 117
securitisation 19, 271–3
    migration as a route to the securitisation
        of social work 271–3
self-care 230–1
separated young people 23
    see unaccompanied asylum-
        seeking children (UASC)
Serco Plc 61, 98, 99, 107, 221
Slough Judgement 213
social care provision 18–19
social justice 28, 29, 97, 144, 157, 267, 269
    Freire, Paulo 190–1
Social Services and Well-Being
    (Wales) Act 2014 124
social work 7–9, 17–24, 95–6
    close proximity to the issues 102–4
    how can social workers support
        destitute asylum seekers? 212–16
    key lessons for frontline support
        service workers 231–2
    key points for practice 104–6
    self-care 230–1
    social work and NRPF (no resource
        to public funds) 106–9
    torture survivors 168–71
    transnational social work 64–5
    unaccompanied asylum-seeking
        children (UASC) 157–9
Social Work Action Network (SWAN) 59
social work without borders 267–8
    collective action 275–7
    migration as a route to the securitisation
        of social work 271–3
    resisting borders in social work 273
    role for social workers with asylum seekers,
        refugees and migrants 268–70
Social Workers Without Borders
    (SWWB) 18, 22, 73
    Calais migrant camp, France 27–33
    family separation 274
    role for social workers 270
    setting up as a charity 33–4
    working as a charity in the UK 34–6
solidarity 90–2

Somalia 206
South Africa 195
Southall Black Sisters 47
Spain 63
Still Human Still Here 215
Sudan 144, 195
suicide 71, 85, 88, 153, 169, 176, 225
surveillance 8–9, 19, 267, 271–2
Syria 27, 86, 88–9, 91, 163

Taking Part? Capacity Building
    Cluster (CBC) 190
Taliban 166, 176
Team Around the Child (TAC) 173
Team Around the Family (TAF) 173
These Walls Must Fall 73
Third Sector Research Centre (TSRC) 190
Tinsley House, Gatwick 223
Tolman, Katy 23, 271, 283
torture survivors 23, 163–5, 180–1
    Amrine – Cameroon 179–80
    creating a framework 168–71
    defining torture 165
    Francois and Alvine – Democratic
        Republic of the Congo (DRC) 171–5
    Hassan – Afghanistan 175–9
    seeking safety 165–8
    women 165, 229
Townsend, Peter 81–2
trafficking 122, 128, 144, 151,
    176, 229, 230, 240
transnational social work 64–5
Trump, Donald 81, 96, 110
Turkey 64, 255
Turner, Anna 23, 271, 283

Uganda 195
UK 17–18, 82, 83, 224
    Calais migrant camp, France 27, 29, 31, 33
    child refugees 117–18
    European Convention on Human
        Rights (ECHR) 1950 122, 125
    European Union Common European
        Asylum System (CEAS) 123–4
    global focus 63–4
    torture survivors 166–7
    UN Convention on the Rights of the Child
        (UNCRC) 1989 121, 124, 145, 223
    unaccompanied children seeking
        asylum in the UK 144–5
UK Borders Act 2007 222
UK Disabled People's Council 77
UK Lesbian & Gay Immigration Group 229

UK Visas and Immigration
(UKVI) 88, 120, 129–30
determination of child asylum
claims 131–4
processing of child asylum
claims 131–4, 138
unaccompanied asylum-seeking children
(UASC) 31, 117, 143–4, 178, 223–4
care and protection 148–54
key messages for social workers 159
National Transfer Scheme 147
policy and legal contexts 145–8
practice issues 157–9
turning 18 154–7
unaccompanied children seeking
asylum in the UK 144–5
see age assessments of unaccompanied
asylum-seeking children (UASC)
UNICEF 146
Union of the Physically Impaired
Against Segregation 82
United Nations 81
UN Convention Against Torture
(UNCAT) 1984 163, 164, 226
UN Convention on the Rights of
Persons with Disabilities 83
UN Convention on the Rights
of the Child (UNCRC) 1989
119–21, 133, 143, 145, 223
UN Convention on the Status of
Refugees 1951 81, 82, 122, 134, 135
UN High Commissioner for
Refugees Vulnerable Person's
Resettlement Scheme 163–4
Universal Declaration on Human Rights 81
University of Warwick 190
Unum 83

Vaz, Keith 98
Venezuela 190, 200
Vietnam 144
Vincett, Jo 23, 283
voluntary organisations 23, 72, 79
Ahmad, Kamil 211
Bristol Hospitality Network (BHN) 205–7
how can social workers support
destitute asylum seekers? 212–16
Mohammad 207–10
Yarl's Wood Befrienders 220, 228–9
vulnerability 87–9, 177–8
detention 223–4
Vulnerable Persons Relocation Scheme 88

Waverley Care 102–3
welfare benefits 7–8, 19, 21, 177–8
austerity 58–60, 83
Immigration and Asylum Act
1999 82, 83–4, 87
NRPF (no resource to public funds) 68–70
rights-based criteria for support 90
Welfare Reform Act 2012 83–4
Windrush controversy 2018 8, 97
Women Asylum Seekers Together
(WAST) 192–3, 200
Women for Refugee Women 229
Wroe, Lauren 279

Yarl's Wood Immigration Removal
Centre 194, 220, 223, 225–6, 227–8
Yarl's Wood Befrienders 220, 226, 228–9
Yeo, Rebecca 22, 211, 272, 283

ZH Tanzania v SSHD [2011] UKSC 4 145
Zimbabwe 195

Author Index

Abdulla, M. 252
Abi-Aad, G. 18
Age of Legal Capacity (Scotland) Act 1991 119
Ahmed, S. 272
Aliens Act 1905 59
Allsop, J. 153
Amnesty International 166
Ang, J. 125
Anzaldúa, G. 42, 44
ASAP (Asylum Support Appeals Project) 101, 102
Association of Directors of Children's Services (ADCS) 129, 147, 240, 241, 242, 243, 245
Asylos 208
Asylum Information Database 240
Asylum Seeker Housing (ASH) Project 104
Aylward, M. 83
Aymer, C. 253
Ayre, P. 100

Bail for Immigration Detainees (BID) 229
Bambra, C. 67
Banks, S. 158
Bashir, C. 163
Bassel, L. 60
Baylis, G. 150
BBC 96, 98, 99
Beale, F. 43
Bean, T. 153
Beddoe, L. 100
Bell, J.M. 277
Berg-Weger, M. 177
Berry, H. 192
Bershtling, O. 275
Bevan, A. 81
Bianchini, K. 241, 244, 246
Birkenmaier, J. 177
Bischoff, A. 253
Blair, T. 83
Borders, Citizenship and Immigration Act 2009 121, 125–6, 131, 145, 239

Bosworth, M. 220, 221, 225
Bot, H. 258
Boyce Davies, C. 41, 42, 43, 53
Boyden, J. 240
Boyles, J. 253, 256
Brah, A. 41, 44
Brämberg, E.B. 253, 256
Bride, B.E. 230
Briskman, L. 28, 158, 159
Bristol Safeguarding Adults Board (BSAB) 78, 80, 85, 88
British Association of Social Workers (BASW) 102, 129, 147, 216, 239, 240, 245, 246, 247, 252
British Medical Association Medical Ethics Committee 225, 230
Bronstein, I. 153

Care Act 2014 36, 79, 213
Care Planning and Care Leavers (Amendment) Regulations 2014 148
Carey, M. 200
Cassidy, K. 97
Cemlyn, S.J. 147–8, 149, 157
Centre for Mental Health 225
Chand, A. 255
Chase, E. 149, 150, 151, 152, 153, 154, 155, 156
Children Act 1989 124, 143, 146–7, 148, 149
Children (Leaving Care) Act 2000 146
Children (Northern Ireland) Order 1995 124
Children (Scotland) Act 1995 124
Children's Society, The 109, 242, 243
Clark, I. 66–7
Clarke, S. 148
Clayton, S. 143
Clifford, E. 80
Cobain, I. 274
Cohen, S. 60, 271
Colling, T. 66–7
Collins, P.J. 67

CommonSpace 99, 102
Community Care 97, 176
Combahee River Collective, The 47
Connelly, E. 225
Connolly, H. 149, 151
Coram Children's Legal Centre 148, 246
Council of Europe 123
Court, J. 67
Coventry Safeguarding Children Board 251
Craig, S. 125
Crawley, H. 128, 147, 152, 153, 158, 175, 176
Crisp, J. 89
Crock, M. 83

Da Lomba, S. 195
Davis, A.Y. 41, 45, 48, 271
De Cleen, B. 81
de Noronha, L. 272, 273
Deepak, A. 64
Department for Children, Schools
    and Families 121
Department for Education 125, 128,
    144, 145, 146, 147, 151, 155, 251
Department for Education and Skills 172
Department for Health 251
Dewees, M. 177
Doctors of the World 239
Dorfman, A. 91, 92
Dorling, K. 147, 155
Drozdek, B. 167

Elsass, P. 166
Elwyn, E. 157
Emejulu, A. 60
Epston, D. 189
Ernst, C. 83
European Commission 123
European Convention on Human Rights
    (ECHR) 1950 122, 125, 274
European Parliament 123
Evening Times 103
Every Child Protected Against
    Trafficking (ECPAT) UK 151, 240

Farmer, N.J. 18, 69, 108
Farooq, S. 256
Fear, C. 256
Featherstone, B. 267, 268, 271
Feldman, R. 68
Ferret, The 108
Finch, J. 271
Foster, V. 200
Foucault, M. 181

Franklin, B. 100
Freed, A.O. 253, 259
Freire, P. 29, 190–1, 196, 200
Friedl, L. 70
Friedman, H.L. 198
Furman, R. 70

Garthwaite, K.A. 67
Geldof, D. 57
George, A. 18
Gilligan, R. 152
Girma, M. 165, 224, 225
Given-Wilson, Z. 133, 135
Gladwell, C. 156, 157
Glasgow City Council Social Work
    Services (GCC SWS) 108
Global Detention Project 221, 224
Glynos, J. 81
Godshaw, D. 223, 224
Goldberg, D.T. 81
Gower, M. 61
Grant, K. 18, 181
Grech, S. 89
Gregg, L. 146
Guardian, The 96, 97, 99, 108, 157, 227, 269

Hadziabdic, E. 252, 253, 254
Hajela, R. 221
Hansard 83
Harrison, R. 178
Hassard, J. 95
Hasselberg, I. 222
Hayes, D. 7, 19, 271
Healy, K. 177
Hek, R. 151–2
Her Majesty's Inspectorate of
    Prisons (HMIP) 225, 226
Herlihy, J. 80, 133, 135
Herman, J.L. 168, 170
Hill, M. 119
Hill Collins, P. 42, 48, 51, 191, 267–8
Hjelm, K. 252, 253, 254
Hodes, M. 133, 135, 153
Home Office 79, 129, 131, 134, 135, 136, 144,
    219, 220, 221, 222, 224, 225, 229, 239,
    240, 241, 251
House of Commons 95, 98, 104
Human Rights Act 1998 34, 125, 252
Humphries, B. 7, 19, 97, 107,
    110, 149, 157, 271
Humphris, R. 151, 156
Hunt, P. 81–2

Ife, J. 158
Immigration Act 2014 61
Immigration Act 2016 61, 137, 148
Immigration and Asylum Act 1999
    7, 19, 59–60, 104, 107
Immigration Law Practitioners'
    Association 240, 243
Independent, The 99, 129
Independent Monitoring Board
    (IMB) 223, 225, 227
International Association of Schools
    of Social Work (IASSW) 21
International Convention on the Elimination
    of All Forms of Racial Discrimination 81
International Federation of Social
    Workers (IFSW) 20, 97, 209
International Organisation for
    Migration (IOM) 122

Jirek, S.L. 230
Johnson, C.V. 198
Joint Committee on Human
    Rights 239, 243, 246
Joint Council for the Welfare
    of Immigrants 61
Jolly, D. 83
Jones, H. 61, 97
Jones, P.A. 201
Jones, R.K. 257, 258–9
Jordan, J. 46, 49

Kaplan, I. 240
Keane, F. 86
Kellezi, B. 220, 225
Khanna, R. 50
King, L. 18, 181
Klein, A. 230
Knight, A. 150
Koch, I. 83
Kohli, R. 128, 143, 149, 150,
    152, 153, 158, 170, 243
Kotsioni, I. 221, 231
Križ, K. 252, 253
Kvittingen, A. 149

Lamb, C. 88
Lampard, K. 227
Larkin, R. 269
Laub, D. 167
Law, J. 95
Lee, J.A.B. 190
Leonard, P. 190
Lodge, R. 21

London Edinburgh Weekend
    Return Group 277
London Safeguarding Children Board 128
Lorde, A. 45, 46, 50, 51–2, 53, 54
Lucas, S.E. 254
Lymbery, M. 277
Lynn, E. 189, 190

MacLachlan, S. 147
Maclean, S. 178
Malloch, M.S. 167
Marsden, E. 227
Masocha, S. 18, 164, 269
Massa, E. 223
Matthews, A. 143, 150
Matthews-King, A. 62
May, T. 88
Mayo, M. 190
Mayo, P. 190
Mazzer Barroso, M. 191
McCallum, R. 83
McGinley, A. 221
McGuinness, T. 61, 222
McKay, L. 230
McKendrick, D. 271
Meagher, G. 177
Meloni, F. 152, 153, 154, 155, 156
Melucci, A. 201
Mendez, J.E. 163
Mendiwelso-Bendek, Z. 190
Migrant Voice 102
Migration Observatory, The 120
Miller, K. 252, 258
Mills, C. 71
Minh-ha, T.T. 42, 44, 50
Missing People 151, 240
Mitchell, F. 143, 150
Moch, M. 190
Modern Slavery Act 2015 239
Mohanty, C.T. 42, 43–4
Mondon, A. 81
Montgomery, A. 176
Montgomery, P. 153
Mougne, C. 240
Mulvey, G. 195
Mustafa, N. 88

Nationality, Immigration and Asylum
    Act 2002 107, 125, 223
Navarro, A. 191, 194
Nayak, S. 42, 49, 276
Negi, N.J. 70
Nelson, D. 29

Ni Raghallaigh, M. 152
North East London Migrant Action
    (NELMA) 62, 72, 109
NRPF (No Recourse to Public Funds)
    Network 107, 108, 213
Nye, M. 147–8, 149, 157

O'Connell Davidson, J. 151
O'Hare, L. 71
Okitikpi, T. 253
Oliver, M. 82
Ortega, R.M. 171

Packham, C. 190
Pannett, L. 199
Parekh, G. 84
Parton, N. 100
Patel, N. 256
Paul, A. 92
Payne, D. 252
Pearlman, L.A. 230
Pinter, I. 149, 151
Price, E. 29
Price, J. 109
Project 17 109

Querton, C. 195

Rainbird, S. 201
Raval, H. 255, 256, 257
Refugee Action 60
Refugee Council 61, 103, 144, 165, 206, 222
Refugee Studies Centre 240
Remen, R.N. 171
Right to Remain 222
Rights of Children and Young Persons
    (Wales) Measure 2011 124
Robbins, R. 276
Robinson, K. 18, 269
Rommel, S. 70
Ryan, F. 84

Safer Bristol Partnership 88
Saleebey, D. 178
Sales, R. 61
Sandman, L. 253, 256
Sawrikar, P. 257, 258
Schrooten, M. 57
Scottish Association of Social Workers 129
Scottish Government 124, 129, 244
Scottish Parliament 107
Scottish Refugee Council 99
Searight, B.K. 255

Searight, H.R. 255
Separated Children in Europe
    Programme 120, 244, 246
Shah, A. 255
Shaw, S. 225, 227
Sigona, N. 151, 155, 156, 157
Silverman, S.J. 61, 221, 223
Simpson, M.K. 164
Skivenes, M. 252, 253
Slough Judgement 213
Smale, G. 170
Smith, R. 177
Soames, R. 107
Social Care Institute for Excellence
    (SCIE) 79, 180, 269
Social Services and Well-Being
    (Wales) Act 2014 124
Spencer, S. 109
Squire, V. 195
Stanfield, D. 100
Stanley, E. 167
Stanley, T. 271–2
Statham, D. 170
Statham, J. 150
Steel, M. 80
Steel, Z. 225
Strier, R. 275
Sullivan, R. 97
Summerfield, D. 167

Talbot, N. 253, 256
Taylor, D. 81
Telegraph, The 27, 60, 100
Tew, J. 179
Times, The 98, 99
Thomas, P. 255
Thompson, K. 253, 256, 257
Thornton, T. 255
Trevena, F. 147
Tribe, R. 253, 255, 256, 257, 259
Turbett, C. 267
Turnbull, S. 219
Turner, S. 80
Turney, D. 181
Tuson, G. 170
Tyler, I. 164, 178

UN Committee on the Rights of the Child 121
UN Convention against Torture and Other
    Cruel, Inhuman or Degrading Treatment
    or Punishment (UNCAT) 1984 163, 165
UN Convention on the Rights of Persons
    with Disabilities 2008 83, 84

UN Convention on the Rights of the
    Child (UNCRC) 1989 30–1, 124,
    125, 133 121, 143, 145, 223
UN Convention on the Status of
    Refugees 1951 122, 135
UNHCR (Office of the United Nations
    High Commissioner for Refugees)
    18, 31, 81, 117, 122, 135
UNICEF 117, 240, 241, 242, 244, 245
UNISON 129
Universal Declaration on Human Rights 81

van Dijk, T.A. 178
Van Parijis, P. 170
Venturini, T. 95
Vincett, J. 229, 230
Vockins, D. 59

Waddell, G. 83
Wade, J. 149, 150
Wadensjö, C. 258
Waite, L. 66

Warren, R. 135, 146
Waverley Care 103
Welfare Reform Act 2012 83
Wemyss, G. 97
Westermeyer, J. 252, 259
Westlake, D. 257, 258–9
White, M. 189
Williams, C. 28, 158
Williams, L. 230
Williams, N. 146
Wilson, J.P. 167
Wilson, K. 177
Withaeckx, S. 57, 64
Women's Refugee Commission 18
Wroe, L. 18, 200, 269, 274

Yarl's Wood Befrienders (YWB) 229
Yeo, R. 77, 78, 80, 84
York, S. 135
Yuval-Davis, N. 97, 109

Zubrzycki, J. 29